Building a Business

Books by Alvin Moscow

Collision Course: The Andrea Doria and the Stockholm
Tiger on a Leash
City at Sea
Merchants of Heroin
The Rockefeller Inheritance
Every Secret Thing (with Patricia Campbell Hearst)
Managing (with Harold Geneen)

Building a Business

The JIM WALTER *Story*

Alvin Moscow

Published by
Pineapple Press, Inc.
Sarasota, Florida

Inquiries should be addressed to:
Pineapple Press, Inc.
P.O. Drawer 16008
Southside Station
Sarasota, Florida 34239

Library of Congress Cataloging-in-Publication Data
Moscow, Alvin.
        Building a business: the Jim Walter story / Alvin Moscow—1st ed.
                p.   cm.
                Includes index.
                ISBN 1-56164-087-5 (hbk.) — ISBN 1-56164-092-1 (pbk.)
                1. Walter, Jim. 2. Industrialists—Florida—Biography.
3. Construction industry—Florida—History—20th century.
4. Real estate development—Florida—History—20th century.
5. Entrepreneurship—Florida.   I. Title.
HD9715.U52W345   1995
338.7'698'.092—dc20
[B]

First Edition
10 9 8 7 6 5 4 3 2 1

Design by Ned Campbell, Bill Smith Studio
Printed in the United States of America

CONTENTS

1   CHAPTER 1
Starting Out Building

21   CHAPTER 2
Building Relationships

39   CHAPTER 3
No Bankers for Shell Builders

61   CHAPTER 4
Building Credit

79   CHAPTER 5
Competition in Building

97   CHAPTER 6
The $15 Million Building Bargain

125   CHAPTER 7
Building for Growth

145   CHAPTER 8
Building for Diversity

167   CHAPTER 9
Building Internally

189   CHAPTER 10
Building Beyond a Billion

213   CHAPTER 11
Beware Building Up Interest Rates

231   CHAPTER 12
Building in Bad Times

251   CHAPTER 13
Building in Good Times

269   CHAPTER 14
Building on a Buyout

301   CHAPTER 15
Building to Survive

331   *Index*

Building a Business

CHAPTER 1

— *Starting Out Building* —

THEY'RE ALL AROUND US, floating in the air, those million-dollar ideas of which fame and fortune are made. Just reach up and grab one, take that calculated risk, run with it, and get rich, famous, and happy. That's the American Dream, the ever palpitating heart of the free enterprise system.

For most people it remains only a dream. And yet, such visions have made multimillionaires of those creative men and women who have given our nation something new and significant, something it needed and never had before.

One of the most opportune times in our history for implementing those dreams, although few realized it at the time, was the period immediately after the end of World War II. Eleven million young American men and women had returned victorious and joyful from the devastation of Europe and the Far East, ready for a new start in the richest and least war-scathed nation of the world. The feeling throughout the country was that in this land of opportunity everyone was starting over, free to make of his or her life anything, or almost anything, he or she chose.

Among those millions of ordinary American veterans was one James Willis Walter, a tall, slender young man of twenty-three, with broad shoulders, an open face, and a ready smile. They called him "Slim Jim" in the navy; back home in Tampa, on the west coast of Florida, he was Jimmy to his friends. Returning from four long years in the navy, he took up his pre-war job: driving a truck for his father's citrus-packing firm. His pay was $50 a week. His home was in the attic apartment of his parents' house. Now, however, with a new bride whom he had met and married while in the service, he was a changed man, mature for his years. The navy had taught him "street smarts." He had learned how to fend for himself in any environment, how to take care of himself and get things done, which went far beyond his high school education and small town upbringing. Now, in the new post-war world, he was looking for something more challenging and exciting than driving a truck for fifty bucks a week. After all, he had joined the navy and seen the world.

So, for reasons deeply embedded in his personality and character, it was James Willis Walter, rather than anyone else, who plucked from the classified ads an idea that would forever change his life and the lives of many others. On this quiet, sunny, Sunday morning in November of 1946 he was sitting in the shade of the front porch with his father, both of them reading the Sunday Tampa *Tribune*. His eye caught a small, two-line ad on a crowded page of agate type:

> NICE little unfinished houses to be moved.
> $895. 9410 11th St., S.S.

How many other people in Tampa saw that ad on that Sunday morning and did nothing about it? No one knows. What caught Jim Walter's eye was the price: $895. The next cheapest house advertised on that page was almost three times as much. With everything in such short supply after the war, especially housing, he wondered why anyone would sell a house at such a ridiculously low price. Musing a while, he then asked, "Daddy, what kind of house do you think anybody could build and sell for $895?"

Ebe Walter, in his midsixties, had been a contractor and

builder many years before and had gone bankrupt in the Florida land bust of 1926. He was a Southern gentleman of the old school: white suit, white shirt, tie drawn up to the neck in the hottest weather, a tall, taciturn man who never spoke about the eye he had lost in a childhood accident. He was a man of absolute integrity who had scrimped and saved without complaint for years to pay back every dime he had owed creditors. He never mentioned that either. His sons, Ebe, Jr., and Jim, adored him. They understood why their hardworking father, who had been forty when Ebe, Jr., was born and forty-five when Jim came into this world, did not play ball or go fishing or hunting with them, as other fathers did. He was always hard at work. But by deeds and example rather than words he had taught them the meaning of integrity, honor, character, responsibility.

As usual, he answered his son's question with as few words as possible. "I don't rightly know, Jimmy; why don't you just drive over there and find out?"

In his father's pre-war pickup truck, Jim bounced over dusty dirt roads to the house on Eleventh Street in Sulphur Springs, a working-class section on the northwest outskirts of town. Tampa, Florida's largest port on the Gulf of Mexico, was not much of a city then. It attracted neither tourists nor industry. Its privileged elite of old, wealthy families owned the land, the citrus groves, the banks, and the utilities. They ran the city while everyone else was working-class poor. With a population of 75,000, the city had never recovered from that 1926 land speculation debacle. Roads half-paved at the time had been left that way, along with the stretches of empty lots where housing developments once had been planned.

The house on Eleventh Street, sitting on concrete blocks, surprised him pleasantly. It was small, to be sure, twenty-by-twenty feet. But it was brand-new, clapboard, gleaming white in the late morning sun, with a black shingle roof, two screened windows on each side, and a tiny stoop, with three wooden steps leading to the front door. Alongside the house was a small shack half its size. The builder, a lean man as tall and perhaps five years older than Jim, emerged from the shack to greet his potential buyer and to introduce himself. His name was Lou Davenport.

Dressed in carpenter's bib overalls, he led Jim through the small, unfinished house. A friendly, open man with a soft, Southern drawl, Davenport was not much of a salesman. What you saw was what you got.

The interior was bare and raw. The subfloor was made of tongue-in-groove pine, the ceiling rafters were exposed, and the rooms were outlined in upright two-by-fours. The living room in the front of the house was no more than ten-by-twelve. Behind that was what would be the single bedroom, about ten-by-ten, flanked by a small kitchen and tiny bathroom. The idea, Davenport explained, was that if you bought the house, he would move it to your own lot, anywhere in Tampa, and then you would finish it yourself. Or, if you did not know how to do one thing or another, you could get a friend to help, or you could hire a plumber to put in the pipes and septic tank, an electrician to wire the place, and a carpenter to put up the interior walls.

Like a first-time buyer kicking the tires of a new car, Jim stamped on the floor and kicked the upright studs. Nothing shook or rattled and he concluded that the house was, indeed, well built. It really was not adequate for his own needs. But it was a house, better than nothing, and he knew that most ex-servicemen, newly married like himself, were desperate for housing. The house, at the very least, was a very good buy. He shook hands with Davenport and said, "I'll be back."

Back home, Jim described the house to his father and said he would like to speculate on it. At such a low price, Jim thought the house would have a great appeal. Most of the men he knew worked with their hands and would be able to complete most of the house, if not all of it, themselves. "That little house sure is worth more than $895," Jim said, adding, "I'd like to buy it and sell it for a profit." His father agreed that it seemed like a sweet deal, adding that he just happened to have two vacant lots in Sulphur Springs that he had taken in exchange for a bad debt, either of which would be suitable for Jim's purpose. Jim had only one more question: "Would you lend me $500 until I sell the house?"

With $900 in hand, Jim went back the next day, bought the house and had it moved several blocks away to his father's land. He put up his own sign: "HOUSE FOR SALE—$1,295." Three days later he sold it.

With the cash in his pocket and a quick analysis of the situation, Jim Walter knew almost immediately what he would do. First, he would return the $500 borrowed from his father, then he would buy another little house from Davenport and sell that one, too. Four hundred dollars profit in three days! That sure beat driving a truck for $50 a week, he assured himself. Aside from his service in the navy, all he had ever done was work for his father. But driving a two-ton truck between New York and Florida was no longer his idea of the good life. He decided to buy and sell another house and then see where this venture led. After surviving the war in the Pacific, he had no fear of taking risks. What had he to lose now? Only money.

Jim Walter had grown up poor during the years of the Great Depression, but no poorer than any of his friends, and never in want. His boyhood had been all fun and games, even with working part-time jobs for spending money. He had been a skinny little kid, full of high energy, a sense of humor, and a devil-may-care attitude. His friends joshed that "they had to burn down the high school to get Jimmy out of it." Six months later, in the patriotic fervor that followed

America's entry into World War II, he and three of his closest friends marched off together to enlist in the Naval Air
Force. Jim, who had just turned nineteen, flunked the physical examination because of a suspected heart murmur. While
his three friends gleefully took the glory route, from which
one of them would not return, Jim signed up for the navy
and, after basic training, was assigned to a new naval station
at Deland, in north-central Florida.

When he got there he saw nothing that resembled a navy
airfield. The Deland Naval Air Station was a swamp, brush-
land, and a few buildings, enclosed by a cyclone wire fence.
His job was to help build the airfield, specifically by driving a
truck. The hidden beauty of the assignment, however, was
that the war was new, the airfield yet to be built, and virtually
every officer and enlisted man there was a raw recruit, too.

One of the "old-timers" who had been there since the
opening of the facility and ran the warehousing of building
materials for the airfield was a third-class petty officer named
James O. Alston. A small, sinewy, tough, outspoken country
boy from Little Rock, Arkansas, Buddy Alston was proud of
his origins: He had been raised on a farm, hunted rabbits in
the foothills of Petit Jean Mountain, delivered newspapers
and bread at four o'clock in the morning, and still found
time to attend and graduate from high school. He was a
brash, self-assured young man who looked with undisguised
disdain upon the young officers at the base, college gradu-
ates who had become officers with only ninety days of training. Buddy was all of nineteen and one-half years old, but he
knew his way around. Taking "Slim Jim" under his wing, he
persuaded him that his life in the navy would be better and
cleaner if he became a storekeeper rather than a cook, even
though cooks got every night off while storekeepers only got
every other night for liberty. They soon became fast friends,
sharing their navy lives together, on the base and off. Jim

Walter began by driving a truck but he went on to learn typing, filing, inventory control, bookkeeping, and administration, earning his petty officer ranking as a third-class storekeeper.

When life at Deland after some eighteen months turned into a bore, the two friends, on no more than a whim, volunteered for sea duty in the Pacific. Sent to the central naval supply depot in Oakland, California, where they awaited orders for sea duty, the two country boys drank deeply of the pleasures of big city life in San Francisco. It opened their eyes to the world around them. Their assignments out of Oakland separated them for the rest of the war: Buddy was promoted to chief storekeeper and sent to Manus Island in the Admiralty Islands where he was put in charge of seven huge warehouses that supplied all the dry stores needed by the Seventh Fleet. Common sense carried him a long way. Jim was assigned to the USS *Newcombe*, the flagship of a squadron of twelve destroyers operating in the South Pacific, where he served as an administrative assistant to the commanding officer. All in all, the navy gave each of these young men a practical education in the real world which far exceeded the experience and knowledge either could have garnered in civilian life. It would be true, but not the whole truth, therefore, to say that Jim Walter was just an ordinary twenty-three-year-old when he returned that following Saturday in November 1946 to negotiate buying another unfinished house from Lou Davenport. This time he spent the day with the builder, both of them sitting on empty nail kegs in the ten-by-ten shack, swapping war stories and talking of building houses. Each of them had seen sea duty, but it was Jim who had lost his ship. Twenty-seven months on the USS *Newcombe* and luckily he had been transferred off the destroyer just prior to the battle of Okinawa, where the *Newcombe* was hit and devastated by Japanese kamikazes. Almost half the crew was lost, including the man who had replaced Jim Walter at his midship anti-aircraft gun battle station.

Davenport explained that he had just started out and was making a fair living building one house at a time, selling it, and then building another on the same lot. He was averaging one house a week. Although he never kept accounts of costs and profits, he figured he made around $200 per house. It wasn't a bad life, he assured Jim; he was his own boss and could take off any time he wanted to go fishing.

Jim told him how easily he had sold the house he had bought and suggested that together they had the makings of a good business here. In driving his truck to and from New York, Jim had seen the kind of tar paper and tin shacks that a lot of people were living in throughout the South. He figured some of those people would prefer to live in a pretty, little white house instead. Where else could they possibly find a home for $900?

By the end of the day, Jim proposed that they go into business together: Lou would build the houses and Jim would sell them. "I've got some pretty good ideas on how we can sell a lot more than one house a week," Jim promised.

It was as informal and as casual as that. Lou agreed: They would pool their money, form a partnership, build and sell unfinished houses, and split the profits fifty-fifty. Each of them assumed the other had savings large enough to launch their new business. When they met early Monday morning at the Springs State Bank, they dug into their pockets and plunked their bankrolls on the counter. They matched funds at $700. It was far less than either expected, but they were builders, not worriers. With a shrug they went ahead and deposited the money. "Davenport & Walter" was in business.

Jim Walter proved his mettle with his very first business decision. He persuaded Lou Davenport that they would attract more customers with a bigger advertisement in the following Sunday's newspaper. A five-inch ad, two columns wide, showing a line drawing of the house would cost $27, but it would be worth it, Jim claimed. It took a considerable amount of persuasion to convince his new partner to spend that much money on a single ad; his two-liner that had attracted Walter had cost only sixty-five cents. But Jim Walter was persuasive.

That Sunday was a day James Willis Walter would never forget. It was the start of a business career of which he had not had the slightest inkling. He could not drive up to the model house on Eleventh Street. Parked cars and pickup trucks were lined up every which way for two blocks. Hundreds of people were crowded into the model house, calling out questions to Davenport, who was standing on a nail keg trying to hold his own in one corner of what would be the living room. Jim scrambled onto another nail keg in the opposite corner of the room and started a sales talk he had been mentally rehearsing for most of the week.

"You can buy this house right here, just the way you see it. Or we'll build you one just like it. . . . The best lumber, the best materials, two coats of quality white paint . . . We'll move it to your own lot, anywhere in Tampa. . . . completely finished on the outside . . . as pretty a house as anyone could buy at this price . . . You finish the inside yourself, any way you want it. Get a friend or two in to help you. . . . Yes, $895 is the total price. Where else could you buy a house for that? First come, first served. Half down and we start construction. The other half when we finish. Then we move it to your site. If you don't have all that money with you today, a $100 deposit will put you next on the list. Believe me, 'cause you know it yourself, you couldn't find a better deal than this in the whole country: A home of your own for under $1,000!"

It was a day of sheer bedlam and pure joy for the two partners. Fielding questions and shouting back answers, they sold houses at the top of their voices. It was like an auction, though the price was the same. "Okay, now, anyone ready to buy this pretty little house?" Walter would ask. "Raise your hand and then follow me next door, sign up, and buy yourself a home of your very own!" The buyers would be led either by Jim or Lou into the shack next door to sign a sales contract, all of it contained on a single mimeographed sheet of paper. If the buyer could pay half cash then and there, he went to the top of the list. The others plunked down the $100 deposit and were instructed to hurry back with the rest of the down payment needed to start construction.

By the end of that joyous day, Davenport & Walter had sold twenty-seven houses! By the end of the week, they had commitments for more than $24,000 in sales. Their new bank account bulged. That was more money than either of them had ever seen in his lifetime—all from a $27 classified ad.

The next day they plunged in and found, like most pristine businessmen, problems everywhere. To build one small frame house was relatively simple, but to build dozens of them set the partners scrambling in all directions. Reliable carpenters had to be found in a hurry. Lumber, doors, windows, roofing, and paint had to be ordered from skeptical suppliers who had never dealt with them before. Even paying in cash did not guarantee results. Building materials, and nails in particular, were in short supply after the war, and Davenport & Walter found itself at the bottom of the heap in the competition with other builders for supplies. Finding and buying the necessary materials was far more difficult than finding carpenters to build the houses. There was no shortage of men who could wield a hammer in Tampa and many of them preferred to work as independent contractors rather than on salary at a 9-to-5 job. Lou devoted most of his time to supervising the construction of the houses, while Jim did the comparison shopping for the needed supplies. Generally it took one skilled carpenter and two helpers to build a shell house, finished on the outside with two coats of white paint and unfinished on the inside. Lou worked with a carpenter until the new worker was able to take over the job himself. For each house they paid a flat rate to the carpenter and he hired and paid his own helpers. As beginners and by inclination, they kept everything as simple as possible. They bought what they needed as they needed it for one house at a time. They avoided buying in advance. Who needed large inventories? The mistakes they made in starting out were small, inexpensive ones, and they learned as they went along.

Jim Walter thrived in the role of entrepreneur, long before that term became fashionable. Customers poured in every Sunday in response to weekly ads. Most of them were eager to buy, once they were convinced that there were no hidden costs, tricks, or misrepresentations involved. Despite a nervous stomach and a slight stammer, Jim Walter excelled as a salesman: it dovetailed with his personality. He enjoyed selling and the art of persuasion. He believed in his product, and his open, straightforward honesty never failed to impress buyers or suppliers. The challenges and uncertainties of running his own business stimulated him as driving a truck never could. He thought he had discovered a gold lode and was eager to work and dig for it. His logic was simple and direct: Shelter was a necessity of life, like food and clothing, and so there would always be people who wanted to buy these small, inexpensive, unfinished houses. Only a tar paper shack or a tent would be cheaper than a shell home.

As time went on, in hundreds of different ways, the two partners changed this and changed that in order to improve every facet of the business, from sales to mortgages to construction. Some of the best ideas came from their customers. When several asked if their houses could be built on their own sites, rather than being moved there, the two young partners tried that and found it to their advantage. Suppliers did not object to delivering directly to the construction site and that saved Davenport & Walter the $75 cost of moving the house. When some customers wanted to buy a two-bedroom house, Davenport sat down and calculated that by adding three feet to one side of the house, he could fit two small bedrooms behind the living room, each of them a bit smaller than the single bedroom in the original model. Jim set the price on the two-bedroom model at $1,250, thereby increasing their unit margin of profit, and gaining new customers who already had one or more children in the family.

Near the end of their first year in business, they were selling about ten houses a week. Then they began to run short of cash customers. More and more frequently, a prospective buyer would ask: "Would you take half down now and let me pay off the rest over time?" The answer had to be yes, or they would lose that sale. With necessity ever the mother of invention, they revised their sales contract. They would build a house for a customer who could pay 50 percent or more in cash, but the customer would have to pledge the land upon which the house was built as part of the mortgage. The remainder of the price was to be paid off in monthly installments over one, two, or even three years, with an annual 6 percent "finance charge" tagged on. If the buyer failed to pay his mortgage debt, he forfeited the house *and* the land.

Installment buying was a remarkably good deal for the customer. If he paid $400 down on a $895 house, his monthly payment on a one-year mortgage came to $44.16, and if he stretched it out to two years, his monthly payment amounted to only $23.33. That was usually less than he was paying for rent. It was a good deal, too, for Davenport & Walter. They sold more houses than before. While they did not advertise or push installment buying, because they preferred and needed the cash, no longer did they have to turn away good customers who did not have the cash in hand. The "good" customers were easy enough to recognize: They were usually the ones who grew up in Tampa, whose families had lived there for years, whose fathers were willing to help out, if needed, with land or money. They came from all walks of life, mostly blue-collar workers, mechanics, carpenters, laborers, storekeepers, clerks, and farmers, men who worked a forty-hour week for a small but a living wage. All of them were eager to buy a home for their new families, eager to "do it yourself" in completing a starter home for their starting-out families. To approve or not approve a mortgage for a buyer, in those early days, was strictly a matter of judgment, but Walter thought he could recognize an honest, responsible man when he saw one.

Gradually, however, the faucet was drained of cash customers, leaving only those who could pay half, or less, of the purchase price in cash. The specter of "cash flow" reared its head. While the actual figures varied from month to month, materials and labor generally ate up approximately two-thirds of the price of the house. With buyers paying only one-half or less in cash, it was clear that the more houses they sold, the less cash they would have in the bank. If they sold enough houses, they would go broke.

Jim made the rounds of the banks in Tampa, seeking loans to finance his new business. He got turned down flat. Even with a new suit and a fresh haircut, he was laughed out the door. They told him, sometimes politely and sometimes not so politely, that his so-called business was too small, too new, too risky. No banker wanted to take an unfinished house as collateral on a loan. If a person was so poor that he could only afford an unfinished house, how could a banker trust him to pay his mortgage? If a bank had to foreclose, what could it do with the shell of a house in the hinterlands of Tampa?

Seeking out the banks beyond Tampa, he received equally definite and equally negative responses. Banks were conservative institutions and not in the business of risking *their* money. What had once looked like a gold mine now began to take on the image of a deep, dark hole which gulped down green dollars, with no end in sight.

Jim's father, his mentor, offered no help. Too much the gentleman to say, "I told you so," he merely repeated his advice to get out of that business. "I think, son, you've sold just about as many of those houses as you are going to sell," he said. "There just aren't any more people who have the money to buy your houses. And if you sell to them on time, you're simply asking for trouble."

Mr. Walter had never been particularly happy to see his son involved in what he considered to be a flash-in-the-pan business. He could see no future in selling unfinished houses to poor people. A conservative businessman of the old school, Ebe Walter did not believe in quick, get-rich schemes, and to his mind unfinished houses fell into that category. He suggested that Jim might do better by joining him in his citrus-packing and shipping business, which was prospering since the war had ended. Jim could make a solid if not spectacular living there, and eventually, his father intimated, the family business would become his.

Jim's wife, Monica, did not think too highly of his business prospects, either. She believed not so much that he might fail and go broke, but that with his drive and determination he would do much better in almost any other business, particularly one that was more stable. Monica had been keeping the books for Davenport & Walter since the beginning; she had put up with her husband leaving the house at five or six o'clock in the morning to get an early start on each day, and his seven-day workweek. What did they have to show for it?

He still drew only $50 a week in salary, drove an old wreck of a car, and was mortgaged up to his neck to pay for the small, three-bedroom house they had bought when Jim, Jr., had been born. But she knew her man well and refrained from advising him about what he should do.

Monica Saraw Walter was remarkably similar in background and personality to the man she had married. Raised in a modest family in a suburb of Buffalo, New York, she had gone to work as a secretary at sixteen and had joined the navy at twenty-two in order to escape a humdrum life. She wanted to explore the "better world out there" that the armed services promised. A tall, lithe, big-boned woman with an abundance of wavy, russet red hair, "Monty" Saraw was every bit as self-sufficient and determined as Jim Walter. In fact, she had considered him an ordinary sort of fellow until she came to know him better. She had been, as others would be, surprised at his mental agility, his high energy level, his humor and pleasant personality, and his ingrained sense of responsibility.

After a whirlwind romance at, of all places, the Jacksonville (Florida) Naval Air Station, which had become a separation center for discharging personnel after the war had ended, they were both on the verge of being discharged. Jim proposed marriage, but Monica had insisted upon staying in the navy for another six months. She was a storekeeper first class, like Jim, but staying in the navy for six more months would gain her that last promotion she wanted: chief storekeeper. Determined to reach the top, she said he would have to wait. They compromised by getting married while she remained in the service. They rented an apartment in Jacksonville, and he commuted from Tampa where he worked for his father. For six months he trucked grapefruits and oranges to New York City, working around the clock, and on his days off drove to Jacksonville to be with his bride. As if that were not enough, he had set up a little business of his own, squeezing orange juice and making baloney sandwiches which he would sell to bored and hungry sailors on the Jacksonville base. He was always looking for opportunities, and he was not afraid to work. That had impressed Monty. That he had phoned his parents on each of his arrivals in Jacksonville, to assure them that he was safe and sound, also touched her. The close-knit structure of the Walter family augured well in her estimation for the future of their own marriage.

In deference to his father's wishes, Jim tried working in the packing plant for a week or so and then came to the conclusion that it was not for him. He did not want to spend his life at something safe and secure; the adventures of a new business appealed to the gambler's instinct within him. Besides, he still believed in those little unfinished houses. They satisfied a basic need of people who could not afford more expensive housing, and he felt he could make a go of the business, even though he did not precisely know how he would do it. It was simply not in his nature to quit.

By the summer of 1947, with the business not yet a year old, Davenport & Walter's monthly sales of one- and two-bedroom houses totaled nearly $30,000, costs were roughly $20,000, and gross profits were $10,000. The basic problem still was that there was no way that the $10,000 profits (minus other necessary expenditures) could possibly pay for the $20,000 costs for the next month. If they stopped their installment sales, they would lose out on growth and profits; if they continued selling with less and less on down payments, they would diminish their cash in the bank and, of course, once you run out of cash, you're out of the game. Davenport wanted to cut back. Walter wanted to expand.

Lou, who wilted under all that stress, pleaded with Jim to go back to their basic business: building houses for cash only. That was what the other fellows were doing who were building similar houses, and that would eliminate all the headaches. But by this time Jim had become the dominant partner, for he was the one who always handled the problems of the business, and so he prevailed. Rather than retrench, Jim decided to branch out into the building supplies business. Their cash flow problems could be solved, he figured, if they could run a profitable retail outlet, selling materials to other builders for cash. At the same time, having their own building supplies company would give them better access to materials they needed for their own construction. Lou acquiesced because he simply did not have the will or stamina to argue with his more dynamic partner. In July, 1947, Davenport & Walter bought the Dixie Building Supplies Company from its proprietor, Ernie Stewart, for $5,000 cash, which barely covered the value of the supplies in stock.

Dixie was not much of a business. Located at 704 East Waters Avenue on the outskirts of town, across from a dog-racing track, it consisted of one old cinder block warehouse which was badly in need of repair and a paint job. Selling hardware and building materials to individual builders and do-it-yourself handymen, Dixie earned a modest profit each month. Alongside the shabby warehouse, Davenport constructed an "office building" which consisted of three of his ten-by-ten shacks strung together. In front of the two buildings, he put up a model home and a hand-crafted billboard sign. Surrounded by sand and loose dirt, with not a shade tree in sight, Davenport & Walter was in business with two ways to win. What Jim did not tell his fearful partner was that Dixie was only the first in a chain of building supplies outlets he had in mind for future expansion.

Jim Walter also believed in luck. He didn't rely on it, but he had faith that more good things than bad would come his way, if he could stay in the game long enough. Jim had just succeeded in having a hard-to-get telephone service installed in his new home when he received a long-distance call from his old navy friend, Bud Alston. As luck would have it, Jim was looking for someone to manage Dixie Supplies, and Buddy, who had gone broke in his own produce business in Little Rock, was looking for a job. Buddy had called on a whim, remembering his old friend, and Jim urged him to pack a bag and hurry on down to Tampa. Pay was $50 a week. James O. Alston, of Little Rock, Arkansas, did not hesitate in changing the course of his own life. He took off the next morning.

Alston's arrival fit in well with Walter's plans and hopes for the future. Walter, ever the entrepreneur, thought it through: If he could not make a go of it with shell homes, he would switch to selling building supplies through his Dixie company. Certainly there was a construction boom in Tampa and all along the west coast of Florida. Acting quickly on his plans, he put his old friend in charge of shaping up the Dixie outlet in Tampa. A few months later, Jim opened a retail outlet in the small but growing town of Madeira Beach, about twenty miles west of Tampa on the Gulf of Mexico, and sent Buddy there to manage that store. A couple of months after that he opened a second Dixie building supplies store there and put Buddy in charge of both stores.

With increased volume and sales, young Walter hoped to bring some more ready cash into his shell home business, and also to strengthen his buying position with Tampa's building supplies wholesalers. Still he failed to impress them. Davenport & Walter was regarded as a struggling, small outfit on the brink of bankruptcy. Naturally, the wholesalers gave priority on materials in short supply to the older, better-established building supply retail stores. The Dixie stores remained too small to make any dent in the market. Nor did they generate the cash flow needed to help finance the houses. Cash poor, Walter was forced to close both stores in Madeira Beach and retreat back to Tampa, where Buddy Alston could tend to Dixie and also lend a hand in selling unfinished houses.

The three of them—Davenport, Walter, and Alston—struggled on through the next year, scratching and scrambling to meet their bills every month. Selling houses was no problem; building them was no problem; but financing them remained a chronic headache. Customers came in eager to buy with smaller and smaller down payments. Cash became more and more scarce. The three men were still taking only $50 a week in salaries. The purchase of needed equipment, like a used truck, became a major undertaking. Jim began to devote almost all of his time to trying to borrow enough money to pay for the houses that Buddy sold and Lou built.

As the second anniversary of the business approached, the partnership of Lou Davenport and Jim Walter began to come apart at the seams. Lou sought to escape the stresses and strains of living on the brink of ruination. Jim insisted upon growth and expansion as the best means of saving what they had built up. But he had to admit the truth of their situation: "We're making money every day and we're as broke as convicts."

Finally, in October 1948, just about two years after they had begun, Jim put it to his partner: "There's just not enough here for both of us to make it worth all this work and worry. So, why don't we split it up? One of us should take the business and the other take the liquid assets. I figure that at about $50,000. And, since I'm the one suggesting it, it's only fair that you take your pick. Which one do you want, the business or the money?"

Davenport scratched his weather-beaten, sun-bronzed face and thought it over. Then he decided, "I'll take the business."

The two men shook hands in agreement, and Jim Walter returned to his parents' home for dinner that night, feeling neither joy nor chagrin. Once a thing had been decided and settled, he tended not to worry about it. What choice he himself would have made, if the choice had been his, he did not bother to figure out. It was a fair split, he thought, and now he would simply have to make his way in some other line of work.

His father was delighted with the choice made, and Monica let out a noticeable sigh of relief. There was no denying that life would be easier without the constant money worries.

The next morning, however, Lou came into the office and rather sheepishly asked, "Jimmy, can I ask a favor?"

Walter replied, "Sure, Lou, anything."

"I'd like to change my mind. I thought it over last night, and I'd sooner take the money and let you have the business, if that's okay with you."

Walter was nonplussed. "Are you sure that's the way you want it?"

"I'm sure now."

Switching roles, once again they parted amicably. Lou Davenport's share of the business came to $53,000 in cash and mortgages, which he subsequently invested in a motel in Alabama. Jim Walter was left with a business of his own, to make of it what he could. Later that week the Walter Construction Company was set up as the successor to Davenport & Walter. Outside of the immediate family and friends, no one noticed the change at all.

CHAPTER 2

— *Building Relationships* —

I N THE DRY, sandy hinterlands of Sulphur Springs across from the Tampa Dog Track on East Waters Avenue stood the Walter Construction Company with the same stretched out wooden office building, a little white model house in front, a billboard with a new name on it, and an old, stucco warehouse/store of Dixie Building Supplies. In the eyes of the Tampa building industry, Jim Walter was still a young, inexperienced nobody, squirming and struggling like everybody else to get a grip on the slippery pole of success. But what the eye could not see was that beneath the surface, where everything looked the same, a significant change had been made in management. Bud Alston had taken over Lou Davenport's role in supervising construction and he, unlike the easygoing Lou, was every bit as ambitious, energetic, and dauntless as Jim Walter.

In Alston's mind there was not the slightest doubt that he and his friend would succeed. Back in the navy, he had reached the conviction that Walter was as smart and as capable as any man he had met, no matter of what rank, status, or educational background. He envisioned the day after the war when he would become a millionaire in one business or another. Observing how his friend Jimmy in his quiet, friendly way managed time and again to get anything he set his mind to, he told himself that Jimmy was a man to watch because Jim Walter would become a millionaire even before he did. Childish dreams? Not for Buddy Alston. He felt he was always a good judge of character, and now with the Walter Construction Company he was more convinced than ever that together they were unstoppable and unbeatable.

Despite his small size, or perhaps because of it, Buddy was a take-command, no-nonsense sort of boss. In his gravelly Arkansan drawl, he said straight out what was on his mind and, like an explosive chief petty officer in the navy, demanded obedience. His saving grace was that he was usually right in his stringent demands. He was endowed with more common sense than the next fellow and his mind whirled and clicked out the answers faster, too. Learning this business, after his wartime responsibilities, was almost child's play. He enjoyed it. Early on, he attached himself to the best of several carpenter subcontractors and watched how they constructed Jim Walter houses. He observed closely each step in the process: laying the concrete base below ground, building up the concrete piers to ground level, and then laying the four-by-four beam which supported the floor plate and subflooring, followed by the construction of the stud framing, the top plates, the ceiling joists, and then the rafters which were covered with plywood, felt sheathing, and roofing shingles. He asked questions: Why this and not that? What's this called? What's that? Why do you do it this way and not that way? How can you tell one two-by-four is good and another bad? How many knots in a pine plank are acceptable and how many are not?

Alston learned how to build houses, though he himself never picked up a hammer. More than that, he judged who was good and who was not so good at his job. The key man was the skilled carpenter, the craftsman who measured and cut the two-by-four studs and the sixteen-inch-wide pine planks for the outer sheathing of the house. His two helpers did the nailing. The amount of lumber used in each house depended largely upon how many mistakes the carpenter made in measuring and cutting. Going from one job to another, Alston did rough comparison studies, though he never called them that, and then told one team what another team had done, and asked why they could not do as well. When he found that the weakest team of men had three or four two-by-fours left over when a house was finished, Alston cut the next lumber order by that many two-by-fours. Like a hawk, he watched material costs. He swore that he could tell within $15 the profit margin on a house on the day the house was sold. In years to come, in hiring construction crews, he let them know his standard for good work: "When you finish building a Jim Walter home, all I want you to have left over is a pile of sawdust." Buddy Alston liked to speak in hyperbolic certainties; it helped get his message across.

As time went on, the carpenters became better and better at putting up a house with less and less waste. They were paid a flat fee on a house, based upon its size, which usually netted the contractor $140 per house (at thirty-five cents a square foot). It would take three men about twelve hours to build a twenty-by-twenty house, seven hours one day and five the next, leaving the rest of that second day to put on two coats of white paint. Working a six-day week, as many did, they could put up three houses a week if they hustled and make very good money, more than they could working for anyone else. Often the construction crews were made up of brothers, sometimes husbands and wives, and later, even thirty years later, fathers and sons. It was a good deal all around and stayed that way down through the years. A good carpenter could build up his own contracting business, using his own relatives and friends and men he could trust, and Jim Walter did not have to keep any of them on his payroll.

Walter and Alston also discovered the advantage of buying supplies, particularly lumber, as they needed them, thereby eliminating the expenses of maintaining large inventories. In choosing a lumber company, for instance, they wanted not only a good price but good, reliable service. A cheap price and no on-time delivery was not much good to anyone. Through trial and error they built up long-lasting relationships with their suppliers that were based upon reliability and personal integrity. Once a relationship of trust was established Walter continued to do business with the same lumberyard, hardware supplier, or paint manufacturer. Blake Lumber, at Temple Terrace Highway and Route 41, for example, began supplying lumber for Jim Walter homes in the Tampa area and went on doing so for years and years. Here again the Walter Construction Company came to a verbal, but binding, understanding with Blake, as it would with other lumberyards down through the years.

"This is a two-way road. You have to make money and we have to make money," Jim or Buddy would say. "We're set up for the long haul, not the short run. Sometimes lumber will be in short supply and sometimes there'll be more on hand than you can sell. We want to pay a fair price, the best price you can give us, but we don't want to be gouged when lumber is short, and we won't try to drive you to the wall when somebody else is selling it cheaper. If you take advantage of us, then it's goodbye; we don't want to do business with you. But if we can trust you and depend on you for price and delivery, then you've got a long-term proposition here, and, you have our word on this, you'll get paid by the tenth of the month, every month, come rain or come shine."

Lumber, of course, was the biggest cost item that went into building a Jim Walter home. Most of the other materials— roofing, windows, outside doors, paint, nails, hinges, sashes—were bought in those early days through their Dixie Building Supplies Company or from Booker and Company, the largest wholesale supplier in Tampa.

Booker was an old, established distributor that controlled scarce building supplies in the Tampa area and beyond. Fortunately, Jim hit it off immediately with one of Booker's key salesmen, Jack Almand, who, like him, was an ex-navy man in his twenties trying to make his way in this new post-war world. They had similar backgrounds and similar outlooks on the future and before long they became fast, lifelong friends. Jim made a particularly strong impression upon Almand when he drove up to the hardware supplier to buy some hinges in his dilapidated pre-war taxicab, the only car he could afford at the time. Jack Almand became a great help in allocating scarce building supplies to Dixie and in guiding Jim and Buddy to the best sources for whatever they might need in their little shell home and building supplies business. Tampa was still a small town where everyone knew everyone else and being accepted, even in the construction business, depended to a great extent upon your reputation and who would vouch for you. Jack Almand was one of the very first men who would vouch for Jim Walter, and more than that introduce him to his own wide circle of friends.

The houses continued to sell, even though the down payments covered less and less of the building costs. Every Sunday they ran their five-inch classified ad and the customers showed up. By mid-1949 the paperwork overwhelmed Monica Walter's ability to keep up with the company's accounts and Jim hired a young accountant fresh out of Tampa University for part-time bookkeeping. William Kendall Baker, who worked during the week for an accounting firm, came in on weekends to handle the Walter books for $50 a month. Two years later the company's bookkeeping became more than Kendall Baker could manage on a part-time basis, and he was not prepared to leave his more secure job. In need of a full-time accountant, Monica recommended one she knew well—her brother.

Arnold Saraw was delighted by the surprise telephone call from his brother-in-law, whom he had met on only two or three occasions. With a recent degree in accounting from the University of Buffalo, he was earning $55 a week at a felt production machinery company in his hometown of Lockport, near Buffalo.

"I can only offer you $50 a week," Jim said, apologizing. "That'd be just fine," said Arnold without hesitation. The decision for him was easy: He hated the bone-chilling cold and deep freezes of upstate New York, and it was warm and sunny in Florida. The money hardly mattered in his decision to move.

He had some serious misgivings, however, when he first set eyes on the Walter business establishment—the shabby office building with its cheap linoleum on the floor, the threadbare second-hand furniture, the small refrigerator in the bathroom, the ceiling about to fall down in the shack they called Dixie Building Supplies—all of it located on a sandlot out in the middle of nowhere. Arnold Saraw was a sensitive, fastidious young man, accustomed to clean, neat surroundings, and what saddened him most was the sight of long-dead, wilted plants in a window box next to the front entrance of the office building. Nevertheless, he moved right in with the Jim Walter way of life. Monica offered him the tiny spare bedroom in their home in exchange for occasional baby-sitting; Jim drove him to work every morning, and before long he, too, was putting in twelve-hour days.

Bookkeeping was the easiest part of his job. He sold houses, drew up mortgage contracts, and tended store at the Dixie Supplies warehouse. Nor was he above sweeping floors when the dirt, dust, and sand became too much for him to live with. Arnold worked in tandem with Buddy, taking turns in the office to sell homes to customers who dropped in and selling building supplies to customers at Dixie. A thoroughly shy young man, Arnold was no match to Buddy when it came to selling, but he could type and draw up mortgage contracts far better than Buddy could. So they installed a makeshift buzzer system between the office and the warehouse by which either one could summon the other for help in writing a contract or selling a bag of cement.

While doing a little of this and a little of that, Arnold's primary role, aside from bookkeeping, evolved into keeping close tabs on the mortgages on all the houses already sold. The other side of the business, equally important as selling shell homes and taking mortgages on them, was selling those mortgages to outside investors. Every week they ran a five-inch double column advertisement in the real estate section of the local newspaper to sell their houses and, back among the truss and miscellaneous advertisements, they also ran a five-inch single column ad to sell the mortgages. For Jim Walter, if they did not sell enough mortgages they would not have money needed to build the houses they sold on credit. It was as simple as that. The price for a basic house was now $995 and if the lot was worth at least 5 percent of the purchase price, Arnold would give 100 percent financing. At 6 percent per year over the usual four years, total finance charges came to $238. He wrote mortgages with a face value of $1,400 and sold them at a discount to investors for $1,000. When buyers sent in their monthly payments of $29.16, usually in money orders, Arnold would deposit the money in a trust account, and since many investors held a number of mortgages, he would remit a check for the total amount due to each investor, along with an itemized list.

As Jim and Arnold worked it out, it was a good deal for the investor. At 6 percent compound interest, the yield came to 11.8 percent, at a time when savings banks were paying less than 4 percent. When their mortgages became difficult to sell, they sweetened the deal further. Walter guaranteed the mortgage, eliminating the risk. "If the mortgage you buy goes bad for any reason, we'll take it back and replace it with a good one," he told worried investors. After all, they were buying the mortgages on sheer trust. They did not know the home owner to whom they were lending money; they didn't know if he would pay his monthly installment or not. Jim Walter did. He had nothing more to offer them than his word. If they would trust him, he promised, they could not lose. If there turned out to be a bad apple in the barrel, he would eat it.

Usually the mortgages were bought by widows with fixed incomes, sometimes by retirees or working people with small nest eggs to protect, and once they learned how regularly the interest was sent to them, they came back for more. Arnold handled the repeat investors, who usually bought $10,000 to $20,000 worth of mortgages at a time. Jim Walter specialized at bringing in new investors, selling them on the concept of providing new homes to worthy people who were so appreciative of ownership that they were not likely to forfeit the house they themselves helped build. These regular investors were like Broadway angels backing an unknown playwright based primarily on their faith in the talent. They often also became friends. One Tampa bus driver invested enough money long enough to pay for a college education for each of his two sons. A retired jeweler from New York, who peddled jewelry out of his pocket to some of the richest matrons in Tampa, was such a good, steady buyer of mortgages that Arnold continued to sell him mortgages long after his money was needed.

Actually, Walter felt that providing full recourse on bad mortgages was not all that great a risk. They had never foreclosed on a bad mortgage, not yet. The people who bought Jim Walter homes were poor but proud people. Owning your own home had long been a goal in life for the ordinary man.

As their most prized possessions, their homes would be the very last things they would give up.

Buddy Alston liked to use that concept as his main pitch in selling Jim Walter homes. "If you're renting a house or an apartment, what have you got at the end of four years? You got a pile of rent receipts. And what can you do with rent receipts? You can put a match to them, you can warm your hands for maybe five seconds. But you put that same amount of money into one of our homes and at the end of four years, when you've paid off your mortgage, you'll own your own home, and then you've got a piece of equity that you can borrow on for whatever you want." A man did not need a college education to understand those economics.

What's more, when an owner finished his home, putting in electricity, plumbing, walls, and landscaping the grounds, he was increasing the equity in that home, not only by the cost of the materials but by the value of the labor he himself put into that house. Jim Walter called it "sweat equity." This sweat equity, once invested, usually doubled the value of the house. Not all buyers finished their homes right away. Some were too poor to do more than string some wires and bare bulbs. A few lived in the bare houses for weeks, sometimes even for months, until they could save enough money to go on with the finishing. But most buyers did manage somehow to bring in electricity, running water, plumbing, and to complete the kitchen and bathroom. Once the interior walls were put up, they were painted, the windows covered with curtains, the floors covered with carpet or linoleum, and then the work began on landscaping and pretty little gardens. Owning one's first home and making it pretty was an innate matter of self-respect.

Jim Walter called on banks in Florida and beyond state lines, as far away as New York, and tried again and again to sell them on this concept of "sweat equity." He had to fight against an ingrained misconception among bankers that poor people were poor risks. Walter knew instinctively and from experience that it was good business selling small, inexpensive, affordable homes to people who, yes, were poor, but who also were proud and honest and trustworthy. Their mortgages were just as good as mortgages on more expensive houses, he told the bankers, because each buyer's credit rating was carefully checked: The mortgage payment could not exceed 25 percent of the buyer's regular income. Walter explained how his home owners had steady jobs, steady incomes, and in no way, except in dire emergency, would fail to send in their monthly mortgage payments. These people bought all their major purchases on time installments, their automobiles, their furniture, their appliances, and, even if hard times came upon them, which would they give up last? Their furniture, their cars, or their homes? Which was, therefore, the safest installment investment?

But it was a hard sell. Bankers shrugged their shoulders and shook their heads. In their minds, lending money to a new company whose only collateral were mortgages on unfinished homes located in out-of-the-way areas where they could not readily be resold was not on the list of acceptable loans in rule books of staid and traditional banks. It was not that Jim Walter was not persuasive. Some bankers sympathized with his plight, even encouraged him, but banks of that day simply did not speculate with their depositors' funds on untested, high-risk ventures.

Some bankers, while refusing to give him a loan, did agree to buy some Jim Walter mortgages. After all, the mortgages offered an 11.8 percent return. The first and most important one to open his arms to the young Jim Walter was a canny, independent banker named Al Ellis, who had just opened his own little bank in the nearby fishing village of Tarpon Springs. That small Ellis bank would over the next twenty-five years grow into a chain of eighty banks which would make Al Ellis one of the richest men in the United States. The two men were introduced by Jim's father, whose fruit-packing company had banked with the Florida National Bank in Lakeland where Ellis had once worked. Jim explained how his homes were built, how they were sold and financed; he described his home buyers and his careful credit checks, and showed the banker a typical mortgage.

Al Ellis, born and raised in Alabama, had none of the prevailing Southern prejudices of the time, and he immediately grasped the essence and vast potential of what Jim Walter was trying to do.

"Jimmy, the way I see it, you have the same idea in housing that Henry Ford had in automobiles. There's a vast, unsatisfied market for the kind of homes you build. There are so many people who cannot afford anything else, and they're the kind of people who cannot walk into a bank and qualify for a home mortgage." He asked Jim to bring in a written proposal and a financial statement of his net worth.

As sole proprietor of the Walter Construction Company at that time in 1952, Jim Walter had a net worth of $23,000. He proposed selling the banker four-year mortgages, which carried a 6 percent add-on annual carrying charge for a total interest of 24 percent over the four years—and as many as Ellis cared to buy. Moreover, the mortgages were being sold with full recourse: If a mortgage was defaulted, Jim Walter would replace it with a good one.

Ellis began buying Jim Walter mortgages by the tens of thousands of dollars. His only regret, as he would tell people later, was that his position as a banker precluded him from investing directly in Walter's shell home business. He did the next best thing, however. Soon after he tested the worthiness of those mortgages, he formed a separate corporation (the General Discount Corporation) of which he owned 75 percent and bought the mortgages at a discount of $24 (the interest), paying $76 for every $100 face value. Then he turned around and using those mortgages as collateral and with his own good credit rating, borrowed $60 on every $100 in face value at 4 percent interest. Thus, he was collecting almost three times the interest he was paying, with only $16 at risk for every $76 invested.

Jim Walter could not do that himself. He did not have the personal credit rating. But at the time he was happy enough to sell the mortgages which would enable him to build more houses. More important than the mortgages, as it turned out, was the relationship he established with Ellis. The astute and earthy banker, who liked to call himself an old country boy, saw young Walter as "a man with a brilliant mind who seemed just born to be a good businessman." In time, the Ellis bank would extend unsecured lines of credit to Jim Walter in the millions of dollars. And, perhaps more important than that, Al Ellis was always there to put in a good word in the banking community about the reputation of Jim Walter of Tampa.

The struggle for cash never let up. The tenth of the month came up quickly every month. That deadline was sacrosanct for Walter, Alston, and Saraw: All bills had to be paid by the tenth for a 2 percent discount and for establishing their reputation for reliability and integrity in the community.

The crunch came the week before, around the second or third of the month, when they would focus all their attention on selling mortgages until the bills could be paid. The doubt and uncertainty played havoc with their nerves and digestion. The sale of every home went hand-in-hand with the need to sell mortgages. It became more and more painful as time went on and Jim Walter came to realize that not only were they struggling to sell these mortgages, they were giving away almost 12 percent profit at the same time.

In 1952, when the still struggling business began to show a profit, Walter did not hesitate to expand the operation. He built his first branch office in the nearest city of decent size: Orlando. Shell homes ought to sell just as well in Orlando as in Tampa, he figured, and the way to develop the business was to branch out to other Florida cities.

Jim found a builder to serve as his first branch manager, hired the manager's daughter as the bookkeeper/secretary, hired a salesman on a straight $50 a week salary, and a truck driver to run building supplies from Dixie in Tampa to the housing sites. Lumber was bought locally. A small cement-block office building and a model shell home were put up on a rented piece of land, the requisite classified advertisement was placed in the local newspaper, and Jim Walter was in business in Orlando, long before Walt Disney brought Mickey Mouse there. The customers flowed in and within months the operation showed a small, but definite, profit. He had made only one mistake, which was pointed out by an irritable farmer who wanted to buy a cement-block shell home. Buddy Alston, filling in there at the time, explained that they only built wooden shell homes. "Then why in the hell did you make your own building here out of cement block?" asked the farmer. There was no good answer to that, except that they were still learning the business.

On one excursion later in 1952 seeking financing in Ocala, about one hundred miles north of Tampa, the president of the leading bank there offered to buy Jim Walter mortgages, but only if he would build his shell houses there. That would be a service to his community. Otherwise he could not bring himself to support housing for poor people in Tampa. Jim accepted the challenge. Common sense told him that branch operations not only would expand his home building but also his sources for financing them locally.

Early the following year he opened his third, new branch

office in Sarasota, some fifty miles south of Tampa. This time both the display shell home and the office were constructed of wood and this time the inauguration of a new branch of Jim Walter Homes was heralded with full-page ads in the local newspaper. Gradually, the company began to pull ahead. Gross sales for fiscal 1952 reached $653,000, and for the first time showed net profits of $15,751. As a sole proprietor, Jim Walter paid $4,000 in income taxes that year and with the desperate need of cash in the company, he consulted with William Kendall Baker and outside accountants. He had the business acumen to know that he would have to do something about that because 1953 promised to be an even more profitable year. The company had grown too big to continue as a sole proprietorship.

In April 1953, Jim sat down with Buddy Alston and Arnold Saraw in his office and rather shyly expressed his gratitude for the hard work they had put into the company and then surprised them with the announcement, "I think we ought to be partners!"

The transformation could be accomplished by his selling each of them 15 percent of the company. They were surprised, delighted, and grateful, but, of course, they did not have any money with which to buy their shares. Jim knew that. He suggested that it be put on the books as a loan, to be paid back out of future profits. As a partnership, he explained, the company could retain more of its profits for reinvestment than it could before. It was all done so casually in those days that not one of the three close partners could later recall the price of the shares involved or if the loans were ever paid off.

In May 1953, the Walter Construction Company was registered in Florida as a partnership. It was a legal change of identity. Nothing else much changed. The three principals worked on as before—around the clock, and on holidays.

Arnold continued to live with Jim and Monica. Buddy and his new bride, Jackie, continued to join them for their once-a-week dinner and poker at Jim's parents' home. Now that their home building was showing a profit, they did agree to raise their salaries. Jim took Monica on a long-delayed honeymoon, their first vacation since marriage, a trip to Europe on the *Queen Elizabeth,* for which he took out a three-year bank loan rather than pay cash. All around, 1953 was a very good year. Home sales reached $874,665 with net profits of $70,296. That was not in cash, of course, but it did allow the company to begin to build up a mortgage portfolio of its own. Now it earned that 11.8 percent on at least some of its mortgages. Cash flow remained as serious a problem as it was before. The only difference was that with increased sales the outstanding bills grew proportionately larger.

In 1954, in order to formalize the handling of the shell home mortgages, the partnership organized a wholly owned but separate subsidiary. Because of the location of Tampa and for the lack of a better name, they called it Mid-State Investment Corporation, and put Arnold Saraw in charge.

The idea was that Mid-State would handle all the credit managing and mortgages, and if they could build up a large enough portfolio, they could then turn around and borrow money from banks using the mortgages as collateral. Approximately one of every six houses was sold for cash. Most houses were sold for 10 percent cash or land value down, with four-year mortgages on the remainder, carrying a flat 6 percent surcharge of interest per year. Walter insisted that a house was not fully sold until the final payment on it was made. It was an important point well taken, and everyone in the company was indoctrinated with that principle. Until that final payment of cash was made, you only had a piece of paper called a mortgage.

The corollary to that principle was that Jim Walter homes

would be sold only to those with the ability to pay. Credit ratings and credit checks were just as important as making a sale. Foolish to sell a house to a man or woman who did not have a job or some other means to pay for the house. Unfair, too, to the unwary or impetuous buyer. Bad business, too, if you had to foreclose and make good on a bunch of bad mortgages. Better to lose a sale than to make a bad one. That became firm company policy, taught to each and every new salesman hired. Another important decision made at this time was to continue charging a straight 6 percent per annum interest rather than employ the usual type of home mortgage in which most of the interest was paid up front and diminished as the years went on. Common sense told them that if they were greedy for the interest in the first one or two years, they would be paying more taxes on the income. By charging an unchanging amount of principal and interest per year, they ended up retaining more cash in the earlier months and years of the mortgage. And that's what they needed, what they always needed— cash and more cash. Not unlike spotting the classified ad that started the business back in 1946, Jim Walter bumped into what promised to be a solid solution to his cash flow problems at a football game in the fall of 1954. The University of Florida was playing its arch rival, Florida State University, at Gainesville. Attending the big game with Alex Kreher, a salesman in his Orlando branch office, Jim quite by chance met Alex's brother-in-law, Ted Meares, a third-generation native Floridian and a power in Miami real estate.

Meares was well-to-do, well connected, sophisticated, and fun-loving, and he and Jim Walter hit it off immediately. Before halftime festivities were over, Walter was telling Meares all about his shell home business. With pride and rising excitement, Jim gave him the facts and figures on the growth of the company and the one factor inhibiting future growth: cash flow. Meares was entranced. The way to raise cash, he suggested, was not to go begging or borrowing from reluctant banks or penny-pinching widows, but to "go public," to sell stock in the company to the general public. Let the public share in the profits and in the risks, Ted Meares advised, adding that he would be the first willing to invest. Furthermore, he added, he knew a good many wealthy Florida families he believed would be quite willing to invest in a company with that much growth potential. There was no shortage of rich Floridians looking for good investments, he told Walter. Ted Meares suggested that he would be happy to put his new friend in touch with the right man to help him. Now Jim Walter was entranced with the possibilities.

Two weeks later Meares came to Tampa and arranged a luncheon meeting where, he promised, he would introduce Jim to "the only true genius I ever met." At Las Novedades, a favorite restaurant in Tampa's Spanish section of Ybor City, Walter was struck with the extraordinary personality of Karl Kreher, a heavy-set man of German extraction who wore thick, rimless glasses and chain-smoked evil-smelling cigars. Kreher was a stock and bonds salesman in the Tampa office of the New York investment firm of Goodbody & Co.

Kreher listened intently, without interrupting, while the young entrepreneur explained step-by-step the building and financial fundamentals of the Walter Construction Company. He reviewed the company's growth year by year and its need for large sums of money for future expansion. After all, this was not just an idea any more; Jim Walter had been building shell homes for eight years.

When he finished, Jim leaned forward. "What do you think?"

"I think that you will remember this as the most important meeting of your life," the enigmatic Kreher intoned slowly. "I'll have to look into this thoroughly, but if everything backs up what you tell me, I'll underwrite a public offering myself." He paused, puffed vigorously on his cigar, and added, "I'll make you a millionaire."

CHAPTER 3

— *No Bankers for Shell Builders* —

G ENIUS, LIKE BEAUTY, is in the eye of the beholder and whether or not Karl Kreher was a genius is hardly subject to proof, not beyond a reasonable doubt. But those who knew him would agree without argument that Karl Kreher was no ordinary, run-of-the-mill stockbroker earning a living in Tampa, Florida. He lived in a mental and philosophical world of his own and he marched to his own personal drummer. His family was old Tampa, tradition-bound German immigrants who came to the sleepy seaport on the Gulf Coast in 1894 and set up the Tampa Shipbuilding and Engineering Company. Karl was a graduate of Carnegie Tech, but instead of going dutifully into the family shipbuilding business, he followed his fascination into the intricacies and possibilities of finance.

While he earned his living selling stocks and bonds, he spent his nights secretly writing an abstruse philosophical treatise which would explain the intrinsic laws which he believed governed the social sciences. In what he called "A Metaphysical System of Metabolism," he tried to use Aristotelian logic to develop a system of absolute truths that would explain the forces upon society of the metaphysical world, just as metabolic processes regulate the human body. In its economic applications, Kreher was confident that his concept would readily abolish such periodic maladjustments of our society as inflation, recession, and unemployment. That was to be his "masterpiece." For relaxation and as a hobby, he collected and studied all the arcane data he could find on the 19th-century financing of the building of the major railroads across the United States. He obviously knew more on that subject than anyone else in the country knew or cared to know. On the other hand, he often did not know where he had parked his car or whether he had driven to a luncheon meeting or walked. He was known to return to his office from a lunch hour, and not remember whether or not he had eaten. But when he talked of the economy or stocks and bonds, Karl Kreher was brilliant. Right or wrong, he had a faithful following of investors who believed in him.

Solving Jim Walter's financial problems would not be diffi-cult to a man who understood how the great American rail-roads of the 19th century were financed. Or, so Karl Kreher said. Walter's need for an immediate and a continuing flow of investment capital to finance the mortgages behind his shell homes was not unlike the need for the immense capital required to finance the laying of cross-country railroad tracks. Kreher delved deeply into the financial problems and potentials of Jim Walter's company, and with his special brand of brilliance devised an ingenious capitalization plan for the company. He explained it to Jim Walter as a "self-financing four-stage rocket."

Rather than capitalizing the company by simply selling stock or bonds, Kreher devised a plan under which they would offer packages, called "portfolios," of a variety of bonds, stock, and warrants that would allow investors to buy more stocks and bonds. Investors could only buy these port-folios, not individual stocks or bonds. The great advantage to the Walter company was that it would get an immediate infusion of cash, and then, as the company grew more prof-itable, investors would convert their warrants into the higher-priced stock, thereby providing a constant flow of new money. Moreover, the influx of this money would increase the company's capital base, which in turn would enable it to borrow more money from banks. Most banks at that time permitted loans up to two-and-one-half times a company's equity which included its subordinated debt. The great advantage to the investor was the potential for an enormous return on his or her investment as the company grew.

Kreher explained the concept and implications of this "self-financing four-stage rocket" to Jim Walter, and Jim, with an innate grasp of numbers, bought it. He understood and marveled at the design of this financial instrument in which everyone profited. Karl Kreher was every bit as persuasive in his way as Jim Walter was in his own. What Jim Walter did not know, never having dealt with capitalization plans, was just how unique, radical, and bizarre the Kreher plan was.

In a series of organizational meetings through the spring of 1955, Kreher tried different combinations of portfolio ingredients. Five law firms were approached for advice on incorporating the company with the Kreher capitalization plan. Three declared flatly that it could not be done. One expressed doubt and hesitated before venturing an opinion. The fifth came through. Norman Stallings, a partner in the old-line firm of Shackleford, Farrior, Shannon & Stallings, opined, "You can't do it this way, but we can work something out for you."

Stallings trimmed, revised, and modified the capitalization plan, making it legally acceptable to the state of Florida, without changing its efficacy in providing what the new company needed most: a constant flow of new money. Working with Kreher and Walter, the attorney became fascinated and intrigued with the concept and potential of selling shell homes to people. His reward was a seat on the board of directors of the new company. Ted Meares, for his efforts, was offered and accepted membership as a founding director, joining the three officers of the company, President Jim Walter, Secretary Buddy Alston, and Treasurer Arnold Saraw.

They decided to name the new company Jim Walter Corporation. Why? Because the two outside directors pointed out that over the previous nine years "Jim Walter" had earned an unblemished reputation in building some 5,000 homes, that the name now had recognition value that was "too good to throw away."

Karl Kreher, marching to his own drummer, declined a seat on the board of directors, but he quit his job at Goodbody & Co. in order to devote full time to underwriting and selling the "portfolios" of the fledgling company to hearty Floridians willing to take a risk on the future. On July 6, 1955, Kreher hosted a party in the Palm Room of the Tampa Terrace Hotel for prospective investors and handily disposed of his 300 portfolios.

Each portfolio, costing $3,994, consisted of twenty-three high-interest bonds, $50 worth of stock and 800 warrants that allowed the investor to buy more bonds and stock. The portfolio broke down as follows:

Twenty $25 bonds paying 9 percent annual interest	$ 500
Two $1,000 bonds paying 8 percent	2,000
One $1,000 convertible bond at 7 percent	1,000
One hundred shares of common stock at fifty cents each	50
Four hundred A warrants at $1.10 each	440
Four hundred B warrants at one cent each	4
Total	$3,994

Built into each portfolio were some very attractive "rocket" offers, based upon the potential of the company's future growth. The convertible bonds and warrants all could be turned into more 9 percent bonds or stock upon payment of various amounts of money. For instance, if the fifty-cent stock rose above $10 a share, it made financial sense to convert the 7 percent bond. It would cost $1,000 to make the conversion, but you got back 9 percent bonds with a face value of $1,000, plus one hundred shares of stock, at $10 each, worth another $1,000. The point was that if and when the stock rose above $10 a share, the stockholder could get one hundred shares of stock at below the market price, and each conversion, in turn, gave the company (JWC) another $1,000 toward its mortgage fund.

If and when the company's stock price rose above $15 a share, the second "rocket" went off: Then the investor could convert one A warrant, which cost $1.10, and pay $40 to receive one $25 bond yielding 9 percent annual interest plus one share of $15 stock. If and when the fifty-cent stock rose above a market value of $30, the holders of B warrants, which only cost a penny a piece, could put up $80 and get in return two $25, 9 percent bonds and one share of stock.

Only the most sophisticated investors could understand all this. One way to look at this proposition was that in an era long before anyone knew of "junk bonds" you were investing $4,000 to buy $3,500 worth of JWC bonds paying 7, 8, and 9 percent annual interest as opposed to triple A corporate bonds paying at most 6 percent. For the extra $500, you were buying $50 worth of stock and warrants that *could* some day be worth a lot of money. It was for the investor a high-risk investment and, like all such venture investments, it was based largely upon faith and trust that this honest-looking, pleasant, soft-spoken man named Jim Walter could, indeed, as Karl Kreher and Ted Meares promised, rapidly build a successful company selling a new product called shell homes in a new, largely untested market. The sale of three hundred portfolios brought in $1,198,000! Jim Walter was ready to go, to expand, and to build and sell more shell houses throughout Florida.

On August 22, 1955, Norman Stallings filed the papers incorporating Jim Walter Corporation as a Florida public corporation, succeeding the partnership of Walter Construction Company.

The three partners were compensated for their share of partnership assets transferred to the new company, valued at $434,500, with portfolios of their own. In aggregate they received 62,500 shares of common stock, 10,000 A warrants, 240,000 A warrant options convertible at $1.10 each, 250,000 B warrants, and a total of $387,500 in subordinated bonds, all of which was split 70 percent for Jim Walter and 15 percent each for Buddy Alston and Arnold Saraw. It would, in time, make millionaires of them all. Karl Kreher, also a true believer, persuaded his family to buy a good many portfolios and he, borrowing money wherever he could, became before long the second-largest shareholder in the new company.

A heady mixture of high energy and euphoria filled the ramshackle offices of the new Jim Walter Corporation on East Waters Avenue. With $1,200,000 in new capital from the sale of the portfolios, and the expectation of borrowing two-and-a-half times that amount from banks, Jim, Buddy, and Arnold laid plans for immediate expansion. Now, they thought, they could grow big. How big, they did not know. They could expand the existing business in Tampa, Orlando, and Sarasota and open new branches, with the same mode of operation, in Tallahassee, Jacksonville, and in the rural outskirts of any Florida city where people needed inexpensive homes. Nor was there any reason why they could not expand eventually throughout the South. They would need to hire new branch managers, salesmen, construction crews. They would do that. They would need to order new building supplies, build warehouses, find dependable local supplies of lumber, and also set up a foolproof system of credit checks, mortgage contracts, and payment schedules, and, of course, everything had to be done at once. What they had done, and done well, in Tampa, they would do in each and every branch of the expanded operation. They tried to anticipate and plan for the future, based upon their past experiences, but they were sailing out upon uncharted waters.

One of their most significant decisions, based upon intuition more than anything else, was that instead of seeking experienced men for the job openings, they would hire young, inexperienced but eager branch managers, salesmen, credit managers, truck drivers. "I want young men who don't know that what we tell 'em to do can't be done," proclaimed Buddy, who was in charge of construction. Jim and Buddy agreed that the company's best policy would be to share the profits with men who had the guts to work hard and take a risk along with them. They would pay a low living wage, whatever the going rate was for the position, but they would offer a profit-sharing plan in the form of stock and bond warrants. Whoever they hired would have to be willing to take the risk they were taking. If the company made it, an employee could build a nest egg. "For every dollar you make for this company, there's a dime in it for you," prospective employees were told. In return, the employee was expected to give his all to the company, to work his tail off, to do what he had to do to get his job done.

Perhaps it was only natural that Jim Walter and Buddy Alston hired men who were pretty much like themselves: young, navy veterans, blue-collar types with more common sense and hard-knocks experience than formal education, who were still trying to find their niche in the post-war America of the 1950s. There was Tommy Hires, who eked out a living selling baby food, and Bill Robinson, who sold ready-mix cement for "fifty bucks a week and all the cement he could eat," and Norman Ziegler, who tried ranching and rodeos and went broke, and Danny Daniels, a bill collector for Sears, Roebuck, and others. Many of them were old friends who had gone to high school in Tampa together. They were all in their middle or late twenties, healthily endowed with energy and motivation, but not really knowing what they wanted to do. In joining this new Jim Walter Corporation they were betting on their own future.

Thomas L. Hires was typical. A big, muscular man of twenty-five with a soft, gentle voice, he looked like a professional football player, but was a Gerber Baby Foods salesman until Jack Almand of the Booker Supply Company, a boyhood friend, introduced him to Jim and Buddy. They all had a great deal in common—growing up in Florida, service in the navy, an inner sense of integrity and a can-do outlook on life. After a social friendship had evolved, Hires was offered a job as a branch manager of Jim Walter Homes. He had never heard of a shell home nor handled a two-by-four in his life, but he liked Walter and Alston, and he accepted the job in October 1955, two months after the public financing.

Alston gave him a week's on-the-job training and instruction, a bottle of rye whiskey, and a used Chevy and sent him off to take over the Orlando branch office, where the previous manager had just been fired. He was on his own, with considerable autonomy.

As branch manager he was in charge of sales, construction, mortgage contracts, supplies. He had to phone the home office only for credit checks on customers taking out mortgages, and to report in once a week on how he was doing. Hires learned on the job, watching the construction of houses, helping the truck driver on his rounds, and typing and retyping the house contracts and sales reports when he was alone in the office. He already knew how to sell. Within a month, he more than doubled sales in Orlando from three or four a week to eight or nine a week, simply by keeping the office open all day Saturday and from noon to six on Sundays. At the end of his first year, he had sold 460 houses, and found his niche in life.

Danny Daniels, a hell-raiser in the navy who had been at Pearl Harbor when it was attacked, had worked as a bill collector for Sears, Roebuck before joining Jim Walter. As branch manager in Sarasota he was a supersalesman, an ever-happy teller of jokes and tall tales, a nondrinker with one kidney, who earned the distinction of selling forty-five Jim Walter homes in one week, a record. He did it by running a full-page ad on Washington's Birthday, proclaiming:

BRING ME A PICTURE OF GEORGE WASHINGTON AND I'LL BUILD YOU
A HOUSE

It was nothing more than a variation on a nothing-down sale: The house would be yours if you put up a lot, which you owned free and clear, valued at 10 percent of the cost of the house. When other branch managers asked him how he did it, he replied, "Hell, all I did was wash the windows on my model house—you ought to try that sometimes." Actually, Danny Daniels was such an indefatigable salesman that he made his forty-fifth house sale that week to the man pumping gas into his car.

The new branch managers started out with the advantage of the lessons learned over the past eight or nine years by Walter and Alston. They now had five different models of shell homes to sell, from the original one-bedroom home to two- and three-bedroom models, ranging in price from $995 to $2,395. But the company's overall policy was exactly as it had been before: They were in it for the long run. They were not there for any short-term advantage over their suppliers, their construction crews, or their customers. A good deal in this company meant that everyone had to be happy with it. The customer, especially, was to be put on a pedestal, catered to, and made to feel that he was getting a fair shake. Branch managers were warned against selling more house than a customer could afford. Credit checks had to be stringent. There was no point in selling a house to someone who could not pay for it. Equally important was that the buyer be satisfied with the house he had bought. Word of mouth sold houses as much as advertising, and every buyer probably had a brother, sister, or cousin who was also a potential customer. To make sure a customer was satisfied, the branch manager himself had go to the house and collect the first mortgage payment, and he had to ask if the new owner had any complaints. If anything was wrong, it was to be fixed. If there were no complaints, the manager handed the new homeowner his Jim Walter mortgage payment book and had him or his wife sign a statement of satisfaction. This policy would later be perfected so that new home owners would be given postcards and "invited" to mail in any complaints to the home office. The company even went so far as to offer seven gallons of free paint if an owner would agree to repaint the outside of an aged Jim Walter home that needed it. Jim Walter wanted satisfied customers: They would help him sell more houses.

Alston instilled in each branch manager his own nononsense philosophy of business. "People try to complicate things in business when they are not complicated," he would say. "In any business, you have a product that people want; you produce the product and then you service the product, and you give them a dollar's worth of product for every dollar they spend. You've got to feel within yourself that you are accomplishing something. If you don't, there's no way you can be successful in this business. And that's the way it is and will always be with our Jim Walter homes."

Business boomed! In early September, a bare two weeks after going public, they opened a new branch operation in Tallahassee, the state capital, just in time to catch the Labor Day crowds. It rained that day and all that week, but the customers came by the thousands to see what kind of one-bedroom home they possibly could buy for $995 or three-bedroom house for $2,395. As it had been from the very beginning, working people wanted a home of their own to live in, and they were willing and able to finish the house themselves to get what they wanted at a price they could afford. That first week JWC sold five houses in Tallahassee, and twenty-three throughout the state. In October they opened a model home, sales office, and warehouse in Jacksonville on the east coast of Florida.

Then in November they acquired a site and began building two model houses and an office structure in Macon, Georgia, just over the Florida border, their eighth location. Dothan, Alabama, was chosen as the next location for Jim Walter Homes, which would make the corporation a three-state operation at the start of 1956. Jim Walter was the driving force. He wanted to spread out from city to city, pursuing the demand for inexpensive housing. It seemed plain to him that the more he expanded his operations, the more money the company would make.

Beyond their fondest expectations, business continued to prosper. By the end of November, completing their third month of operations, they were selling an average of forty shell homes a week, double the sales of the previous August. Revenues were up, earnings were up, interest on the corporate bonds was paid, a monthly dividend of ten cents a share was declared, and, best of all, thanks to the new financing, the company now was able to hold on to home mortgages in excess of $1 million, earning 6 percent a year.

The troublesome thorn in this rosy picture was that their bold expansion plans gobbled up money voraciously, their burgeoning mortgage portfolio was all deferred income, and once again they found themselves running out of cash. It was the same old story: The more houses they sold and the more mortgages they kept, the closer to the brink of bankruptcy they ran. Their expectations of borrowing against company assets hit the proverbial brick wall of traditional banking. Jim Walter traveled far and wide visiting financial institutions throughout Florida and in New York and Chicago, and each time he got in to make a half-hour pitch for money, he spent twenty-five minutes answering questions about his company's self-financing capitalization plan. It was so complicated that most bankers and securities analysts simply could not understand how it could or would work. They could not believe the company could grow at the rate predicted. Several analysts voiced the suspicion that for the A and B warrants to be worth anything, as one put it, "the conversion points (of $10, $40, and $80) have been set percentagewise so astronomically high that the corporation is discounting not only just the remote future but veritably the hereafter!" Brilliant as it may have been and premature for its time, Karl Kreher's capitalization plan became a headache and heartache for Jim Walter. Little did the skeptics know what a $4,000 portfolio would be worth in years to come.

Nor did bankers give any credence to Walter's rosy prediction that his company was capable of selling one hundred or more houses per week. They accused him, as one put it, "of reaching for the moon and gazing at the stars." They thought the company would go bust. Politely and impolitely, they turned him down. None were interested in lending money on the collateral of mortgages held by poor people in rural and remote locations. They were not a good risk, said the bankers again and again; how in the world could any bank follow up on such mortgages if Jim Walter did go bust, and what value would such houses have in the event of foreclosure? It was a bitter and frustrating experience for an eager entrepreneur still in his twenties who just *knew* he had a winning concept in shell homes and was not able to sell it to the financial world. He realized that he was frequently looked down upon as a country bumpkin from Tampa by the city men in their three-piece suits, but that, too, was a keen learning experience that would one day pay dividends.

To make matters worse, a worrisome flaw that everyone had apparently missed was discovered in Kreher's plan: The warrants did not have to be converted into stock until the year 2001. That meant that the owners could convert them at any time forty-six years into the future, while the company could not redeem them until 1961. Consequently, in those first few years many of the warrant owners chose to hold on to them in anticipation of a higher stock price. As a result, the much-anticipated flow of conversion money was erratic. And that in turn meant that the company could not plan to spend what it did not have: cash.

In the seemingly never-ending search for cash, the indefatigable Walter came upon an article in a financial journal describing how the risk-conscious Walter E. Heller & Company of Chicago had made a fortune extending credit in places where banks feared to tread. That was his kind of company. He sat down and wrote the credit company a long, persuasive letter, describing in great detail his situation and his desire to borrow $1 million with his mortgages as collateral. Back came the hoped-for reply: "Come up to see us and bring a sample of your paper."

Jim prepared for that meeting as though the life of his company depended upon it, and perhaps it did. He learned that the Heller company charged 10 percent interest on its high-risk loans, but he thought he could live with that. The most perplexing question was: How many of his mortgages should he take with him as "a sample" of his collateral?

After much thought and many consultations, Jim decided to take all of them. The night before he left for Chicago, a small staff stayed late to copy the hundreds of account cards in the entire mortgage portfolio. The next day he was ushered into the large, plush office of the executive vice president of the Heller company, carrying in each hand a large cardboard carton, tied with rope. "I thought you might like to see *all* our mortgages, because I didn't want you to think that maybe I only picked out the good ones." The crux of his presentation, he knew, would be to convince the credit company that the people who bought his shell homes, mortgaged their land, and invested their "sweat equity" were not only good but excellent credit risks.

Harry Abrahams, who at age sixty had been with Heller for thirty-five years at that time, took an almost instant liking to this young, sincere man. Why? Having seen many loan applicants over the years, he was impressed with the straightforward, no-nonsense honesty of the man. Unlike so many others, Jim Walter did not beg or boast or make promises. Although the shell home business which Jim explained in detail was new and intriguing, Abrahams believed in lending money on the basis of the trust and integrity of the borrower more than on the potential bottom line. That did not stop him from sending a team of investigators into Tampa to check on Jim Walter's operating procedures, to interview home buyers, and to take a close look at the quality of the home construction.

The reports back to Abrahams were glowing with unexpected praise. The Heller people were impressed with the close supervision of construction, prompt fielding of complaints, and the honest effort to see that buyers got what they paid for. Heller's investigators also gave high marks to the management of the mortgage collections, saying that Jim Walter Corporation was operating like a small lending institution of its own. Harry Abrahams approved a loan of $1 million at 10 percent. When that $1 million was immediately used up, Jim Walter asked him for another $500,000.

Before the loan was finally approved, however, Abrahams caught hell from his boss. Walter Heller returned from an extended Christmas vacation in Europe, took one look at the proposed loan, and exclaimed, "What kind of nonsense is this?" The autocratic Heller questioned Abrahams closely on the large, unusual loan to an unheard of, off-beat business in Tampa. "We don't want that kind of business," he declared. "I want you to get rid of this."

"I've given the man my word," Abrahams retorted. "I've already promised him one million, and I'm ready to give him a half a million more. I'm well within my authority as executive vice president, you know. So, if you really want to get rid of this loan, you'll have to get rid of me, too."

Walter Heller approved both loans and, like Abrahams, became one of Jim Walter's close personal friends and staunchest backers down through the years. In time, he would propose merging their two companies, which Jim Walter declined, and then he invited him to join the Heller company's board of directors, which Jim Walter accepted.

With the new $1 million line of credit from Walter Heller, and another $500,000 promised, Jim and Buddy plunged ahead with their month-by-month expansion, opening new branch operations in Pensacola, Panama City, and Fort Myers in Florida; Mobile and Birmingham in Alabama; and Albany and Atlanta in Georgia. The procedure was simple and inexpensive: Put up one or two model homes next to a small office building, and, if necessary, a warehouse for needed building supplies. Run a full-page ad in the local paper announcing the opening, staff the new branch office with managers from other divisions, and then wait for the rush of new customers.

When they opened in Pensacola in March of 1956, they advertised:

JIM WALTER CORPORATION

WORLD'S LARGEST BUILDER OF SHELL HOMES

COMES TO PENSACOLA

Not only was JWC the largest builder of shell homes anywhere, they were the *only* corporation in this brand-new, untried field. Their only competition came from scattered individual builders working by themselves, including some who had learned the business working for JWC. Home sales went up proportionately week by week: thirty a week in December, fifty in January, sixty in February, seventy in March, and in June they broke the magic number—one hundred houses sold every week of the month! They were on their way.

In June 1956, they took another giant step in expansion and integration of operations: They started their own insurance agency, called Best Insurors, as a wholly owned subsidiary, to handle all the fire and title insurance required on JWC homes. The agency was the forerunner of their own insurance company which they set up to underwrite all the insurance needs of a JWC home owner. Why give that money to someone else? Now Jim Walter Corporation could advertise itself as "the Pioneer and Largest Designer, Seller, Supplier, Builder, Insurer, Guarantor, and Financier of Shell Homes in the World!"

Open communications was an integral and essential element of their early success, a policy initiated from common sense which continued through the years. Jim Walter, knowing that they would be moving very fast, started from the very beginning sending progress reports every month to the company's stockholders. With confidence that he would succeed, he wanted to keep the stockholder informed frequently rather than on the usual quarterly schedule. They were folksy newsletters, full of facts, telling shareholders the latest:

PROGRESS REPORT, February 11, 1956:

National figures for the month of December showed a more than seasonal decline in home building. However, we just completed another record breaking month for January even better than our BLOCKBUSTER month of November. Our volume per week was unusually steady, exceeding forty houses per week for the month of January.

Many of our Stock Holders visited our Model Home Exhibit at the Florida Fair. We exhibited our "Capri" model which was especially erected right on the fairgrounds full size complete just as we always sell them. We received lots of direct orders and down payments for homes right at the fair, enough to pay for our exhibit many times. One man was so impressed he insisted on paying cash for the "Capri" we had on exhibit so we could move it out of the fair intact directly on his lot on an "As Is" basis. Moving it is far cheaper than tearing it down and besides, we made a nice profit on the house.

PROGRESS REPORT, July 10, 1956:

. . . June was in a class all by itself. It was an EARTH-QUAKER! We averaged 107 houses per week or one house every 22 minutes for the entire month. At that rate and building three in every block we could build a row of houses from Tampa to Jacksonville in one year.

PROGRESS REPORT, August 11, 1956:

During July we paid out our monthly Bond Interest and our 10th consecutive regular monthly dividend of 10c per share.

The month of July, just completed, was another GREAT month for Jim Walter Corporation. With the exception of June which was in a class all by itself, we ROCKED AND ROLLED over every previous record month we had ever established, selling on average 80 houses per week. On the construction front we did even better. We actually built and completed more homes during the July month than any month on record—even more than during the fabulous month of June. Results so far for August indicate we will close our first fiscal year to end 8/31/56 with another GREAT month.

We note with pleasure—TAMPA, which was pretty much of a laggard in June, perked up to good SOLID business during July—ATLANTA, which has been steering a course steady as the Rock of Gibraltar for each of the six weeks since it opened, suddenly burst out with a SMASH week in the seventh.

—VERO BEACH, which didn't even get out of the box in the previous week, suddenly got off to a FLYING START last week.

—AVON PARK, which has been sitting back with the boys, all at once CLOBBERED its way up to a place with the MEN during July.

—MACON, the mighty battering ram from Georgia and from which we felt nothing but EARTH TREMORS during June rested on its laurels during July, but it had plenty of LAURELS on which to rest.

—JACKSONVILLE, which set the woods on fire during June, kept them going FULL BLAST in July; seemingly you just can't burn up the whole of Duval County in one month.

—The reason we do not mention spots like OR-LANDO, which did a BANG-UP JOB last month, is that ORLANDO always does a bang-up job.

—Last but not least, DOTHAN, which we had almost forgotten was still in the league, during July had a WHALE of a month all month.

That August report, coming at the end of the company's first fiscal year, paid tribute in its way to the keen competition among all the branch offices, and particularly the branch managers, to be best in selling and constructing Jim Walter homes. That competitive spirit was honed to a fine edge by Buddy Alston, who was brilliant in his leadership. For instance, Buddy installed teletype machines linking all branch offices to the home office in Tampa. At first, the teletypes were used simply to save money on the telephone bills. But then Buddy inaugurated his unique Saturday morning teletype conferences, which have remained a tradition in the company to this day, even though computers have now replaced the old teletype machines. On each and every Saturday morning, without fail, all branch managers were required to be at their teletype machines to report the number of houses sold, houses under construction, houses completed, weather reports, crowds, and other details of the business for the previous week. Each branch manager could see instantly what the other fellows had done that week. Buddy would comment on each report, congratulating those who had done well or implanting barbs of caustic comment to the laggards. There was no place to hide. Alston cleverly played on each man's sense of pride and fostered personal rivalries so that branch managers would look forward to a Saturday morning teletype conference to find out if Danny Daniels in Sarasota or Tommy Hires in Orlando had sold more houses that week. The teletype conference calls came to be seen as Buddy Alston's special psychological weapon that he wielded like the toughest football coach. The branch managers came to realize what he was doing, but they could not help but play along. They *had* to compete for Buddy's weekly prize of a box of cigars or a bottle of whiskey, and his acknowledgment of who was the number one branch in the company.

By the end of its first full year of operation, Jim Walter Corporation had expanded phenomenally. It had twenty-six branch operations in Florida, Georgia, and Alabama. It had plans for twenty additional branches in Mississippi, Louisiana, and eastern Texas. The company was building and selling shell homes at the rate of more than five thousand a year. Business volume from the first to the fourth quarter of that year quadrupled. Total sales revenues topped $10 million. Net earnings topped $1 million. Such growth would have been unbelievable at the beginning of the year. In fact, the banks and power structure of Tampa were somewhat startled to learn that the little-noticed Jim Walter Corporation, located near the dog track on the wrong side of town, was the first company in Tampa to earn more than $1 million in net operating income in one year, and, at that, its first year.

The first annual shareholders meeting of Jim Walter Corporation was held on Saturday night, October 6, 1956, in the Palm Room of the Temple Terrace Hotel. The five directors of the company were duly reelected for the ensuing year, and that took care of the business at hand. All the rest was a gala celebration and extravagant party expressing the company's gratitude and appreciation for all the efforts of so many people over the past year. Nor did it start and stop that Saturday night. Jim Walter loved a good party in which people from different spheres of the company's activities could meet socially and get to know one another. That first annual meeting, setting another tradition, started Thursday night and ended Sunday morning. The company's charter stockholders turned out en masse, 110 out of a total list of 122 stockholders. Wives and husbands were invited, too; and the branch managers and home office staff; and the suppliers; and, most particularly, the bankers who had extended credit or were contemplating extending credit, and even some who were not. What did all these people have in common to talk about? As Jim Walter so shrewdly anticipated, they talked about the company's great financial first year and its bright prospects for the year and years ahead.

CHAPTER 4

— *Building Credit* —

T HE FLEDGLING JIM WALTER Corporation wasted no
time in moving to the right side of the tracks in
Tampa. One year after incorporation, ground was
broken on North Dale Mabry Highway, a major north-south
thoroughfare on the west side of town, for a new, two-story
headquarters building costing $350,000.

With considerable foresight, while still in a partnership,
Jim Walter and Buddy Alston had personally bought a twelve-
acre parcel on North Dale Mabry on the hunch that Tampa's
business district would expand there eventually. When the
company had outgrown its ramshackle offices on Waters Avenue, Walter and Alston sold 25 percent of the property, with
50 percent of the frontage, to the corporation at cost. With
the usual shortage of cash, they had to mortgage the land
heavily, so the transfer essentially took place on paper.

The new, modern glass and stone building, no matter how
heavily mortgaged, was a pure joy to the thirty-eight young
men and women who had moved away from Waters. Now
they could spread out in the 16,000-square-foot working
quarters that looked and felt like an office building. To be
sure, Jim Walter Corporation building stood alone on a
vast expanse of vacant lots and it would be years before
Tampa would catch up with forecasts. But in time the city's
major interstate highway would cross in front of the building, the new Tampa Stadium would be erected on North
Dale Mabry, and the city's new principal business section

would extend to within ten blocks of the company's head-quarters. Most important, the new site would amply support the future growth of the company. As Jim Walter Corpora-tion grew and expanded, it would build first one eight-story tower and then a second eight-story tower behind the origi-nal structure. What the company was trying to say to all who would heed it was that it was here in Tampa to stay.

Inside the new building with its new, simple office furni-ture, Jim Walter Corporation was still an informal, shirt-sleeve operation. Executives had their own private offices, but they kept their doors open. Communications were eye-ball to eyeball. If you had something to say to someone, you walked over to his office and said it. Writing memos seemed silly and a stupid waste of time in this closely knit commu-nity. Office workers had their own desks and space around them, yet they enjoyed a sense of equality in trying to get things done and done right. Everyone pitched in. They con-sidered themselves charter members of this new, vibrant en-terprise which built homes for people who needed them. Everyone was on a first-name basis. The work atmosphere was friendly but frenetic. With more work to be done than daylight hours could accommodate, when necessary, they worked nights and some holidays, too.

Bud Alston ran the home-building operation from the first floor. Now he had two telephones on his desk and two tele-type machines outside his office, and a calm and efficient secretary, Daisy Collins, who was invaluable as a buffer when his zeal for speed and perfection was thwarted by the less than perfect world outside.

Arnold Saraw, with his growing staff of young women who handled the ever-growing stockpile of mortgages and credit reports, occupied most of the second floor, along with the accounting department, headed by William Kendall Baker, and a small, diligent group of people, headed by Joe Kelly who checked the credit ratings of each and every customer signing up for a mortgage on a Jim Walter home.

Jim Walter occupied a corner office on the first floor, but he was out traveling more than half the time, for days and weeks on end, searching everywhere for the hard cash needed to keep the home building going. From the very start the company seemed to be on the threshold of success. Morale was high, customers were flocking in, and they were not just looking—they were buying Jim Walter houses. Every new branch was a thriving financial success in three to six months after its start-up date.

And yet behind the spectacular sales figures was the daunting realization that this was still a company that was devouring itself. Month by month, they were living hand-to-mouth, ever short of cash. The lack of ready capital imposed a restraint upon their optimistic expansion plans. They really did not want to slow down. Every impulse told them to charge ahead. Every operation of the company was profitable and successful and there were many more people out there who wanted to buy a Jim Walter home. No one had any idea of the heights their further expansion might take them. But, with all his optimism and self-confidence, Jim Walter was still a realist. In dealing with money matters, he exercised caution. It was the part of him that was not by nature impulsive. In this instance, he decided on a balancing act: Expand and grow, but not too fast. It was indeed a very good lesson to be learned early on. He feared his company would suffer the fate of overeager companies trying to expand beyond their financial blood supply and go belly up for the lack of cash. It made no sense to him for JWC to open a new branch in Montgomery, Alabama, until the company found cash to support the mortgages on houses sold there. So of necessity the decision was made: Slow down on opening new branches but do not handcuff your existing branches and risk losing the all-important gung-ho spirit and momentum of the company.

As time went on, it became clear that the future success of the company depended on finding some better way of financing the mortgage portfolio so that they could fill the seemingly unlimited market demand for their shell houses. Jim had already scoured almost every banking source in the country. In the financial section of lower Manhattan in New York City, he walked the streets and dropped in on banks cold, without appointments, and made his pitch. He visited one Chase Manhattan branch so often that the loan officer there wondered aloud, "Tell me, Jim, are you picking up your mail at this bank?"

Jim Walter persisted, pleaded his cause, and perfected his sales pitch. He visited bank after bank, saying the same things over and over again: His company now had ten years of experience in selling custom-built, not prefabricated, one- and two-bedroom homes at a price people could afford. Unlike an automobile bought on credit that decreases in value over the years, a Jim Walter home, finished and improved by the owner, increases in value. If foreclosure was necessary, his company had always made a profit on reselling the house. But foreclosures were rare because the company was stringent on checking the credit and ability to pay of its buyers, screening out irresponsible buyers who might be attracted by price alone. Contrary to popular opinion, mortgages were given to qualified buyers with higher-than-average incomes who already owned a building site free and clear.

"Our profits are free and clear and our books are open to your inspection," Walter would say. "We now sell more than a hundred houses a week! The demand for low-cost housing is so great that we've been growing well over 50 percent a year. What we have here is a largely untapped market for low-cost housing. With proper financing to support our mortgage portfolio, we could double or more than double our growth and profits in the years to come."

He could reel off all the facts and figures relating to his company, his product, his market, his financing, his good credit rating. He knew every wrinkle in the cloth. After all, he had grown up with all of that since leaving the navy. He knew every man and woman working for the company, every sales branch, every model home, every bit of financial data. There was no question a banker could pose that he could not readily answer. When he caught a glimmer of interest, he would invite the banker to Tampa to see the company in operation. "Isn't it worth a trip?" he would say, "I'll be happy to give you your plane ticket, if you'll come down and look us over. Just do that before you make a decision."

The toughest part of his sales job was to persuade a banker to take that first step, to make the trip to Tampa, Florida, to see Jim Walter Corporation in action. Once seen, more than half the job was done. Most of the bankers who made the trip made the loan, even if only against the collateral of home mortgages, and then only at a discount, usually sixty cents on the dollar. That amounted to a loan of $600 for every $1,000 in mortgages held in escrow for the lender. With that kind of mortgage loan, even now in million-dollar denominations, it was just as difficult to get ahead as it had been selling $1,000 mortgages through the back-page ads.

What Jim Walter really wanted was an unsecured line of credit, backed by his company's assets, experience, and future potential, a line of credit that would expand as his company grew and proved its creditability. That's the business banks were supposed to be in. But what the staid and cautious banks saw before them was an eager, young man in his early thirties in a store-bought suit and new haircut from some vague city in Florida selling ridiculously cheap houses to poor people whom the bankers considered poor credit risks. It was just too hard for them to believe and not the sort of thing that city banks loaned money on. Of what value was an unfinished house as collateral to a bank? Besides, if the government's Federal Housing Authority (FHA) and the Veteran's Administration (VA) would not back unfinished houses, why should private banks take that risk by themselves?

Shell homes with their built-in "sweat equity" were an entirely new concept, a new product with an appeal to a new type of home buyer, and while the business world extols innovation and pays it full lip service, very few bankers or businessmen are willing to be first in risking hard-earned cash on something new and unproven. Jim Walter was hardly surprised the thousand or so times he had heard the line: "Sorry, no, but thank you for coming in."

Another man might have given up and rested contentedly with the existing size and scope of his company. But Jim Walter looked upon his financial situation as a kind of puzzle to be solved: How to get that first olive out of the tightly packed bottle? Banks obviously had plenty of money to lend, and JWC could build all the shell houses that its customers clamored for, if only it could get the needed bank financing. Karl Kreher's capitalization plan, as ingenious as it had been, had not made the company truly public. It had signed up 122 stockholders and raised over one million dollars, but that had not been enough, obviously, to convince the nation's bankers of the intrinsic value of the company. What to do?

Jim Walter kept knocking on doors, making inquiries everywhere, and when it came, the answer he sought was simple, quick, unexpected, like the experience of the tired and overworked scientist who stumbles by pure chance on a new drug or cure. At a casual lunch one day in early 1957 with Karl Kreher and Barney Prescott, Kreher's fellow stock sales-

man in Tampa, Jim was pouring out his woes in finding some
new way to finance all the homes the company could sell and
build. The company was operating at its financial maximum—about 650 shell houses a month. One month they
had topped seven hundred homes and they had to cut back.
They simply did not have the cash to finance more houses
and grow. And he did not want to cut back. That would be a
slow death. Any ideas?

Barney Prescott, a mild-mannered, easygoing man, offered
a suggestion almost meekly. "Why don't you call or go see my
brother Ned? He's an investment banker in Cleveland, but
he knows the Florida terrain pretty well because he has a winter home down here in Daytona Beach. He always has lots of
good ideas, and he just might be able to help you."

Edward P. Prescott turned out to be the biggest investment
banker in Cleveland, head of Prescott & Company, and a
man nationally known for his acumen and integrity. Jim Walter did not wait for Ned Prescott to come down to Florida;
he phoned him and flew up to Cleveland before the week
ended. In his usual straightforward fashion, Jim laid out all
the facts and figures of his young company, its past history,
its future potential, and its need for long-term financing to
support its mortgage portfolio. Unlike other bankers,
Prescott listened and asked for *more* information. He was positively intrigued with shell homes. The facts and figures recited by Jim Walter were the same, but investment bankers
are a different financial breed from bankers who work in
banks. Listening with a different ear, they seek out the
young, vital companies with great earning and growth potential. They don't invest their own money. No, investment
bankers earn their living and reputation by finding and
putting together those who need capital with those who have
the capital and need a place to put it profitably. JWC fit the
mold.

Prescott put the young man from Tampa at ease, and before the end of their first day together the two men were on a first-name basis. They talked for hours that first day, and Jim stayed on in Cleveland for the better part of a week. Almost from the very start, Prescott intimated that he thought he could help Jim Walter solve his cash flow problem.

He explained that he and John Loeb, the head of the prestigious investment banking firm of Carl M. Loeb, Rhoades & Company in New York, had recently helped a Cleveland man named Ernest P. Knapp sell off all the assets of his company, Ferro Machine & Foundry. Ferro now was nothing more than the shell of a company, 51 percent of which was owned by Knapp, and the other 49 percent owned equally by Ned Prescott and John Loeb. Ernie Knapp now was a rich man. Prescott thought Knapp, who was very well connected with the banks of Cleveland, would be interested in getting involved in this business opportunity. Knapp could afford to invest heavily in JWC and also arrange for substantial lines of credit from Cleveland banks. The second piece of advice offered was to explore the possibility of taking the company public nationally, with a new bond issue and an offering of the sale of company stock. This offering could be done through Prescott's firm in Cleveland and John Loeb's company in New York, and that would establish the true market value of JWC stock in the eyes of the financial community. If JWC grew and expanded as rapidly as expected, the company should have no trouble attracting investors, and with the shareholders establishing the stock price of the company, JWC should then be able to qualify for bank loans based upon its assets and stock price value.

Jim Walter realized in his gut that he stood now on the threshold of a new, wider world of finance. As Prescott explained details, Jim nodded in agreement. His company would have to "pay" for these two courses of action; it would be expensive, but then risk capital is never cheap. Throughout the world money is an expensive commodity, especially when you really need it. Jim already knew that.

Over the next few weeks, with the introduction and intercession of Ned Prescott, Jim met with Ernie Knapp in Cleveland and with John Loeb on Wall Street. Knapp was a self-made man, much like Jim Walter, only older and more experienced. His success and wealth were not worn on his sleeve. A stable, solid Midwesterner, he put on no airs of superiority and offered solid advice only when his advice was sought. His interest in Jim Walter's business was genuine and only because the two men took to each other easily were they able to advance to the next stage of their proposed merger.

John L. Loeb, to all outward appearances, clearly belonged to a special species of man. Tall, thin, austere, almost glacial, impeccably attired in a Saville Row suit, starched white shirt, and dark silk necktie, John Loeb was regarded far and wide as "the aristocrat of autocrats." Powerful men who had difficulty getting to know him well held him in awe.

He was the dominant head of the prestigious firm he had founded with his father in 1931 to take care of their own investments in the depths of the Great Depression, and it had grown into one of the most powerful and respected investment banking firms on Wall Street. Its twenty-three partners, all chosen by John Loeb, sat on boards of more than sixty large and medium-sized corporations. The firm held memberships on seventeen securities and commodities exchanges and served as a clearinghouse for twenty-two correspondent brokerage and investment firms operating in 140 cities in the United States and Canada, of which Prescott & Company was one. It underwrote new issues, managed investment funds, and maintained its own venture capital portfolio in the hundreds of millions of dollars. In years to come, Loeb Rhoades would eventually merge and become part of one of Wall Street's giant investment banking firms, Shearson Lehman Hutton.

As Jim Walter described the struggles and achievements of his company since the day he saw that classified ad and bought that first shell home for $895, John Loeb focused his attention as much upon the manner as on the words of the man from Florida. Facts and figures were easy to follow and to verify, but this astute New York financier also could grasp what came through between the lines: the integrity, keen mind, enthusiasm, good humor, and solid, no-nonsense personality of the man telling the story. That counted for a great deal. Wall Street invested as much in the man proposing a deal as in the deal itself, and John Loeb was deeply impressed with what he called "the innate ability" of the young man from Tampa. Innate ability is next to impossible to discern or describe or guarantee, certainly not on short notice, but judgment and experience indicates whether it is there or not. In Jim Walter, John Loeb discovered a man who had worked hard, thoroughly understood his own business and its financial underpinnings, and had demonstrated the courage to take risks and grasp opportunities. This was a man to invest in, a winner; besides, the financier concluded that the shell home business had the potential for rapid growth and huge profits.

In shaking hands with Jim Walter on a public offering of JWC stocks and bonds, John Loeb was essentially putting his own personal seal of approval upon Jim Walter Corporation. Wall Street would take notice.

The deal with Ferro and Knapp, once the details were worked out in mid-December 1956, was almost as complicated as Karl Kreher's original capitalization of the company. In essence, Ferro guaranteed to secure for JWC lines of credit from Cleveland banks at one point above the prime rate of interest in the amount of $6 million! In return for arranging such financing, Ferro wanted to buy from the major stockholders—Walter, Alston, and Saraw—stocks and warrants which, if fully exercised, would give Ferro ownership of fully 20 percent of the company—at the original cost!

Was it worth 20 percent of the company to secure $6 million in bank loans? That was the $6 million question. The details of the deal were what made it complicated. Ferro was getting in return not so much stock as A and B warrants which allowed him to convert the warrants only at the expenditure of a considerable amount of money. Basically, Ferro agreed to lend JWC an immediate $650,000 as an advance on the $6 million bank credit, which had to be made available by the end of the fiscal year in August 1957, and to pay Walter, Alston, and Saraw $300,000 for 20,000 shares of their stock, plus $1,000 for 100,000 A warrant options and $1,000 for 100,000 B warrants.

The warrants had a special destiny. Ferro was to exercise 15,000 of the A warrant options and their underlying warrants immediately, paying JWC $615,000 for the conversion. This would result in JWC issuing Ferro 15,000 of its $25 bonds at 9 percent interest and 15,000 additional shares of stock at $15 a share, which was half their current value. The remaining 85,000 A warrant options and the one hundred B warrants, as protection for all of them, would go into a joint trust account along with all the options and warrants owned by Walter, Alston, and Saraw. No one could exercise any of these warrants without the consent of all the others. Thus, Jim, Buddy, and Arnold were not in any danger of losing ownership or control of their company.

The Ferro offer was argued up and down and sideways at an all-day meeting of the board of directors, attended by Karl Kreher as a major stockholder. The cigar smoke was so thick none of them could see across the room. Kreher and Ted Meares were vehemently opposed to the deal. They thought

Jim was being too "soft hearted" and giving away too much of the company in return for a mere loan. They argued the company would be better off struggling along without paying that high a price for the infusion of needed capital.

Jim's line of reasoning was that without the needed $6 million in lines of credit, the company might never get off the ground to a point where all the warrants and options of the company would be worth anything at all. In order to fire the next stage of Karl Kreher's four-stage rocket, they had to pay the going price for venture capital. Jim believed it was a fair deal all around. Furthermore, he pointed out, it was his and Buddy's and Arnold's holdings in the company that were being sold. There was no need to be greedy. If JWC was to become the success they all hoped for, everyone would make enough money to keep him and his family happy for a lifetime. It was time to move into a bigger, more substantial pond. Buddy Alston and Arnold Saraw, the cofounders of the company agreed. The motion carried. In exchange for JWC stock, bonds, and warrants worth, when fully exercised, 20 percent of the company, Ferro Machine & Foundry (owned by Knapp, Prescott, and John Loeb) agreed to secure for Jim Walter Corporation $6 million in lines of credit before the end of fiscal year, August 30, 1957. Ernie Knapp was elected to the JWC board of directors.

The next part of the financial restructuring was every bit as important. Ned Prescott and John Loeb agreed to underwrite a public offering of $2,750,000 JWC stocks and bonds created by the conversion of 100,000 A warrant options and 100,000 B warrants out of the trust account. Their firms in Cleveland and New York would buy the stocks and bonds and sell them on the open market to the public. Not only would that raise almost $3 million for JWC, it would also make the company truly public. Its stocks and bonds would be traded nationally on the over-the-counter market in New York on a day-to-day basis. Its stock price would now truly reflect the public's assessment of the company's market value and future potential. That in turn would help JWC secure bank financing at a reasonable rate of interest.

However, before the company could be listed on those regional "pink sheets" used by the over-the-counter traders, it would have to satisfy the registration requirements of the Securities and Exchange Commission in Washington. What should have been a small, routine registration turned into an ulcer-creating, frustrating miasma of bureaucratic red tape.

With the responsibility of protecting the public from misleading or fraudulent stock offerings, the SEC demands full disclosure of all pertinent facts concerning a company desiring to offer its stocks or bonds to the public, and in this instance, the SEC knew nothing about the product called shell homes and even less about a company called Jim Walter Corporation. Norman Stallings, acting as the company counsel, filed the necessary legal papers, disclosing the company's business history, capitalization, financial condition, officers and directors, et al. Three weeks later, on August 14, 1957, the SEC replied with fourteen chilling pages of questions and requests for technical changes in the submissions. Some of it was nit-picking of high order, such as a twenty-cent error in calculating the registration fee.

But the heartrending impact of the important questions was the indication that the SEC, or whatever bureaucrat was handling the registration, simply did not believe how sound the company was from the JWC prospectus. The SEC wanted to know, for instance:

Why had sales and earnings increased so much in the past nine months? Was it one or two big (and nonrecurring) buys from a single customer?

Are the JWC homes qualified for VA or FHA loans and, if not, why not? (No government agency could lend money on unfinished homes because the law was set up that way, before shell homes were on the market.)

Could there be any assurance that the level of current sales, now at six hundred homes a month, would continue in view of possible competition and the cyclical nature of the economy? (The answer was that JWC anticipated selling more than six hundred homes a month and already had reached a level of 750 homes in one month.)

Did they use any pre-cut materials, as other low-cost builders did? (The answer was simply no.) Was a shortage of materials possible? (Anything is possible, but this was unlikely.) Would unions object to putting up pre-cut sections? (No, there were no unions involved and no, there were no pre-cut sections.) Did JWC or the lumberyards help buyers finish their houses? Did the price of the house include the cost of finishing it? If not, where would the buyer get the money to finish the house? On and on went the questions, legal and perhaps pertinent, and each and every one of them had to be answered accurately and with restraint.

Clearly there was the need for Jim Walter and his colleagues to explain to faraway Washington the soundness of a business based upon the character and honesty of the JWC people building and selling shell homes and the reliability of the people buying and finishing those shell homes. The bottom line had to be, as reported to the SEC, that Jim Walter Corporation in its first two years had sold 8,550 shell homes, 10 percent of them for cash, the other 90 percent for credit, and in all that time had to foreclose on only ninety-seven homes—a delinquency rate of only two-thirds of one percent. Furthermore, every one of those ninety-seven houses had been resold at a profit.

The public offering was approved by the SEC on August 23, 1956, at 12:30 p.m. and before that business day was over,

Ned Prescott and John Loeb had sold 50,000 shares of JWC stock and $1,250,000 of JWC 9 percent bonds. The two investment bankers had no trouble at all selling the stock and bonds to steady customers and friends who relied upon their acumen and integrity in buying new stock offerings. In fact, both men took healthy chunks of JWC stock for their own personal portfolios. Walter and Alston were in John Loeb's office that happy day when they overheard the financier say on the telephone, "I don't fully understand their capitalization myself; don't ask, just buy it."

This offering turned out to be the start of a long, fruitful association between JWC and John Loeb as its underwriter and also a lifelong friendship between two men who came from such diametrically opposite backgrounds: one a wealthy, sophisticated, Harvard-educated descendant of a prominent German-Jewish family in New York, the other a relatively poor, small town Southern boy with a public high school education, a former truck driver who now sold plain, unfinished houses to people who could not afford more. And yet . . . these two men were not as different as one might think from their outward demeanor and regional accents. A close friendship that spans more than thirty years has to be based upon shared values that transcend social class, religion, and economic background. Behind that austere public facade, John Loeb had a personal warmth and a keen sense of wit that he revealed only to close friends and associates, while behind the country boy demeanor of James Willis Walter was a sharp, quick mind that absorbed information, nuances, and the world around him as readily as any man's in the business world. Besides, there were a great many things they could learn from one another. Over the years John would grasp the finer points of hunting and fishing, and Jim would develop a taste for caviar and fine wines. What they shared was a sense of personal integrity, decency, curiosity, and a joy of life.

The infusion of ready cash and 479 new stockholders reaped from the public offering, plus the substantial new lines of credit, was like the uncorking of a bottle of champagne at JWC. Effervescence bubbled up and flowed through the corridors of the headquarters building on North Dale Mabry in Tampa. Word spread throughout thirty-six branch office operations: Branch managers who had accepted warrants instead of high salaries were reassured that they would share in the company's new prosperity.

Now there was no holding Bud Alston back. He set to work on his plans for building new branch operations. So hectic was his work week that he took on Tommy Hires, his top branch manager, as his second-in-command and in the new company two-engine Beechcraft they flew hither and yon, adding fifteen new branch operations to the previous thirty-six. This expansion took JWC into two new states. In Tennessee, branches were opened in Memphis and in Nashville. In North Carolina, they rapidly began selling shell homes in Charlotte, Greensboro, Fayetteville, and Rocky Mount. The company now had branch operations throughout the entire southeastern section of the United States—and as far west as Houston, Waco, Freeport, and Corpus Christi in Texas. Along the highways on the outskirts of major cities in nine states billboards announcing "Jim Walter Homes" became a familiar sight.

The branches all looked alike: a small office building and two to four model homes open for inspection. The buyer saw what he got before he bought: simple and attractive white, clapboard houses with pitched shingle roofs and one, two, or three bedrooms. The house model could be altered or enlarged at extra cost.

And the people bought! Every new branch office in all nine states sold more and more houses as the months rolled by. By the end of fiscal 1957, the company had more than doubled the 3,015 homes it had sold its first year. In 1958, JWC sold 8,094 homes for a gross profit of $6,740,970. They no longer were a small-time operation.

The following fiscal year, which ended August 31, 1959, when expansion plans were in full swing, JWC's sales territory and coverage increased from fifty-one branch offices in nine states to seventy-six offices in fifteen states. Jim Walter Homes moved into Kentucky, Virginia, Oklahoma, Arkansas, and Arizona. That year they sold 10,958 homes for a gross profit of $9,840,812. In addition, JWC's other operations began to kick in with substantial profits. Earnings on the mortgages held by the JWC subsidiary Mid-State Investment Corporation, rose from $100,886 in 1956 to a whopping $2,152,586 in 1959. Fire and theft insurance premiums added another $1 million that year.

These were happy days. The company was doing better than Jim Walter or anyone had expected. Net profits for 1959 topped $2,820,000, 46 percent higher than the previous year, and with seventy-six profitable branch operations in fifteen states, some of them just getting started, the future looked brighter than ever for "the world's largest builder and seller of shell homes." Twice during the year the board of directors raised the dividend, reaching a record eighty cents per share per year. The price of JWC stock, split three for one the previous year, was still rising. Shareholders were smiling and converting their warrants into stock, thus giving JWC *more* working capital to further expand its home building. The officers and directors of the company were exhilarated with the company's progress. "Truly, 1959 has been a banner year for Jim Walter Corporation and your management foresees another great year ahead," declared Jim Walter in the 1959 annual report.

Indeed, with such clear blue, sunny skies in Tampa, Florida, what could possibly go wrong? It is precisely then, when everything seems to be going smoothly, that a company, any company, is most vulnerable to disaster.

CHAPTER 5

— *Competition in Building* —

COMPETITION IN ITS most virulent form reared its nasty head for the first time in 1960, and then, like a pestilence, got worse. But that is the price one often pays for fame and fortune in the business world.

Much as Jim Walter had foreseen, the $6 million in bank lines of credit, the $3 million from the sale of stock and another $3 million from the sale of bonds had served to uncork the flow of cash, which allowed the company to expand its home building in 1958 and 1959. Sales and profits surged, JWC stock soared, and Wall Street sat up and paid attention to the astounding growth of this hitherto unheard of company in sleepy Tampa, Florida.

The national media quickly made a celebrity of the former $50-a-week truck driver who had become a millionaire selling shell homes. *Newsweek* magazine was the first to take notice of Jim Walter in March 1958:

> James W. Walter is a Tampa, Fla., home builder who has scored a spectacular success in the past few years—without ever building a complete home. Since August 1955, despite rising costs, tight money, and now recession, Walter's firm has sold 20,000 houses. During the fiscal year that ended last summer, he grossed about $11 million.

A few months later, *Florida Trend* magazine featured Jim Walter as "riding the crest of the nation's wave of home building," adding:

Of sizeable new Florida industries, the Walter Corp. probably is reigning champion in percentage gain in profits. This company and its subsidiaries has managed to more than double its profits in nearly every period to date.

Finance magazine in 1959, reviewing the company's progress since 1952 as well as its unusual capital structure, concluded:

Barring the unforeseen, the momentum of growth seems almost certain to continue. In addition to expanding sales through a steady broadening of its marketing area, the company is rapidly building its mortgage income, with consequent dual expansion of earning power . . . . On the basis of careful, continuing study, it emerges as an outstanding speculative possibility for long-term major capital appreciation, for those experienced investors who have learned to investigate before they invest.

In June 1960, *Business Week* featured James Willis Walter on its cover and ran a five-page story on JWC's phenomenal achievements. "Success has actually increased Walter's confidence in himself and his company," said *Business Week*. "He thinks the going will be much smoother in the future simply because the spadework and slogging of his pioneering days is over."

Soon after that the *Wall Street Journal* put Jim Walter and Jim Walter Corporation on the front page, and later featured his personal success in the *Journal's* book, *The New Millionaires and How They Made Their Fortunes*. *Time* magazine carried a story on the company and *Barron's*, the financial magazine, carried a long, prominent story, proclaiming that "Shell homes have become the fastest-selling houses on the market."

Throughout the financial community, Jim Walter was hailed as a pioneer in home building, a self-made millionaire, a poor boy who had made good. And, in 1961, the American Schools and Colleges Association presented him with the prestigious "Horatio Alger Award," which put him in the lofty company of the nation's most famous self-made successful men who possessed the high personal ideals of that fictional character.

By the end of 1960, however, there were hundreds of others trying to duplicate what Jim Walter had done with shell homes. It looked so easy, so lucrative. No technology was involved, no special skills required, no big factories or equipment needed. Not only had Jim Walter shown how to build the shell homes with contracted outside labor and materials bought as needed, but he had also revealed how to finance the homes profitably. It was all laid out for anyone to see in the company's 1957 prospectus that accompanied JWC's public offering of stocks and bonds.

The competition started in 1958, mostly by individual builders or small companies, and grew exponentially through 1960 and into 1961 when a number of large, well-financed home improvement companies went into building shell homes. "We just stole Jim Walter's prospectus, and just improved on it a little here and there," one competitor frankly admitted to inquiring journalists. By the end of 1961 the total number of competing companies reached 213. They flooded the market.

Everywhere that Jim Walter homes were sold, competing companies opened up for business next door. Along a one mile and a half stretch of Bankhead Highway, just west of Atlanta, for instance, there were no fewer than fifteen shell home builders displaying model homes. In Atlanta itself, there were thirty-one shell home builders, some small and struggling and some large and well financed by major banks and finance companies. Stretched out along highways on the outskirts of town, they looked like new and used car lots. In fact, the shell home builders had lured away the used car salesmen to sell their shell homes on a commission basis, ranging from $200 to $300 for every house sold. These nattily dressed, suede-shoed salesmen, as they were commonly known in the South, hardly waited for customers to drop in; they went out knocking on doors and making their pitches. No one actually counted them, but it was estimated that 50,000 shell homes were built in the United States in 1961, and 100,000 the following year. It was not unlike the gold rush days of yore.

Competition was fierce and unscrupulous, and it cut deeply into the Jim Walter operations, sales, and profits. Jim and Buddy ordered all their branch managers to hunker down, to cut overhead but not quality in building or credit requirements. They knew something they thought the new shell home builders had not yet learned: the business was not as simple as everyone thought.

To the public and to the financial community, Jim Walter issued this statement: "We've come down the road all by ourselves, and we've stumbled into every hole along the way. Now, there may be thirty or fifty or a hundred or two hundred shell home builders in business, all trying to profit from our mistakes, but none of them has our experience, organization or our backing. What they do have—and we were spared this at first—is competition. *We are the competition.*"

Over the previous two years, before the competition in shell housing began in earnest, Jim Walter and his colleagues had been busy getting their own house in order. By 1960, it is fair to say, they had a smooth, clean, thriving operation. While Buddy Alston cracked the whip perfecting the home-building operations, Jim Walter diligently made the rounds of banks and lending institutions around the country. He had become acquainted with more bankers than any other man in the country. He had made friends among them, dined and drank with them, played golf with them, and established lines of credit for loans, still backed with JWC mortgages, in excess of what the company needed.

The big breakthrough came in 1958 when the Chemical Corn Exchange Bank of New York (now Chemical Bank of New York) granted JWC its first *unsecured* line of credit for $1 million. The man responsible was William G. DeWitt, vice president of the bank, who said memorably one day, "Oh, what the hell, it isn't worth all this trouble securing those mortgages, and I'm sure you're good for it." Jim Walter beamed. At long last, his company was deemed sufficiently strong and solvent to borrow money on its word.

Of course, in the fine print, there was a sticking condition: Chemical insisted upon attaching a "negative pledge" to its unsecured line of credit. That meant that all of JWC's future loans would be unsecured, not backed by mortgages as collateral, and on an equal basis with the Chemical loan. The inherent risk for Walter was that he might lose more lines of credit than he was gaining if other banks would not renew their loans without the backing of specific mortgages. Jim had to take this to his board of directors for approval. There, the board decided to forge ahead and take the risk.

A week after Chemical Bank made its loan, Chase Manhattan Bank and the Manufacturers & Trade Trust of Buffalo followed suit. The National City Bank of New York (later Citicorp) came through with a $1 million line of unsecured credit, and before long all of JWC's bank loans and lines of credit were made on that basis. Unsecured borrowing eliminated the time, effort, and expense of physically depositing mortgage papers with the banks extending the credit, and it also cut the loan rate by 1 percent. When not one previous lender backed away from extending credit to JWC, Jim Walter, Buddy Alston, and Arnold Saraw had good reason to smile and to sigh with relief.

With a keen eye on the future, Jim Walter began looking for someone to help him with the varying and increasing financial dealings of JWC. His eye lit upon the young CPA from Price Waterhouse who had audited the company's books for 1957 and 1958. Joe B. Cordell was a sturdy, stable, and down-to-earth native Floridian of thirty-one, a graduate of the University of Florida, whose father and uncle were bankers. Jim Walter felt that Cordell would fit right in with the company's way of doing things; he also knew that the young man had just been promoted to audit manager in the prestigious accounting firm's Atlanta office, and that he was happy there. So, he took the oblique approach.

"Joe, why don't you look around and see if you can find me a young man who dresses right and can talk to bankers to help me on these bank loans and some deals I have in mind," he said.

The following Friday, he phoned Cordell in Atlanta, and asked, "Have you found that guy I need yet?" Joe answered that he had not. "Well, keep looking." It was not an unusual request to a public accountant who regularly made the rounds auditing several companies.

The calls went on for three or four weeks, with the same question and the same answer. Then, at 7 o'clock one Monday morning when Joe had come in to work on JWC books, Jim stopped in to chat with him. A little while later, he telephoned and asked him to come up to his office "for a minute." When he arrived, Walter rose from his desk and closed the door, an unusual occurrence. Joe sensed what was coming. Walter offered him a job as assistant to the president at $25,000 a year with the prospect of becoming JWC's chief financial officer.

Although he liked the free-swinging style of the company,

Joe Cordell had some concern over giving up a promising career at prestigious Price Waterhouse for a niche in a small home-building company with assets of about $8 million. "Tell me, Jim, how big do you think this company is going to get?" he asked.

Jim thought for a while and said sincerely, "Now you may think I'm crazy, and don't laugh at this, Joe, but I think we're going to be a fifty-million dollar company someday."

The thirty-one-year-old accountant didn't laugh; he took the job, the smartest career move he ever made. For years afterwards both men would chuckle at this gross underestimation of the company's future potential by its own founder and chief executive.

Within a few months, Cordell was promoted to vice president and chief financial officer of the corporation, the first outsider—and a college graduate and professional man at that—to join the slim ranks of managers of JWC. As such he took a great deal of joshing from the lusty field men of the company who delighted in referring to him as the "shiny-pants bookkeeper." It was a sign of acceptance in the ranks of the company where Bud Alston was known as the "He-Boar," a fuming, cigar-smoking razorback boar from Arkansas, and Tommy Hires was referred to as "the Bald Eagle" because of the lack of hair on top of his head.

Actually, Joe Cordell, with the instinctive caution of a certified public accountant, provided a good balance to some of the more impetuous notions of Walter. He often served as a needed brake on the natural enthusiasm of Walter and Alston, who were accustomed to quick decisions and fast action. To the decision-making mixture at the top of the company, Cordell added a touch of caution.

A sense of prudence, however, need not prevent one from taking the initiative, and it was not long before Cordell realized that the two largest banks in Tampa had never extended credit to the company. He promptly called upon a college friend who worked at the city's largest bank. "You know, this is embarrassing," he pointed out. "We're a pretty good size company and we borrow money from a lot of big banks all over the United States, and here you are, the biggest bank in our own hometown, and you won't give us a line of credit."

Before Cordell got back to the office, the president of the bank telephoned Jim Walter and personally offered the bank's legal line of credit. After that, the second-largest bank could not wait to give JWC a loan. If nothing else works, shame them into doing business with you.

There was always a need for more cash. The company always needed bank loans to support the mortgages taken in on the homes they built. At one point, Joe Cordell decided to hit all the banks too small to warrant a personal visit in the eight states nearest Florida. Consulting bank directories, he wrote to every bank that could lend more than $100,000, sending them an annual report, proxy statement, 10-K, and a list of banks like Chase and National City already extending credit to JWC. With that simple and direct approach, he raised more than $50 million.

Keeping everything simple and direct, or as simple and direct as humanly possible, was the unspoken and elemental management policy of the young Jim Walter Corporation because it reflected the personalities of the company's leaders. Both extroverts with full measures of self-confidence, they had no need or time for office politics or ego gratification games. Whatever was on their minds they said directly. They made decisions fast and easily, based upon the facts available and their instincts, without any deep soul-searching, and they acted without fear upon their decisions. They had no reason to doubt their instincts. The company was growing by leaps and bounds and they had successfully surmounted the cash crunch which had become part of their business life.

With Cordell aboard, Jim Walter began mapping out a business plan for JWC. It was not a formal undertaking, nothing was put down on paper. But with his innate ability to look into the future and see clearly around corners, Walter decided that he wanted the company to diversify beyond building shell homes. JWC was barely three years old and at the time diversification was not a well-known management strategy in corporate America. Nevertheless, Walter realized that the company needed a better balance in its earning power. He assigned Cordell the primary task of searching and finding companies that JWC could purchase. He wanted businesses within their field of knowledge, preferably ones which enjoyed a good cash flow. Adding equity would also further increase JWC's ability to borrow greater amounts of money.

That was the strategy. Putting it into play, however, was difficult because no one was offering companies for sale to JWC. The shell home building company was known, where it was known at all, as a company eager to borrow money, not one with excess capital for acquisitions. But by 1959, with the great increase in sales and profits, people began converting their warrants into stock, and an unexpected stream of cash flowed in.

JWC's first acquisition on January 30, 1959, was a relatively small, consumer finance company called the M. A. C. Corporation which operated sixteen small, storefront offices in Florida and southern Georgia. The price was $540,000. The consumer finance operation, borrowing money from banks and lending it out at a higher rate of interest, was not all that different from the handling of JWC's home mortgages, and by opening several new storefront offices and injecting a little more push in the daily operations, JWC managed to double the equity value of M. A. C. in less than a year. Over the next year, with nine new branches, M. A. C. was even more profitable.

When the eighth-largest bank in Florida was put up for sale in August 1959, it was just too good to resist. With all his experience as a borrower, Jim Walter felt familiar with banking, and he knew, too, that the area served by this bank was growing rapidly with the influx of retirees from up north. Strictly as an investment of corporate funds, JWC bought a majority (54.3 percent) interest in the First National Bank of St. Petersburg, founded in 1936 and located in downtown St. Petersburg. To make sure that, as he put it, everyone kept his hands out of the cookie jar, the bank was put under orders that it was never to lend a dime to JWC or anyone working for it. Even so, it did not hurt to have a bank of your own when you went out to borrow money from other banks.

As chairman, Walter brought William DeWitt down from New York to run the St. Petersburg bank as president. It was in large measure a display of his gratitude to DeWitt, who, as vice president of Chemical Corn Exchange Bank, had granted JWC its first unsecured line of credit. In three years, DeWitt and Walter had increased the bank's capital surplus by $2 million, moving First National from second to first place among banks in St. Petersburg.

While Walter was out of the office, wooing and winning over the banks and bastions of Wall Street, Bud Alston became a commanding presence in running the nuts and bolts of the home-building business. Like a fighting bantam rooster, he ruled his roost with an iron claw. Everyone out in the field selling and building Jim Walter homes was answerable to him, and he met them all straight on, hiring and firing, eyeball to eyeball. He fussed and fumed and fought, was frequently overbearing, and insisted upon the "right" way to do everything: his way. But everyone knew that he cared deeply for the company, appreciated a job done well, and protected and helped the men who shared his loyalty and drive. His men characterized him well with the oft-repeated line, "Bud's fault is that he doesn't know anything about humility; he thinks it's a weather condition."

As JWC operations spread throughout the Southeast, Bud never strayed from his original concept of hiring young men in their twenties, preferably right out of the armed services. He wanted honest, eager men who had experienced rough times and would respond to a genuine opportunity to make something of their lives. Educational or economic background did not matter; he would teach them what they had to know. He'd give them the chance to work twelve to sixteen hours a day to prove themselves. He told them to try things that they didn't know couldn't be done. The company had been built on that philosophy. Both Alston and Walter liked to explain that philosophy. "This company is like the bumblebee. Aerodynamically, the bumblebee can't fly. Its body is too heavy and its wings too small. And yet, somehow, it flies. It does the impossible, every day." It's surprising what a man can do if he sets out to do it, not knowing that no one had ever done that before. If a new man could not hack it, he simply did not last long in the company.

"This business is won or lost on blood and guts," Bud would exhort his salesmen and branch managers. "You put the blinders on, and like a racehorse you run. Nothing can't be done. You got a problem, you improvise. You come up with a solution. This job is your life, it's what you make of it." He often forewarned a newly hired branch manager to consult with his wife on the long and arduous hours involved before he took the job. While the men worked long and hard, they also enjoyed the camaraderie that was part of the Jim Walter operation. Wives suffered alone and lonely. They sensed their men were playing like boys, enjoying it all. More than one loyal but torn JWC manager had occasion to caution his wife, "Please don't make me choose between you and Jim Walter."

As the company grew larger and more prosperous, neither Bud Alston nor Jim Walter forgot their earlier penny-pinching days. Walter checked every bill that passed his desk, and Alston read expense accounts and petty cash vouchers from the field religiously. He fired one manager who submitted an expense account item of $5 for three-cent stamps, and never stopped recounting that story for the benefit of others. "Hell, there ain't no way a man can use five dollars' worth of three-cent stamps in this job. I don't give a damn if it's five dollars or a loaf of bread, if you steal it, you're a thief, and I won't have you in this company."

The seventy-six branch operations spread out in fifteen states were divided into five regions, and once a month Alston and his home-office entourage would fly in and spend a full day in meetings with each of the regions for five days straight. He would exhort the troops, clear up difficulties, spread the word on that month's sales slogan and thrust, and at the end of each meeting confer privately with each and every one there. At the personal conference, each of them had the opportunity to complain, ask a question, or to say anything directly to the boss. Once a year Bud would personally hand out the appropriate bonus check and then ask if that check was satisfactory and fair. If anyone could convince him that he or she deserved more, Bud would write out an additional bonus check on the spot. It was not long before many of them realized that Bud Alston kept score by the checkbook.

Branch managers were given considerable independence and flexibility on how they chose to do things, but each was held totally responsible for whatever went on within his realm of authority. Bud told them that power comes from respect and not from any corporate organizational chart, and as a result, JWC branch managers ruled their domains with much the same domination and personal care that Bud Alston wielded over them.

For him, there were no shades of gray; things were either black or white, right or wrong. The man who cheated or took advantage of a customer was fired. "Don't anyone try to tell me you didn't know something you did was wrong. That's no excuse. Worse, it's a damn lie. Nobody can be so damn dumb he doesn't know right from wrong. Even my seven-year-old son knows that. In this company, we do things right, or we don't do them at all. If it's wrong, we ain't goin' to do it. Now that's not so complicated, is it? It's real simple. Right? Right!"

Salesmen were on a straight salary basis, so that they could feel and say that they worked directly for the company and not strictly on commission. Later, when it became necessary to add commissions to the salary, the commission was the same no matter what the price of the house. No salesman was to make more money by pushing a more expensive house on a customer. Every sale had to be approved and written up by the branch manager, who was responsible for making a credit check on the customer. Again and again Alston insisted that the customer was always king, to be served and not taken advantage of. Word of mouth sold homes. A satisfied customer brought in other potential buyers; a satisfied customer was a salesman without pay for the company.

Alston could and often did fly off the handle, but he got things done. At the opening of the branch in Macon, Georgia, they were selling so many one- and two-bedroom houses, the new manager there started to make appointments with customers to come back later if they wanted a three-bedroom house. Bud caught him doing this and screamed, "You're crazy as hell. You don't make customers come back at your convenience. I don't care what the hell the customers want, we're going to have somebody here to talk to them."

Bud played to the pride as well as the pocketbooks of his branch managers and their salesmen. He was always running contests pitting branch office against branch office and later region against region. Prizes for the best salesmen ranged from a free personal car to free vacations to free gasoline, and they were awarded with great fanfare at festive occasions. More important than the material prizes was the competition to determine which region was the best in selling and building the most Jim Walter shell homes *that* week—the Carolina Tigers, the Mississippi Rebs, the Florida Gators, the Oklahoma Cowboys, the Texas Longhorns, or the Virginia Generals. Alston and the company's new advertising company subsidiary, headed by Larry Bankston, provided the slogans, the posters, the rallying songs, and the convention skits. It became important to know who was the best regional manager, best branch manager, best salesmen. Why? Because the men who were the best could razz all the others.

When the shell home market became flooded with competitors in 1960, it seemed like the beginning of the end of the good times for JWC. Where once JWC had been virtually alone selling shell homes, now it seemed like Jim Walter Homes against the world. Competitors were everywhere, selling shell homes cheaper or with easier mortgage financing over longer periods of time, or selling partially completed homes which appealed to many buyers, or giving away prizes and special inducements that ate into profits but did lure in prospects. The bigger companies spent heavily on advertising and marketing gimmicks to gain a greater share of the market. JWC's gross dollar sales on shell homes began to slide. From an increase of 61 percent in fiscal 1959 over the previous year, it slipped to a 43 percent increase in 1960, and to only 16 percent in 1961. In fiscal 1962, JWC shell home sales decreased for the first time in the company's history, from $42 million in 1961 to $30 million in 1962.

It hurt. But Jim Walter and Bud Alston were of one mind on meeting and withstanding the ferocious competition. They decided deliberately that they would *not* try to match the offers and practices of the competition. They would *not* reduce prices or mortgage requirements or quality of construction on their homes. Instead, they would emphasize that they were the biggest and best builder of shell homes with the most experienced personnel and the best quality of materials used. For their own good they began to pay even stricter attention to qualifying their customers before extending credit.

Their strategy was to continue to cut costs and outlast their competitors. It was based upon their belief that most of their competitors were woefully lacking in construction and credit experience and although some of them were well financed they would, in the end, all go broke when the people buying their homes could not pay for them. Walter reminded his employees that a house was not sold as far as he was concerned until the last payment on it was made. To those who voiced dire predictions that JWC was not expanding fast enough to meet the new competition, Jim Walter recited one of his pointed homilies: "I don't want to build this company fast; I want to grow it good."

Competition did force some changes in the product offered customers. There was a legitimate consumer demand for partially finished homes, where the buyer did not have to do everything himself. By mid-1961, Walter and Alston agreed to bring on the market a variety of options the customer could buy. At a price, the customer could order the package for installed plumbing, electric wiring, interior wallboard, or all of them. Walter and Alston agreed to stop short of installing kitchens or painting the interior of their homes. They knew well that the key to their success in building shell homes depended on the speed of building the same basic house over and over again, painting it white, satisfying the customer, and moving on to the next sale. Designing kitchens was a different business altogether.

The partially finished shell home turned out to be immensely popular and opened an entirely new market for the company, appealing to middle-class families who wanted a second home, usually a simple vacation retreat tucked away in the woods somewhere. Because of the added cost of the partially finished homes and because competing companies offered longer-term financing, JWC was obliged to extend its usual four-year mortgages to six years, then seven years, and later, for the more expensive homes, twelve years. The idea was to keep the monthly mortgage payment down to what the customers could afford, usually $40 to $50 a month.

When it came to the basic business, Walter and Alston kept close tabs on branch managers, insisting that they tighten their controls on building costs, office overhead, and credit checks on new buyers. In the face of severe competition, they spread the word to their own people that they would tolerate no diminution of company standards. Repeatedly they insisted that their salesmen remember that in the shell home business Jim Walter Corporation was heads above all the competition in experience, in financing, and in the quality of their homes. "Take Advantage of Your Advantage" became the sales slogan and rallying cry of the company as it faced down its competition. Every month Alston sent a two-by-three-foot poster to be hung in each JWC branch office with the slogan. In one poster, called "Operation CAKE," he spelled it out:

Start with a lot of COURTESY in answering the telephone, courtesy in meeting your prospects, courtesy by showing appreciation of their interest in your product.

Mix thoroughly with good APPEARANCE, appearance of your branch, the personal appearance of everyone associated with the company.

Add to this KNOWLEDGE, knowledge of your product by everyone in contact with a prospect or customer, knowledge of what you can do and what you can't do, what you will do and won't do.

Serve with a lot of ENTHUSIASM, enthusiasm by everyone to get for your customer the very best that can be had for the money he is spending, enthusiasm in treating your customer as you would have him treat you.

Operation CAKE—Put it to work for you. It can't help but give you satisfied customers, and satisfied customers are an advantage. When you have an advantage . . . TAKE ADVANTAGE OF YOUR ADVANTAGE.

As Ever,

BUD

The men at JWC gritted their teeth, watched the shenanigans in the industry going on, and waited out the storm of competition. Where JWC had instilled a spirit of loyalty to the company among their salesmen, stringent credit rating requirements for their buyers, and highest quality materials and labor in their houses, almost all the other shell home builders, in their haste to catch up with Jim Walter, did little or none of that.

New companies invading the field opened five, ten, and sometimes twenty branch offices in a single month, rushing headlong into the business they knew little about. They indiscriminately hired commission salesmen who were more interested in earning $200-300 per house sold, depending on its price, than in fostering a company reputation. They peddled houses to anyone who wanted them and could sign his or her name to a contract. They sold to people with poor-paying jobs or no job at all, to relatives, and even to each other. When necessary, they falsified credit applications and they pocketed their commissions; collections were someone else's problem. For a customer who did not own a site for a home, a salesman would buy him the land, for about $50, sign him up, and collect his $200 commission. These salesmen knew and used all the slick tricks in the book, and most company managements were too new or too eager to check carefully on a customer's ability to pay. When buyers failed to keep up with mortgage payments, the salesmen did not mind handling the repossessions and selling the houses again for another commission. "I know of one house that was repossessed and resold seven times," recounts Alston. "The salesmen were selling it back and forth to each other."

By mid-1962, the small builders began to fall by the wayside, and a year later the vast majority had gone out of the shell home business voluntarily or through bankruptcy. Few of them left with any money in their pockets. Most had gone broke by not paying attention to the financial side of the business. The banks and finance companies which had backed the larger of these firms lost millions of dollars. Many of them now turned to JWC to take over the sale of the thousands of repossessed shell homes. JWC sales climbed to more than 14,000 homes in one year. Now the company, begun in 1946 with one $895 shell home, maintained 157 branches in twenty-eight states, stretching across the country, from Tampa, Florida, to Fresno, California.

By mid-1964, five years after the much-heralded competition had begun, it was all gone. The only company left was the original "World's Largest Shell Home Builder"—Jim Walter Corporation. By this time, it was a vastly different company in size, structure, and product line.

CHAPTER 6

The $15 Million
Building Bargain

I T'S A KEEN EYE that sees what others miss. Just as he noticed that classified ad for an $895 house sixteen years
before, Jim Walter, a voracious reader, became intrigued
with newspaper accounts in 1962 of a world-famous company
supposedly worth $36 a share one day and only $25 the following week. He investigated that anomaly and out of that
came the biggest single achievement of his business life.

The woes of one Eddie Gilbert, a young man in a hurry in
the canyons of Wall Street, had been well publicized. Edward
M. Gilbert, a poor boy born and bred in the Bronx, seemed
to have come out of nowhere and astounded the traditional
financial community with his bold stock speculations. An
early version of a corporate raider, Gilbert scored his most
spectacular success by actually cornering the market on the
stock of the E. L. Bruce Company, of Memphis, Tennessee,
the nation's leading manufacturer of hardwood flooring. It
was something that had not been done on a regulated stock
exchange since the wild days of the 1920s. Dubbed the "Boy
Wonder of Wall Street," Gilbert became a celebrity with his
high living in the social whirl of New York and nightlife of
Paris. His spectacular success in the stock market won him
acceptance in the financial world.

In 1961, Gilbert tried to repeat his coup. Borrowing heavily
and buying stock on margin in New York and on even lower

margin in Switzerland, Gilbert quietly began accumulating a major holding in a major American company called Celotex, a world-famous name in fiberboard and other building materials. Aiming for 500,000 shares which would give him control, he wanted to merge Celotex with his E. L. Bruce Company.

This time, however, his stock manipulations did not go unnoticed. The price of Celotex in early 1962 began to climb steadily. Gilbert kept buying. Buying on margin, he was essentially using money borrowed from his bankers. Then, in May 1962, in the midst of a housing slump and a strike at its largest plant, Celotex reported a six-month loss of more than $1 million. The stock tumbled from a high of $42 to a record low of $16 a share. Eddie Gilbert was called upon to cover his margin.

Scrambling desperately for the millions he needed, he began negotiations to sell out his Celotex stock to the Ruberoid Company, another building supply firm interested in merging with Celotex. They reached or almost reached agreement on $36 a share. While waiting for Ruberoid to bail him out of trouble, Gilbert began dipping into Bruce corporate funds to cover his personal margin. That's embezzlement. When Ruberoid delayed on closing the deal at $36 a share and the unauthorized use of Bruce funds was discovered by his board of directors, Gilbert panicked and fled to Brazil, which had no extradition treaty with the United States. That business story hit the front pages of the nation's newspapers. Wall Street went into an uproar over the Gilbert scandal, and the attendant publicity focused attention on Celotex as a company in trouble.

Celotex had had a remarkable history. Founded in July 1920 by a group of intrepid men in Minnesota, headed by Bror Dahlberg, the company succeeded a year later in producing a new and superior insulation fiberboard made out of a leftover product called bagasse. Bagasse was what was left of the sugarcane stalks after the juice had been crushed out of them; in effect, it was the waste product of sugarcane mills. It also was an amazingly tough, resilient material and the sugarcane industry produced mountains of it every year. What the founders of Celotex did was invent the machines which compressed the bagasse into long, hard sheets of fiberboard. Their first operation site, across the Mississippi from New Orleans, came to be known as the Marrero plant and is still operating today. The first insulation board for commercial use, a half-inch thick and eight hundred feet long, was run off the new machine in August 1921, and then cut into eight-by-four-foot building boards. Eighteen months later, the Marrero plant was producing eighteen million square feet of cane fiberboard a year.

The product was ubiquitous. It could be used everywhere, and was. Its primary application was as an insulation between the outer and inner walls of homes and commercial buildings. But Admiral Byrd also used Celotex board to build a village of huts at the South Pole. A maharajah shot tigers from a stand insulated against India's searing heat with Celotex. Five layers of Celotex carpet lining were used for resiliency beneath the padding of the Madison Square Garden boxing ring for Gene Tunney's last fight, an eleven-round knockout of Tom Heeney in 1928.

Celotex became a household name, a generic term for all fiberboard. Even the sophisticated *New Yorker* magazine remarked on something being "as American as apple pie and Celotex." The company went on to develop new building products, such as roof insulation, acoustical tile, and lath. Its profits soared with the Roaring Twenties, and then sank along with so many others in the depression years of the Thirties. When World War II ended, a multimillion-dollar expansion program revived Celotex's annual sales from $21 million to $76 million over the next fifteen years. Then in 1961, a drop in construction and depressed selling prices reduced revenues to $62 million and profits to a minuscule $700,000. The company appeared to be on the skids. That's when Gilbert, perhaps knowing something others did not, began buying Celotex shares.

When the bottom fell out of Eddie Gilbert's portfolio some eighteen months later, the Ruberoid Company had the inside track on acquiring Celotex. But Ruberoid made the tactical error of trying to buy too cheaply. Its public tender offer for Celotex stock at $25, when all of Wall Street knew Ruberoid had been prepared to pay $36, raised a lot of eyebrows, and particularly piqued the curiosity of one James Willis Walter in Tampa.

How could a company the size and scope of Celotex lose one-third of its value in one single week? If Ruberoid had been willing to pay $36 a share, Celotex probably was worth that much, if not more, he figured. He began to weigh the possibilities of buying the nationwide company with the famous name. If he could get the company by raising the offer to $26 or $26.50 a share, it might well be a steal. Walter had been looking for acquisitions to help diversify JWC's operations beyond shell homes, although he had not been looking for anything as large as Celotex, a listed company on the New York Stock Exchange. With the new competition in shell homes flooding the market, Walter realized that he could not continue the dramatic growth of his company if he limited it to shell homes. He wondered about Celotex: What was it really worth? Could he afford to buy a company twice as big and a hundred times as complex as JWC? He decided to check it out with his favorite investment banker.

At lunch about a week later with John Loeb in the firm's exquisite dining room at 42 Wall Street, Walter brought up the matter, expressing his interest, and asking, "John, do you know anything about Celotex? What do you think of the company?"

Loeb chuckled. "Well, I do know something about Celotex. It so happens we own a very meaningful position in it. We used to be one of Eddie Gilbert's bankers and we have some Celotex stock, and Lazard Frères (another big investment banking firm) has some, and we have friends in Switzerland who have a big block of stock." It turned out that Loeb could put his hands on fully 34 percent of Celotex's stock. He thought it might be available.

Jim outlined his interest in acquiring Celotex. "Does it make any sense to try to put a deal together?" he asked. Loeb was intrigued with the possibilities. "I have just the man who can tell you all about Celotex," he assured him. Back in his office after lunch, Loeb asked Gene Woodfin, a senior partner in the firm, to join them.

Woodfin, a fourth-generation, hard-driving, dynamic Texan, had left one of Houston's leading law firms three years earlier to join the Loeb firm as a senior partner. He had hesitated at first, saying, "I'm an attorney and I've had absolutely no financial training," but the wily Loeb, who had observed him in negotiations, won him over by saying, "We don't need your financial training, we need people with brains." Woodfin, a deal maker, handled most of Loeb Rhoades's mergers and acquisitions business. He had written the book on Celotex for Eddie Gilbert and he wasted no time in explaining to Jim Walter that Celotex, then still selling below $17, had a stated book value of $30. But that book value grossly undervalued extensive stock and land holdings of Celotex at their original cost and not their current market value, Woodfin said. He estimated the total assets of Celotex to be at least $48 a share, and "probably were more than that." Woodfin explained that the current depressed price of Celotex on the market was due largely to a cyclical down-turn in the building industry, a price war in fiberboard, plus that long labor strike at Celotex's major plant in Marrero, Louisiana. All in all, the dealmaker said that Celotex would be a good deal for any lucky buyer.

Jim Walter returned to Tampa with a copy of the Loeb Rhoades financial analysis of Celotex. Joe Cordell, apprised of Walter's keen interest in Celotex, called Price Waterhouse in Washington for copies of all public documents pertaining to Celotex, its annual reports, its 10-K forms, et al., and he checked and prepared his own analysis.

It was all there in black and white on public documents for anyone to see: Celotex's balance sheet in its 1961 Annual Report listed total assets at $28,382,477. That figure did not include Celotex's outside investments. It owned 48.3 percent (307,992 shares) of the South Coast Corporation, a sugar company that owned some eighty-nine square miles of sugar-cane land in Louisiana. Celotex listed that asset at what it had paid, $438,541, and noted that its current market value was $9,119,398. It also owned 11 percent of the South Shore Oil and Development Company, which drilled for oil on the sugar company's land, and that holding was worth $1 million more than it was listed in the books. Celotex also owned 242,000 acres of timberlands in northern Michigan, valued at close to $9 million.

The two men spent most of July 4th examining, reviewing and analyzing all the data, and in the end they agreed that the total equity value of Celotex was just about $60, or, to be exact, $59.40 a share. Ruberoid was offering $25, less than half. Jim was positively excited. He reached for the phone and called for a special meeting of his board of directors on Friday, the day after next.

A meeting of the JWC board of directors in those days was like a meeting of a clan: familiar, informal, friendly. Jim made a straightforward presentation of the facts and figures he had gathered. Buying the Celotex Corporation for just about half of its real value was a great bargain, not to be resisted, Walter exclaimed. With this one acquisition, they could move their still small, one-business company into the big time. Buying control of Celotex would insure JWC a place on the New York Stock Exchange and give it national prominence. Besides, Jim pointed out, it was the closest thing to a no-lose deal. With Celotex's ownership of half of the sugar company, a part of an oil company, and all that timberland in Michigan, if worse came to worse, they could sell off the pieces and still come out ahead. Walter told his board of directors that he would begin, with their approval, by offering $26 a share, one dollar more than Ruberoid offered.

The eight-member board—Bill DeWitt, Ernie Knapp, James E. Holmes (investment banker of Alex. Brown & Sons), attorney Norman Stallings, and Ted Meares, as well as Walter, Alston, and Saraw—scrutinized the proposed deal from all angles of their own individual expertise. That Friday afternoon he telephoned John Loeb and made an appointment for early Monday morning.

In New York on Sunday, the day before the all-important meeting, Walter and Cordell went to see the St. Louis Cardinals play the New York Giants in the Polo Grounds, and saw Stan ("The Man") Musial, the Cardinal slugger, establish a new record by hitting his fourth consecutive home run for as many times at bat. They took it as a good omen. Jim Walter fully intended to hit a memorable home run of his own in the world of business.

The next morning they went over columns of figures once again with Loeb and Woodfin, and it all looked better than ever. It was disclosed that because Loeb Rhoades, along with Lazard Frères and a group of Swiss investors, had been backing Gilbert's efforts to gain control of Celotex, Loeb could

gather up in a few phone calls some 350,000 shares of Celotex, constituting 34 percent of the outstanding Celotex
stock, enough for control and enough to stop anyone else
from trying to outbid them.

With just a slight catch in his throat, Jim Walter suggested
that he and his board had agreed to offer $26 a share for
the stock. John Loeb leaned forward and said, "Jim, if you
really want to get it, you should offer $30. At $30 you're
going to get it. Now you might do it for $26, but I'm not sure
they will sell at that. If you really want it, pay $30. That's my
advice."

That was $1.4 million more than he had expected to pay at
the outset and a full $2 million more for the 500,000 shares
he would ultimately need for majority control of Celotex, but
Jim rolled with the punch. "If we can find the money, I want
to buy it," he bravely announced. At $30 per share, 350,000
shares would come to $10.5 million and the full 500,000
shares would cost a total of $15 million.

Woodfin smiled and announced he already knew where he
could find that kind of money. He had already apprised a
banker of the situation and felt reasonably certain that First
National City Bank of New York would come up with the full
$15 million. "I've got a good buddy over there named Bill
Spencer," said Woodfin.

Walter remarked that he had some credit lines with City
Bank and was in good standing there. Woodfin laughed good
naturedly at the naivete of the newcomer, saying, "Jim, this is
a different department of the bank and a completely different kind of deal."

At First National City Bank, Walter met a different kind of
banker. William I. Spencer, a senior vice president in the
chemical and petroleum department at the time, was a big,
burly, pipe-smoking, fun-loving man who wore tweeds as
often as banker's grays, but he had a no-nonsense approach

to business matters, especially loans. He called in two associates to help him evaluate the oil properties, the sugar company, and the timberlands, as well as the balance sheet of Celotex. Jim Walter recited his well-rehearsed story of shell homes, sweat equity, the financing spread on mortgages, and his company's fifteen years of increasing sales and profits. He explained, too, the recent wild competition in shell homes and JWC's stunning slump of the first and second quarters of that year, and the recovery of the third quarter of 1962. JWC was a young company with considerable growth potential, he explained. Of the 450 people in the company, only five were over forty years of age, and he himself was thirty-nine. Walter held nothing back. That was his way of doing things: "What you see is what you get."

The banker in Spencer was obviously impressed. After three hours together, he assured Walter, "I'm going to recommend this loan, if the numbers check out. Let me do my homework, and come back to see me at 9 o'clock tomorrow morning and you'll have your answer."

For a loan above $1 million, Spencer needed the approval of two executive vice presidents above him, and his recommendation of approval was met with astonishment by his seniors. They considered it too risky to lend that much money to an unproven company such as JWC in order to enable it to buy a failing company twice its size. Wholly competent men can view the same facts and come to different conclusions. It depends so much on one's point of view. Spencer did not back down. He insisted that Jim Walter and his company were a worthwhile risk for the bank because of their record of accomplishment and the underlying value of the company JWC was buying. "I believe in this man, Jim Walter; he's got what it takes, and I think this will turn out to be a very good deal for him and for us."

The two senior officers of the bank decided not to overrule him, but they warned him, "If this deal goes sour, remember, we warned you: it's your ass!"

Spencer realized the risk, and it was this kind of courage that elevated him over other senior officers when several years later he was promoted to president of the First National Bank of New York. The loan to Jim Walter for Celotex remained one of his all-time favorites. Spencer enjoyed explaining why he took that kind of risk. "Hell, anyone can lend money to Exxon," he would say. "Making loans to men on the rise like Jim Walter is all the fun there is in banking. Recognizing that this guy, and not that one, is going to make it, and if you help him, he's going to become a customer for life, that's what it's all about." Jim Walter became more than that: He and Spencer developed a fast friendship that has lasted a lifetime, far beyond the banking or business needs of either man.

After spending an anxious night of uncertainty, on the dot of 9 o'clock that Tuesday morning, Jim Walter presented himself at Spencer's office, accompanied by Cordell and Woodfin. The banker was all smiles. Congratulating Walter, he handed him a letter of intent committing the bank to a $15 million loan. "Great!" exclaimed Walter. "We certainly appreciate this, but, I've got to tell you, there are two things I want to do before we commit to the loan. One, I'd like to offer a piece of this action to other banks that we do business with. Is there any problem with doing that?" Walter had already thought of the long-term value of maintaining good relationships with as large a number of banks as possible to ensure ample sources of future borrowing.

"Fine with us," replied Spencer, understanding the situation, "but we want a minimum of $5 million, although we'd like $7 million."

"One more thing," added Walter. "Before we go ahead, I want to tell Henry Collins [the president of Celotex] in

Chicago what we are doing. I don't want him to read it in the newspapers. I wouldn't want to do an unfriendly takeover. I want a working relationship with the man. So, if he has strong objections, I want to hear them, and reconsider the whole situation."

That noon, after checking with several other banks in New York on parceling out portions of the proposed loan, Walter and Cordell flew to Chicago. They were two happy, young men flying high on the biggest adventure of their careers, with a piece of paper in hand worth $15 million. Jim Walter was a bundle of nervous energy, a mixture of happiness, confidence, and apprehension. It was a great opportunity to expand his own company, possibly to make a lot of money, and yet he realized that he really did not know what he was getting into. Of course he knew that a deal is never done until final papers are signed and that almost anything could go wrong, but he hardly expected the scare of the day to be the plane hitting an air pocket and bouncing about in the sky, sending kippered herring to their laps and their hearts to their throats. "What an inappropriate time to die," thought Cordell, who retained a special awe of flying ever since he had bailed out of a crashing navy plane on a training mission during World War II.

In Chicago, the Ambassador Hotel had only one suite available on short notice, a living room and a bedroom with twin beds, and so for the first time these two business colleagues shared a bedroom. In the morning, Jim announced with mock solemnity: "Joe, we're going to have a long business relationship and I hope we are going to do a lot of things together, but I'll tell you here and now, for damn sure, I will never sleep in the same room with you again." Joe nodded, not needing an explanation. He knew he snored.

The first stop of the new day was at Celotex's leading bank, the First National Bank of Chicago, which was down the street from Celotex headquarters. Wanting to establish good relations with Celotex's bank by offering it a portion of the loan, Walter asked to see Richard Willer, who had been an enthusiastic supporter of JWC, lending the company one, two, and three million dollars at a time for the past four years. He was the only friend JWC had at the bank, but Willer was on vacation at a cabin in Wisconsin without a telephone. Walter was referred to Willer's superior, James Badger, and when Badger, the bank's credit manager, heard Walter's plan to buy Celotex, he quickly led the two men into the office of the bank's chairman, Homer Livingston.

Neither Walter nor Cordell had ever met the chairman of Chicago's biggest bank, nor did they have any idea that the chief executive had long regarded all shell home builders as incipient crooks. He had approved each of Dick Willer's loan recommendations on JWC with the dire warning that he was doing it only to teach the young man a lesson on how easily a banker can be fooled by a fast-talking salesman. Walter and Cordell were not to know this until a long time afterward, for on this day Homer Livingston did a complete about-face and greeted them with open arms and the apparent warmth of the Florida sun.

The chairman was delighted to learn that Jim Walter was about to acquire a controlling interest in Celotex; he thought it an excellent idea. From his point of view, the two Floridians had arrived at First National like unexpected saviors. The bank was in a terrible bind with Celotex. Even though Celotex had been a longtime customer and kept millions in checking accounts that drew no interest, when Eddie Gilbert showed up one day, the bank had loaned him money to foster his takeover of the company. Bank officials had taken the pragmatic view that it was a ripe candidate for acquisition. Henry Collins was righteously furious at the treachery, and told Livingston in no uncertain terms that he intended to move Celotex's business to another bank. In order to preserve the Celotex account, Homer Livingston offered Walter $10 million, or two-thirds of the money he needed.

"Thanks, but no thanks," said Walter. They settled on $3 million from First National of Chicago. The bank's attitude reinforced Walter's opinion that the acquisition was a good idea and held no hidden glitches.

Henry Collins, the handsome, silver-haired president of Celotex, received Walter and Cordell graciously with just a touch of condescension, expecting them to open negotiations on purchasing some Celotex building materials. He was visibly surprised when Walter announced, "Mr. Collins, I have the opportunity to buy 34 percent of Celotex by the close of this business day. The stock is available to me, and I believe it would be a good fit between Celotex and my company. I hope we can work well together. But if you have any objections, I think you ought to speak up now, before I make my decision."

Collins, who was almost twenty years older than Walter, shrugged his shoulders in resignation. He had feared Eddie Gilbert and then had accepted the inevitability of a merger with Ruberoid, and now was suprised with Jim Walter coming out of nowhere. With a sigh, he said, "Celotex has been losing money, and I know somebody is going to own us, so it might as well be you." That was as close to approval as Jim Walter could expect from a defeated man.

Walter, who had kept his board of directors informed by telephone, called each one again to take a telephone vote authorizing him to sign the loan papers with the First National City Bank and to buy control of Celotex. He phoned the go-ahead to John Loeb, and then he and Cordell rushed to the airport to get to the bank before it closed at 3 o'clock.

The flight was delayed, New York traffic was as bad as ever, and they rushed through the bank's revolving doors at 445 Park Avenue just before closing time. The cab driver raced in after them and caught them at the elevators. "Hey, you forgot to pay the fare!" Walter tipped generously and on the way up to Spencer's office mused, "Here we are closing a $15 million deal and we almost beat a cabby out of ten bucks."

In Spencer's midtown Park Avenue office, Jim Walter signed loan papers while John Loeb, on Wall Street in lower Manhattan, worked the phone to confirm the verbal agreements on the purchase of 350,000 shares of Celotex stock at $30 a share. Spencer agreed to advance the whole $15 million and then, that week, apportion the $15 million among the banks on Jim Walter's list. Cordell mentally calculated all the offers Jim had received from the banks he had called, and the figure came to $57 million. Jim Walter Corporation, which had had so much trouble borrowing money in the past, now could borrow $57 million for one single deal. Shortly after 5 p.m. Woodfin phoned to announce, "The deal is done; we've got 34 percent."

It was an amazing turn of events. From start to finish, Jim Walter had taken control—with borrowed money—of a $60 million company in fewer than ten days. He did have to wait another day to receive confirmation on the stock rendered by the investors in Switzerland, only because of the time zone difference. Jim and Joe spent hours over the next two days in the Loeb Rhoades trading room, enjoying the actual buying of all the Celotex stock that came on the market for $30 or less. They left instructions to keep buying at that price, $30 or under, until JWC acquired 49 percent, but not 50 percent, of Celotex. As long as he did not own a majority of Celotex's stock, JWC would not have to carry Celotex's substantial losses on its books.

The announcement on July 12, 1962, shocked some of the traders in the financial world and surprised them all. No one on the outside had had an inkling of what Jim Walter had been up to. Reactions ran the gamut of opinions on Wall Street. Some saw it as a brilliant, courageous coup: A young, energetic company with assets of $30 million had acquired control of an old-line, well-established, national company with assets of $60 million. Others speculated that it would prove to be the worst deal of the year: an inexperienced management taking on a money-losing company in a cyclical industry, and paying too much for it. As usual, opinions on Wall Street depended largely on points of view and which facts which people knew, like blind men feeling different parts of an elephant. And there were many who simply read the news stories and wondered, 'Who the hell is this Jim Walter?'

They returned to Tampa for the weekend and when the celebrations were over, Joe Cordell flew back to New York to sign for bank loans covering the purchase of Celotex stock and then on to Chicago. Wasting not a day, Jim Walter flew directly to Chicago to get right to work with the senior management of Celotex, but not before taking his elderly and now frail father for their customary Sunday morning drive around Tampa. When in town he never failed to share his business affairs with his father and to seek his advice on these drives that had replaced the Sunday morning porch talks at his father's house.

Truth be told, Jim Walter fully understood without advice from anyone that he had his work cut out for him. All of a sudden, he felt as though he were starting all over, poised at a new beginning, with his career, his reputation, and perhaps even his own company at stake. Now he would start running a nationwide manufacturing company that employed six thousand workers in twenty-three huge plants scattered from Pennsylvania to California, and from Michigan to Louisiana. He had never done anything like that before. He and his people had never owned a factory, never manufactured anything, never managed a highly structured organization. They had been customers, not manufacturers. JWC simply bought and supplied the materials their carpenters needed, while most of their own employees handled little pieces of paper called mortgages. Everyone knows it is cheaper, easier, and more efficient to buy an existing business than to start up fresh from nothing in a new field. But like buying an old house, no matter how much care you take, you never really know what you've got until after you've moved in.

Bud Alston packed a suitcase and flew up to see what his partner had bought and to lend a hand. But Walter told him to get back to Tampa and mind the store: Celotex was to be his own personal project; he would handle it with Cordell's help. Buddy was to run JWC along with the home building as long as Jim and Joe were away at Celotex. No one then knew how long that would take.

What they found in Celotex, to put it simply, was a company that had grown fat, dumb, and unhappy. Doom pervaded the ornate and somber offices and hallways of company headquarters on La Salle Street in downtown Chicago. Everyone was worried about his or her job, and resentful of the "know-nothing, country bumpkins" from Florida who had come north to take over.

No two companies could have been more unlike one another. Celotex's top managers were men in their fifties and sixties, most of them marking time until retirement; at JWC, only one man was past the age of forty. Where Celotex was bureaucratic and overstaffed with lawyers, accountants, managers, and vice presidents, JWC operated with little staff and few layers of management.

Jim Walter Corporation reflected the personality and character of its founder and namesake. By temperament Jim Walter, the man, was down-to-earth, straight-talking, reliable, and trustworthy, and he prized those attributes in those who worked with him. He inspired a sense of urgency; there are so many things to be done and done quickly because they could easily pile up and overwhelm you. He urged those around him to examine a problem carefully and objectively and have confidence in their own God-given common sense. The primary caveat for all JWC managers was a simple one: "Don't do anything stupid." That meant: Use your judgment, take due care, and be prepared to explain the reasoning behind your course of action.

Supervising an unstructured company, JWC management had tried to keep things simple. Fancy words and elaborate charts and communications were shunned in favor of one-on-one relationships. If you had something to say to Walter, Alston, Cordell, or anyone, you walked over to his office or called him on the telephone. You did not write memos which required the other man to reply with a complicated answer. Of course, an intrinsic matter of integrity was understood. You trusted one another to remember what was said and agreed upon. One's reputation depended upon being a man of one's word. In most companies memorandums are written primarily to cover one's backside in the event of future trouble, and at JWC they wanted none of that.

At Celotex, one had to write a memo to ask to see a superior down the hall. And then your name would be put on a list. Sometimes it would take a week to get in to see your superior. Some memos never were answered. Managers were known to slip a troublesome memo into a drawer and hope the problem would somehow go away. Bad news did not travel far at the company, and as a result, few top people there knew what was going on. Decisions were put off. Managers just rocked along as long as they got paid, and the company showed a profit, however small, each year. The Marrero strike in early 1962 hit the company in the solar plexus and before that fiscal year ended, Celotex would show its first loss, and that was in the millions. By then it was too late to remedy the situation.

By the end of their first week there, Walter and Cordell sized up the overall situation fairly well and were appalled most of all by a simple fact: Celotex was losing money, more than $1 million that year, and no one seemed to be doing very much about it. Rather than swing an axe around wildly, they decided to dig down deep into the specifics and find out who the real players were and what kind of game they were playing. Cordell delved into Celotex's internal financial statements to find out where the money was being spent, which divisions of the company were making money, which were losing money. The whys and wherefores involved, and what they could do about it, would come later.

The Floridians rented a two-bedroom apartment on Chicago Avenue, above a steak house where they would eat many a dinner, and settled in for the long haul. There late into the night, night after night, they would compare notes on the day's activities and plan their strategies for the next day. Their goal was clear: to turn Celotex around from a losing operation to a profitable one.

At the beginning they deliberately walked softly through the corridors of power at Celotex, asking questions, seeking advice and explanations, and trying to learn how things worked at the company and who made them work. Everyone there knew they carried a big stick, knew that these two young men with their Southern drawls had come to clear away the cobwebs that had been strangling Celotex.

Walter moved more cautiously than was his custom, examining the different sides and dimensions of a problem before attempting to solve it, finding out and differentiating who was deadwood that had to be swept away, who was salvageable and needed nurturing, and who deserved promotions and power. That took time. Celotex was a big, tradition-bound company. No single solution could possibly cover the multitude of problems that beset it. Walter needed and kept Henry Collins and his top management officers for the continuity and stability they provided. Collins had joined Celotex as a salesman in 1923, the company's third year of existence, and he had risen slowly through sales and marketing to executive vice president in 1948 and president in 1957. While not an inspiring or aggressive leader, he was well known and respected in the industry and willing without bitterness to help the new owners revamp the company he had failed to manage effectively. Walter, in turn, consulted with Collins frequently and relied on his firsthand knowledge of the company and its people.

In restructuring the management, Walter added on Joe Cordell as vice president of finance and a director of the company. He also appointed seven new members to the thirteen-member board of directors, including Buddy Alston and Ernie Knapp.

In the process of learning the operations, Walter and Cordell were constantly making judgments on the people who worked there. Sometimes they could size up a man in the first five or ten minutes. More often, they would work alongside a Celotex manager, take him out for dinner and before the evening was over, they would get the full measure of the man's energy level, motivation, courage, ability, and personality. They knew they not only had to get rid of the deadwood, but they had to persuade others that there was a point to working hard and working smart in the Jim Walter way of doing things. This was far from simple. What motivated one man did not necessarily motivate the next one. Each manager was different and needed different handling.

But Walter and Cordell did have the advantage of coming in with a clear view; they had no emotional attachments that prevented them from doing what they thought best for the company. They had no sacred cows. If a cow did not give milk, sell the cow, and get one that does. That was their policy. They were humane about it; they gave early retirement, severance pay, and time enough to find another job, but they were determined to clear the way for younger, more eager men to move up. Henry Collins helped point out the assets and liabilities of the various top managers, but many of the old-timers there were his "sacred cows" and he just did not have the heart to do what he knew had to be done.

Cordell, with his accountancy background, was dismayed by the financial operations of the company. By the end of the first week, he sought help from the Chicago office of his old firm, Price Waterhouse, and hired the firm to replace Celotex's former auditors. Kenneth Matlock, who had been with the accounting firm for fourteen years, was assigned as manager of the account, with William Weldon to assist him. The two CPAs moved into Celotex's accounting department and took over.

The very first thing Cordell wanted to change was the antiquated system of keeping the company financial records. No one person seemed to know what was going on throughout the whole company. Matlock and Weldon were put to work on a complete, in-depth, internal audit of every company plant and operation in order to get a grasp on the company's hidden assets as well as the profitability of each of its parts. Incredibly, for instance, the accounting department had purchased the latest model IBM computers, but no one there knew how to use them. They were calculating the payroll by hand, using the same old punch cards, and operating the fancy, new IBM computers merely to write the checks. Believing in the shock value of the unexpected, Cordell ordered a meeting of Celotex's accounting department with

IBM sales and technical staff for 8 a.m. the following Sunday morning.

Sunday morning?

Yes, Sunday morning.

That got their attention. At the meeting, Cordell complained, scolded, and served an ultimatum on the IBM people for having sold new, state-of-the-art equipment to Celotex without training its staff how to use it. "Now either you send some of your people in here to straighten this thing out or we are going to throw your computers out and start all over again with somebody else." The IBM people came through with some good ideas to meet the level of sophisticated accounting demanded by Cordell, and Cordell even agreed to buy some additional equipment needed to accomplish his purpose. He warned them this time, however, "I just want you to know my friends from Price Waterhouse over here are going to monitor all this for me and the company."

Gaining insight into the overall situation at Celotex from their first go-around at headquarters, Walter and Cordell, accompanied often by Ken Matlock and sometimes by Weldon, toured every plant and facility of the company. Asking question after question, sizing up plant managers, staff, workers, and production facilities, more often than not, they were welcomed heartily. It had been years since anyone from Celotex headquarters had visited the outlying factories and plants and shown an interest in what was going on. In the middle ranks of management throughout the company, they found a great many good men, eager to get down to real work, who had felt blocked and frustrated by the men above them.

The team returned to Chicago with long lists of people and facilities that needed to be trimmed or severed. Late into the night, sometimes into the early hours of the next morning, the two men worked together, comparing notes, searching for what they needed to know, and then making commonsense decisions. Celotex, they discovered, was half the size of its principal competitor, U.S. Gypsum, which had its headquarters just a block away in downtown Chicago. But Celotex maintained the same size staff and the same amount of overhead as its competitor, and that was a stupid way to keep up with the Gypsums.

Seven or eight months were spent just learning Celotex's varied businesses and then the new directors began cutting overhead, trimming excess staff, giving early retirement to tired executives, and cutting production of low-profit or no-profit items. They did it gradually, but not slowly, cutting into layers of fat once, twice, even three times. At the huge Marrero fiberboard plant in Louisiana, for example, Cordell spent five days there and trimmed a cool $1 million in annual costs, mainly by shutting down old, unprofitable product lines only to return six months later to cut another $500,000 in waste and overhead he had missed the first time. At each and every plant, they found fat to cut. To reach out to all the plants and factories, Walter and Cordell divided the places to be inspected and visited them separately. There seemed to be no end to the decisions that had to be made almost daily. Gallows humor, however, helped relieve the personal stress and loneliness of having to make so many decisions that affected so many lives. "Who'd you fire today?" was their standby greeting at the end of a workday, or "What are we going to sell off today?"

The two accountants from Price Waterhouse, Ken Matlock and Bill Weldon, earned their weight in gold and were rewarded subsequently by a change in careers that altered their lives. But at the time, while still employed by their accounting firm, they spent all their working hours going over and analyzing the books of Celotex. Deep in those records they discovered unpaid accounts receivable of more than $2 million going back several years. Henry Collins, president of Celotex, was flabbergasted when the figures were put in front of him. He didn't know what to say. The company's controller put in for early retirement. The accountants also found parcels of real estate, unused facilities, and all sorts of bits and pieces that could best be sold or written off as losses. They compiled detailed analyses of profit and loss statements for each of the company's manufacturing plants, which helped immeasurably in the decisions of Walter and Cordell in shaping the future of Celotex.

With the company showing an operating loss of $1.7 million for the 1962 fiscal year that ended October 31, Walter and Cordell decided to write off the old unpaid accounts as well as the facilities that were shopworn, outdated, and unprofitable. Combining all the losses in that one year gave Celotex a tax refund of $4.4 million. That was a good tidy sum in those days—the equivalent perhaps of $40 million today—and it gave the company a good head start on the next year, its first full year with James Willis Walter in the driver's seat.

The workload was enormous and the demands on their time unrelenting. The two Florida men toiled singlemindedly twelve to sixteen hours a day, day after day, and sometimes through Saturday and Sunday. For the better part of three years, they became commuters, leaving Chicago late Friday afternoon, spending the weekend in Tampa, and flying back up early Monday morning. Celotex became their whole lives, and their lives were made miserable by Chicago's notorious winter weather. When they left the office late at night and walked up dark and deserted La Salle Street, the freezing wet wind off Lake Michigan would whip through them to the marrow of their bones. The two Florida natives bought heavy overcoats and shivered. Cordell succumbed to wearing earmuffs (which Walter disdained), and they suf-

fered through one Chicago winter in which for one month
the temperature never rose above zero. There was not much
to like in the long hours, the frustrations, the grinding dull-
ness of numbers upon numbers, and particularly the frigid
winter weather. But they felt they had to do it, and, surprisingly enough, it was doable.

From cutting costs and increasing profit margins they
moved on to measures designed to boost sales, revenues, and
actual profits. Competition was mainly in price. Further, with
a slump in housing and building and the need to keep the
factories going, the competing building materials companies
were driving prices down to where the red ink flowed.

With the help of Cordell, Matlock, and Weldon, Jim Walter chartered a new course for Celotex, shifting the company's focus from sales to profits. Above all else, the most
important task during all of 1963 was trying to change the
mental attitude of the men and women who worked for Celotex. Particularly in the ranks of top management, Walter had
to put some gumption, some sense of loyalty, some sense of
caring back into company. At JWC he had long believed that
no matter how good the product was, no matter how low the
price, the success or failure of any company depended upon
the spirit, verve, and motivation of its people.

Just about every week Walter and Cordell gave pep talks to
small groups of headquarters staff, salesmen, or plant managers and foremen. Their talks never lasted more than twelve
minutes and they were right to the point. They demanded a
full day's work for a full day's pay. They promised to reward
those who could produce profits, not just more sales, for the
company. They sought to instill a new sense of purpose and
a new beginning throughout the operations of the company,
and they bluntly urged all of them to join in or get out. And
they followed through with an incentive bonus plan similar,
although smaller, to that at JWC. Word flowed through the

ranks of management that as the company prospered, the people responsible would also prosper. Celotex had had nothing like that. That first year, in addition to $100,000 for bonuses, Walter offered stock options in JWC to the key management people in Celotex. Appalled to learn that no one in the management owned any significant shares in the company, he wanted them to have a personal stake in the results. He wanted to be able to tell them, "Hey, if we cut you, we bleed; when you cut us, you bleed."

Walter and Cordell, even with the help of Matlock and Weldon, did not turn around Celotex by themselves. There never is one button to push or one lever to pull to change the direction of a company employing more than five thousand workers. What they did was set a new tone and pace to the management of the company, and people responded to it. They came to see that Walter and Cordell were in their offices every working day at about 7 a.m. and stayed late, with one or the other available and reachable at all times. Before long people began coming in earlier and working later and later into the night. And after the first full year when they began seeing the results of their labors, the inner sense of accomplishment was as satisfying as the increased earnings. It helped, too, that the construction business in general picked up that second year and Celotex was in there reaping its share of the rewards.

For fiscal 1963 Celotex reported sales of $81 million, a 25 percent increase over the previous year, and operating profits of $1.7 million, which represented a complete reversal from the operating loss of $1.7 million in 1962. Celotex had been "turned around" in just thirteen months! During the year, Walter had continued buying Celotex stock on the open market, accumulating 624,500 shares, or 61.3 percent of the company. With Celotex out of the red, and now owning more than 50 percent of the company, JWC could cheerfully consolidate its Celotex sales and earnings with those of its own for 1963.

Now Walter proceeded with the plan he had in mind from the very start. He wanted to acquire 100 percent of Celotex's outstanding shares, and then move it out of the frozen canyons of downtown Chicago to the sunny climes of Florida's west shore. Moving a company of that size required the highest order of strategy and secret planning until it was revealed to employees only at the last minute; otherwise current work would have been seriously disrupted. The proud Chicagoans of Celotex had to be wooed to leave familiar grounds and friends to take up life in the far-off tropics of Tampa.

There was no hint of what was to come when Jim Walter Corporation fulfilled the SEC requirements of size, sales, assets, and shareholders to be listed on the New York Stock Exchange with the symbol JWC. That day, March 9, 1964, was indeed a proud, symbolic day for the company which had begun business with an $895 shell home.

The listing of JWC was essential in Walter's plan to acquire Celotex. With both stocks registered on the Big Board, Walter (who for the time was chairman of two listed companies) could acquire Celotex in exchange for JWC common shares of established value. The purchase agreement of August 31, as complex as any, required outside Celotex shareholders to accept 1.1 shares of JWC common stock for each share of Celotex. They, of course, had the right to sell the JWC shares they received on the open market, but JWC did not have to lay out any more cash for Celotex stock.

Still, the people at Celotex did not perceive the implications involved. Walter and Cordell went about their ways, drawing up lists of people essential to Celotex in Tampa. They divided Celotex management and staff into three groups: those who were so essential that Celotex would pay all moving expenses and do almost anything to get them to move; people who could come if they wanted to pay their own moving expenses; and finally, those who were to be given severance pay and no invitation at all. Cordell enlisted the services of the Tampa Chamber of Commerce to produce an information kit on life and living costs in Tampa and Florida, the housing, the schools, the shopping, and the leisure activities, with a tourist brochure filled with color photographs of graceful palm trees, white sandy beaches, sparkling blue water, and clear sunny skies. The cost of moving Celotex came to $1.5 million, and Cordell took an insider's delight in charging those expenses to Celotex's accruals in such a way that no Celotex accountant detected the surgical extraction of $1.5 million from company earnings.

The night they hosted a hotel banquet to announce the move, the worst snowstorm in twenty years hit Chicago. Outside the wind howled and snow drifts grew mountainous while inside Jim Walter waxed eloquent on the good, healthy life of sunny Florida, where Ponce de León sought eternal youth.

The next six months were spent winding up affairs in Chicago, flying Celotex people back and forth for a tour of Tampa, helping them make the adjustment of moving their families, finding temporary office space for the newcomers, and making endless arrangements. Finally, in July 1965 the venerable Celotex Corporation, founded in 1921, was closed down in Chicago and started a new life as a subsidiary of the Jim Walter Corporation in Tampa, Florida.

The time was fitting. It was just one decade since the shell home building company had incorporated with $443,000 in assets. In its tenth annual report, JWC listed assets of $259.5

million, sales of $159 million, and earnings of $34 million. With the acquisition of Celotex, the shell home company that had started with fewer than one hundred full-time workers now employed more than six thousand people nationwide. In ten short years, it had grown up and joined the big boys in American business.

CHAPTER 7

— *Building for Growth* —

N OW THAT THE smaller company had swallowed the larger one, how was it going to digest it? Not easily, to be sure. Upset stomachs, heartburn, and headaches were the usual signs of indigestion when the Celotex executive and administrative staff began to arrive in Tampa in July 1965. Not only did they have to adjust to the new, strange environment of Southern living, they also came face to face with the rough-and-ready style of the "old-timers" in the shell home business of JWC, who, frankly, resented the "invasion from the north."

Integrating different corporate managers and staffs, each with their own traditions and values, is never easy, but moving urban, white-collar Chicagoans into the essentially blue-collar, country boy culture of JWC was almost volatile. It was like mixing caviar and catfish.

The physical transfer of all the worldly goods of the Celotex headquarters in Chicago—the furniture, file cabinets, computers, typewriters, paper, and paper clips—was accomplished in seven weekend moves spread out over some six months. Workers in two or three departments at a specified time would pack up, leave the office at the end of a Thursday, and report to work the following Monday in Tampa. Over the weekend, six or seven vans would move everything and set up the offices as they were before.

Their new workplace was hardly what they had expected. The promised eight-story tower for the company headquarters on North Dale Mabry was barely off the drawing boards. For the time being (which lasted more than a year) they had to conduct business in an old, windowless, four-story warehouse in downtown Tampa. Though remodeled and freshly painted, their quarters were plain and overcrowded compared to the sedate corporate accommodations they had left in Chicago. It was hardly an interior decorator's delight. Jim Walter moved in with the Celotex people. He was not abandoning his allegience to JWC, but Celotex was where he felt he was most needed. If you expect your people to endure hardships, he believed, you had better be in that boat with them.

Henry Collins had chosen to remain in Chicago to represent the company, and Marvin Greenwood, the longtime executive vice president who had headed the daily operations of Celotex for more than ten years, was put in charge of Celotex in Tampa. Greenwood, an engineer by training and not particularly adept in handling people, was as set and stubborn in his ways as was Bud Alston, who ran the home-building division of JWC. The two men simply did not get along. Their styles of management, which permeated the attitudes of the men who worked for them, were totally different, and, whatever the merits of either side, working together was a constant battle for supremacy. The Celotex people, for instance, were paid more than the JWC employees because the Chicago pay scale was higher than that in Tampa and Walter chose not to cut salaries when he had to persuade the Chicagoans to move south. Alston resented what he perceived as the higher pay for less work, the bureaucracy, waste, and frills of the Celotex operations: he feared that they would ruin the lean and hungry values he had personally instilled in the JWC workforce. Greenwood undoubtedly hated what he considered encroachments by the less experienced Arkansas hillbilly who happened to hold the title of president of Jim Walter Corporation. Jim Walter worked hard to keep the peace.

What made the combination of these two companies and two cultures so difficult was the appearance of the tail wagging the dog. At the time of the move in 1965, Celotex was providing about three-fourths of JWC's consolidated sales volume. The subsidiary was not only bigger than its parent in assets and revenues, it had the corporate staff of attorneys, accountants, tax experts, labor relations and personnel people, and specialists of one sort or another, all of which JWC lacked. The Homes people, led by Bud Alston, bristled at the "intrusion" of so many lawyers, accountants, and professionals. With his lifelong antipathy for college-bred professionals, Alston liked to point out that while Celotex accounted for 75 percent of sales, the old Homes Division produced 90 to 95 percent of the company's profits.

Jim Walter knew better than anyone else that it would take years to reconcile the corporate culture of Celotex with the smaller shell home business he had founded. He wanted to change the Celotex people and give them the drive, spirit, and motivation that pervaded JWC. But he realized that attitudes and feelings of people are not changed by the boss's demand or a set of corporate rules. He didn't believe in ordering subordinates to do something—not unless he absolutely had to. The Celotex staff would absorb JWC culture just by being there, he believed, and he preferred teaching by example. He had himself assimilated a wealth of business knowledge since the Celotex acquisition, and he looked forward with his natural optimism to the day when the Celotex newcomers, with their old ways of doing things, would blend in with the old-timers in the Homes Division, who were more young at heart.

Recognizing the need for competent and creative staff ever since the acquisition of Celotex, Cordell hired Ken Matlock away from Price Waterhouse and put him in charge of all of Celotex's financial affairs. Bill Weldon remained with the accounting firm and when Celotex moved to Tampa, Price Waterhouse moved him there as its auditor of Jim Walter Corporation. Five years later, he too would join the company.

Walter was very careful in choosing new men for his top management team. He preferred to hire men he already knew well, who, beyond their professional competence, would fit naturally into the friendly but driving corporate atmosphere of his company. James W. Kynes was a case in point. A native Floridian, center and captain of the University of Florida football team, a successful lawyer, a prosecuting attorney for the city of Ocala in central Florida, and then the attorney general for the state, Jimmy Kynes was, beyond being a knowledgeable attorney and keen judge of people and situations, a big, warm, congenial man with a good sense of humor. When he campaigned for reelection in the Democratic primary of 1964, he stopped in to see Walter, whom he knew well.

"Jim, I need your help financially," he said. "How about a campaign contribution?"

Writing a personal check for $1,000, Walter said, "I'm going to give you this money, but I hope you lose, so you can come to work for me."

When Kynes lost the statewide primary by 599 votes, he got a prompt call from Walter, saying, "Okay, now I want you to come to work for us."

"You must have put the jinx on me when you gave me that money," said Kynes with a laugh, but when he finished his term in office, he joined JWC as general counsel and vice president, and was there until he died more than twenty-five years later.

Longevity and loyalty were not unusual at JWC. People

who came and prospered stayed on, not that there were no better jobs or better offers on the outside, but rather because Jim Walter inspired an intense personal loyalty. From top management men to the original branch managers in the shell home business to the secretaries who worked there from the beginning, some of whom rose to become top administrators, all stayed on. Some said Walter was loyal to a fault, meaning that in their eyes he would put up with many a fault that others would not. But more than that, he extended himself on a personal level to help someone in need. He was there at family crises, he extended advice and sometimes loans, he was approachable, and he did those extra little things not as a good business practice or as a special favor, but because he was that kind of man. It was a small, intimate company, and the men and women there appreciated their boss and reciprocated that loyalty, extending themselves so as not to disappoint the man who had shown in his own natural way that he had faith in them.

By the time Celotex moved to Tampa, Jim Walter personally was on a roll, the adrenalin flowing, his optimism and self-confidence rewarded: He had survived three years of backbreaking work and worry in Chicago and now stood at the helm of the nation's oldest and largest builder of shell and partially finished homes and one of the largest, best-recognized building materials companies in the United States. As one among many financial analysts reported in August 1965: "The company, with 1964 sales of $151.8 million, and after-tax profits of $6.5 million, is an American success story in the finest tradition."

Given normal rates of corporate growth, the development of this company had been phenomenal. In 1947, Jim Walter and Lou Davenport were happy to sell ten shell houses a week. In 1957, after incorporation, JWC annual sales had climbed to just under $12 million; five years later sales had quadrupled to $30 million. One year later, consolidated with Celotex, sales leaped to $133 million, and with some added zest to the management, JWC had grown to almost $152 million for 1964.

But for Jim Walter that growth was in the past, and only a prelude of what was to come. Ever the pragmatic dreamer, he was not satisfied merely to preside over the normal, albeit treacherous, transition from small company to large one. He viewed the Celotex turnaround as a new beginning. In another sense he had turned his own company, JWC, around, too. In the shell home business, he was the big fish in a little pond; now, in the building supplies business with Celotex, he was a little fish in a big pond.

His success with Celotex had given him and his company two essential things: capital and credibility. JWC's equity ownership in Celotex gave it greater borrowing power in the financial community, and the turnaround proved to the whole business world that Jim Walter and his team could run a complex manufacturing and distribution business as well as anyone, without any hocus-pocus bookkeeping or liquidation of assets. With the obvious success of Celotex, Jim Walter earned a large measure of credibility and respect in financial circles. Acquisition and merger propositions began to flow in as JWC was now seen as an affluent buyer rather than a borrower or a beggar for money. However, before Walter or his company could venture out on the acquisitions trail, he had to answer the looming question: "Now that we've got Celotex, where do we go from here?"

The expected synergism of the shell home division using Celotex building materials had not worked out as envisioned in 1962. Shell homes simply did not use that many products manufactured by Celotex, nor could Walter from on high order his branch managers to buy Celotex products. The branch managers always had the autonomy to make their purchases on the local market, depending on the best products at the best prices. Celotex would have to make it on its own, once the fat and waste had been trimmed away and low-profit items were replaced with more profitable building materials. That meant largely switching from overproduction of insulating fiberboard to increasing production of acoustical ceiling tiles, gypsum wallboard, and interior wallboard panels.

The next logical step was to increase the diversity of building materials manufactured by Celotex so that it was not so dependent upon one or two products in the field, like fiberboard. In that vein, before the move to Tampa, Celotex bought two companies. The first was the Crawford Door Company, a well-established, profitable outfit in a suburb of Detroit with annual sales in the $9-11 million range. The company had pioneered the upward-swinging (overhead) door as far back as 1929. The other was the Vestal Manufacturing Company, a small but very profitable, family-owned foundry in the tiny town of Sweetwater in eastern Tennessee. A leader in its field with annual sales of $3 million, Vestal manufactured cast-iron stoves, fireplace units, and some 150 other metal products widely used by builders and home owners. After the acquisition, Walter probed the managements of the companies on what he could do to help them increase sales and earnings. For Vestal, he had Celotex invest $2 million for the construction of a new semiautomatic foundry. The modernization increased Vestal's output by some 50 percent. For Crawford, he authorized replacing the company's split operations in two old plants on one side of Detroit with a large and modern facility on the other side of the city. That well-laid-out plan boomeranged. One year after moving into the modern plant, Crawford suffered a 100 percent turnover of personnel and never had another truly profitable year. The planners, with the best of intentions, had neglected to consider that Crawford workers lived near the old buildings and would not want to drive across Detroit to get to work.

In streamlining the Celotex operation, Walter already had made the tough decision to acquire full ownership of South Coast Corporation, the sugar company, and of The South Shore Oil and Development Company, which leased sugar company land in Louisiana for oil exploration and drilling. Both companies had great potential, along with considerable risks down the road. But even as majority stockholder, Celotex could not run the companies without the consent of other shareholders. Walter felt uncomfortable with sizable investments in partially owned companies. Wanting either all or nothing, it took Celotex until 1968 to buy out the other shareholders and acquire 100 percent of South Coast and South Shore.

JWC's core business—the selling, financing, and building of shell homes—was a source of deep satisfaction to the company's original founders, Walter, Alston, and Saraw. By the mid-1960s, Jim Walter Homes was supreme in the industry with some 150 branch sales offices in thirty-eight states, selling between eight and ten thousand homes a year. Almost all of the ferocious competition of the early 1960s was gone, and the few remaining large shell home companies would close shop before 1970.

The competition, in retrospect, had done two important things for the company. First of all, it had forced JWC in 1962 to offer partially finished homes to the public in order to meet the competition's product. Walter and Alston had gone into the more elaborate homes reluctantly, wanting to keep their basic shell home as simple as possible. To their surprise they found partially finished homes, with customers buying some or all of the option packages, becoming more and more popular. By 1966 or 1967, more than 90 percent of sales were for some form of partially completed homes.

Times had changed in America. The American working man now either had enough money for a more expensive home or he no longer had the time or inclination to put in "sweat equity."

The economics of that change in buying habits was significant. Jim Walter homes, which once sold for $1,000 to $5,000, depending upon size, now were priced in the range of $2,000 to $8,000. The average price in the mid-1960s was $4,500. Of course, the bigger the home and the more completed it was, the higher the price and the profits that flowed into JWC coffers. In order to keep the monthly mortgage payment low and affordable, always a key selling point for Jim Walter homes, the company stretched the mortgages to twelve years where needed, and that, with the interest of 6 percent each year, further increased the revenues and cash flow of the company. By the end of 1966, the company's mortgage portfolio had grown to a whopping $204.8 million dollars, with about $25 million of that due that year. That $25 million was coming in no matter how many or how few homes were sold that year. As home sales increased, however, the number and face value of the mortgages increased and provided the all-important cash flow needed for further expansion. It turned out to be a wonderful cycle.

Competition in the early 1960s also served to hone JWC's home-building operations to a higher degree of sophistication, if not near perfection. Bud Alston, ever the perfectionist, involved himself in just about every detail of selling, financing, and building homes, even down to working out how all the auxiliary materials needed for a home could be loaded on one truck for one run from the warehouse to the homesite. By the mid-1960s, JWC was buying building materials in huge cost-saving amounts, mostly through the Booker Company, with which it had started doing business back in 1946. Warehouses were built to serve branch and sub-branch offices within a radius of one hundred miles. As the branches reported each Saturday on the numbers of houses sold and built, the figures were passed on to Jack Almand at Booker, who now devoted just about all his time to this one account, and Almand would direct the flow of inventory from the manufacturer to each warehouse, as needed.

Competition and the furious rate of foreclosures also had tightened up the credit operation of the company. Now JWC required that the buyer's ability to pay be based upon a mortgage payment no larger than 20 percent of his monthly income, a figure far below that required by the FHA or VA. Pursuing Walter's original concept that a house is not sold until the final payment is made, the company was vigorous in chasing down its mortgage payments. It maintained a force of more than one hundred bill collectors who went out and knocked on the doors of delinquents. Telephoning was not enough. A knock on the door and a thirty-day notice usually brought forth the money due. If not, foreclosure proceeded. Forfeitures were relatively rare, based more often on divorce, death, or other family trouble than on a buyer having been a poor credit risk.

Home building had grown big enough to support cost-saving consolidation of some operations which had once been handled locally at the branch level. In the mid-1960s Alston decided, against the wishes of almost all the branch managers, to consolidate the company's advertising. He formed JWC's own advertising company, a wholly owned subsidiary, Coast-to-Coast Advertising, and appointed Larry Bankston, who handled local advertising in Tampa, to head the new company. Bankston, then in his mid-twenties, protested that he was too young, too inexperienced, and did not know enough about advertising to take on that assignment. Bud Alston rose from his desk, his face turning red, the muscles in his neck bulging and shouted, "Are you telling me I don't know how to do my job? I picked you. Get your ass down to that office and do the job I gave you!" Bankston continued doing that job for the next thirty years until his retirement in 1993.

The home-building operation through the years had had almost uninterrupted growth in sales and revenues since incorporation, with the one exception of 1962 when shell home competition had been at its fiercest. The beauty of JWC's core business, which had not been planned at the start, was that it was countercyclical to the rest of the home-building industry. Housing is perhaps the most interest-sensitive industry in the American economy. When interest rates go up, the cost of mortgages and monthly payments go up, and sales go down. The ups and downs are volatile, immediate, and extreme. And, no one can predict what general interest rates will do from year to year. On the other hand, Jim Walter homes were financed by Jim Walter Corporation through its Mid-State mortgage subsidiary. Thus, when the money supply became tight and bank mortgage rates went up, the potential home buyer came to Jim Walter where the mortgages were financed in-house and at attractive, below-market rates of interest. In years like 1966, when money was tight, economic conditions depressed, and housing starts low, Jim Walter Homes flourished. On the other hand, the building materials operations of Celotex suffered along with the rest of the housing and construction industry in the downturns.

In its 1966 annual report the company duly noted: "General economic factors of course played a decisive role throughout the year. Higher interest rates coupled with private and public apprehension over the state of the national economy have had their greatest effect in the fields of finance and construction, which are the principal areas of operation for the Company. In light of these developments, it is especially gratifying that the Company was able to maintain its sales and earnings rate, since this indicates penetration of its several markets." In other words, JWC held its own in a bad year. It actually did a great deal better than its competitors.

Fiscal 1966-67 was a kind of watershed year, the beginning of the end of bad times for the construction industry. Total housing starts in the United States had been declining steadily since the boom years right after the end of World War II, when millions of returning servicemen were out looking for a place to live and Jim Walter began building low-cost shell homes. In 1950, for example, housing starts reached almost 2 million; in 1955 they had slumped to 1.6 million and in 1965 had slid even further to 1.5 million. Economists were crying "mini-recession," and the predictions and forecasts were generally for more gloom and doom.

Looking ahead, however, Jim Walter saw a great deal of pent-up demand for new housing in the years ahead. "It doesn't take a genius to see that all those babies born right after World War II will be coming of age in the late '60s and early '70s, and those are the people who will be buying houses." Despite all the talk of recession, this was no time to cut back, thought Walter; it was a chance to go forward and build, to acquire new companies and expand Celotex so that it could become the leading building-materials company in the industry when the construction recession ended. Of course, there was no guarantee of a housing boom in the near future, or any way to predict general economic conditions, or to forecast the all-important interest rates in the coming years, but Jim Walter, by instinct more than anything else, wanted to choose the high road for his company.

He stated the company's future intentions very clearly in the 1966 annual report:

The philosophy and character of the Company, which has attained its present size and eminence in but twenty years of existence, are so growth-oriented that no consideration is ever given to an interruption or even a slowing down of the corporate program for internal expansion and improvement.

The population of the United States will continue to increase and over the long run the economy will expand. Young couples will require homes, growing businesses new plants; both of these fundamental needs will generate demand for builders, building materials and financing, all of which the Company will be asked to help meet.

It is the intention of Jim Walter Corporation, undeterred by temporary pressures on the economy, to be thoroughly prepared for an expanded market.

In preparing for that anticipated market, Walter hired two different consulting firms to survey and analyze Celotex's potentialities. What new businesses could and should Celotex get into? That was the key question. With a nationally known name, a well-established chain of distribution and sales offices, and its own administrative staff, production engineers, marketing experts, and research facilities and personnel, Celotex could develop, market, and sell other products with little if any increased costs.

The two consulting firms came back with almost identical lists of just about every product that goes into any residential or commercial building. Carpeting headed both lists. Almost every building needed carpeting and there was no one company that dominated the market. Paint was high on the list. So was roofing.

Walter digested the material, consulted with others, compared notes with his colleagues in Celotex and JWC, and decided to acquire companies that presented good opportunities for growth, so long as they somehow fit in with JWC and Celotex's area of expertise. He knew he wanted to buy companies that were well established, profitable, and had a depth of management that could carry on the business under the JWC aegis. He wanted companies that could be acquired either with an exchange of JWC stock or with borrowed money. "The road to success is paved with borrowed money," he repeatedly advised his colleagues. That's how his shell home business had grown in the first place. Above all, he preferred acquisitions that would add to JWC's equity base, knowing that the more assets owned by the company the more it could borrow from banks for future growth.

The company had followed that basic concept in 1964 when acquiring Warren Industries of Miami, one of the country's largest manufacturers of steel and aluminum window screens for residential and commercial buildings. The product fit right in with JWC since all Jim Walter homes came equipped with screens. Warren Industries was run by three energetic young men who had taken their company, founded in 1948, just about as far as it could go by itself. They proposed a merger, promising future expansion, wider markets, and more bank credit under the JWC umbrella, and they promised to stay on to run the company. JWC bought Warren Industries without hesitation, moved it into a new 200,000-square-foot plant in Hialeah, a suburb of Miami, and Eugene Katz, who headed the company, aggressively expanded product lines, sales volume, and profits the very next year, as promised.

As luck would have it, while searching for acquisitions that would enhance Celotex, Walter was approached by Gene Woodfin of Loeb Rhoades, with an "opportunity" to buy a savings and loan institution that was underpriced. He explained that the Brentwood Financial Corporation, a holding company which owned and operated the Brentwood

Savings and Loan Association, with three branches in the affluent west side of Los Angeles, was for sale. Brentwood had
$158 million in assets, rather meager earnings of $1.43 million
the previous year, a management that pledged to stay on,
and, above all, an unusually good potential for future growth
with the flood of people moving to Southern California. Los
Angeles was one of the fastest growing areas of the country.

The fit was good, Walter and his board of directors agreed.
Brentwood Savings and Loan dealt in home mortgages; JWC,
with its Mid-State subsidiary, certainly knew the ins and outs
of the mortgage business. They had done well with the St.
Petersburg bank since 1959, more than doubling its resources to $160 million. Above all, the price was right: $9 million in preferred and common JWC stock, with no outlay of
cash. So, on January 5, 1966, JWC acquired Brentwood as a
wholly owned subsidiary in exchange for 390,650 shares of
$1.20 voting preferred stock and 141,200 shares of common
stock of JWC. If housing increased, as Jim Walter expected,
then the Los Angeles-based Brentwood would reap the benefits along with the whole building industry.

Fundamentally, Jim Walter believed in grasping opportunity whenever possible and feasible. Formal strategic long-
range planning, he did not believe in. How could anyone
know what was going to happen in the next five years, and if
you didn't know, how could you plan for it? He consulted
with management consultants, as he had been advised to do,
and he came away unconvinced and with thoughts of his
own. "I think a five-year plan is not worth the paper it is written on," he told his colleagues and his board of directors. "I
never saw anybody who's going to write a five-year plan that
says four years from now we're going to be in a depression
and we're going to lose our butts. The guy who forecasts that
gets fired. What he will do is put in some multiple of increase

over present figures, and if you look at that five-year plan you can be in Utopia."

As with so many best-laid plans, no sooner was the Brentwood S & L acquired than the money supply grew tighter, competition for the savings dollar became more fierce, and housing starts continued to decline. For the next two years the Brentwood S & L lost so much money it almost went broke. In 1967, the nationwide money squeeze became so bad that the bank had to borrow from the Federal Home Loan Bank in order to cover withdrawals and suspend all its lending until it could repay the FHLB. Nor could anyone predict the weather. For three years in a row, 1965-67, the sugarcane fields of the South Coast Corporation in Louisiana were hit by hurricanes, crops were lost, and earnings tumbled.

At the time the closest thing approaching Utopia was the move into the gleaming, new, eight-story headquarters building on North Dale Mabry Highway, facing the new Interstate 275. Rectangular in shape with eight thin vertical columns of windows which appeared slate gray against a white brick facade, it was a large, modern high-rise for Tampa, containing 120,000 square feet of office space. The $1.5 million tower, wrapped around and incorporating the two-story headquarters building erected ten years earlier, was characterized by "simplicity, economy, ease of maintenance, and attractive appearance," which is what Jim Walter had requested at the outset. It fit the personality of the company. The first five floors were devoted to various administrative and communications functions, the sixth and seventh floors were left vacant for future expansion, and the eighth floor contained the executive offices. Contemporary simplicity was the interior decorating style, no fancy frills or luxury trappings, and the chairman's office reflected the open, easy decor of the rest of the building in its beiges and browns, light walnut paneling, and spare, contemporary furnishings. Celotex building products were used throughout the headquarters, of course.

For the formal dedication of the building in December 1966, Joe Cordell had a friend track down the original shell home that Jim Walter had bought from Lou Davenport in November 1946. It was still standing where the buyer had moved it twenty years before, and now it cost Cordell $3,200. Freshly painted and refurbished, the tiny clapboard house was moved to the front of the new headquarters building. It was the star of the dedication ceremonies, for this little $895 house—built 150,000 houses ago—had given birth to a new idea. From this shell house evolved the eight-story office tower and the $164 million company, now one of the largest home builders in America.

A company's headquarters is more, much more, than a mere building, and the brand-new office tower on the west side of Tampa served as a symbol of a company coming of age, reaching a new maturity. More than that, it gave the workers of Celotex a completely fresh start in life with JWC. It was more than four years since Jim Walter had acquired Celotex, and his personal imprint was becoming more and more evident in the changes in the company management. The move into the new company headquarters put the Celotex people on a more equal footing with the old-timers. They were no longer second-class citizens in the company. They belonged. It was a new beginning for Celotex.

In time for the opening of the new headquarters, Jim Walter made some significant changes in the Celotex management. Henry Collins was moved "upstairs" to vice chairman of Celotex and a director of JWC, but stayed in Chicago; Marvin Greenwood, the executive vice president, was elected to the JWC board, but not made president of Celotex. To run the company, Walter chose Eugene Katz, the aggressive head

of Warren Industries. Katz, a short robust man with bound-
less energy, was a take-charge, hands-on kind of manager. In
short order, he cut through even more layers of fat than Walter and Cordell had found. He energized Celotex's sales and
service departments on the fundamental theory that since
most building products were of equal quality and price, it
was the personal services, dependability, and integrity of the
company itself, and particularly its sales force, that attracted,
won over, and held the customer. The Celotex people rose
to the occasion, responded to the change in management
style, and progressed year by year to increased sales and earnings and greater shares of the market in their various product lines.

With a firm belief in the future of home building and all
the related building supplies, JWC did not stint in support-
ing the growth of Celotex. In moving the subsidiary to
Tampa, it made no sense to keep Celotex's research laboratories housed in an ancient red brick building in Des Plaines,
Illinois. Instead, the company built an up-to-date research
laboratory complex of five buildings on a college-like cam-
pus in nearby St. Petersburg, only a fifteen-minute drive
from the Tampa headquarters. It became one of the outstanding research and development centers in the building
and construction materials industry. The professional staff
of about one hundred scientists represented more than
twenty-one disciplines in the physical sciences, including
chemistry, physics, ceramics, plastics, and more. The twenty-
three laboratories and four built-in environmental control
rooms with all the latest testing equipment gave the center
the ability to develop and test just about any element of all
the building materials available to the industry. The staff did
basic and applied research on new materials and elaborate
testing on the wear and tear of all their products. The research center would in time be responsible for developing

new kinds of insulating material, new kinds of acoustical tiles, and new kinds of wallboard that more than paid for the cost of the well-endowed facility.

Call it luck or being smart, or a little bit of both, but the Homes Division and Celotex were poised, prepared, and ready to surge ahead when the economy of the United States did an about-face in 1968-69 and began one of the greatest housing booms since the end of World War II. The tight money situation eased, cash and credit began to flow once again, and the pent-up, deferred demand for housing burst forth. At the same time, personal income, savings, and expenditures reached all-time highs. It seemed that all those people who had put off buying a home now wanted to buy. The economists reversed themselves and predicted a genuine housing boom lasting well into the 1970s; the only thing in doubt was the home-building industry's ability to keep up with the demand.

With the economy booming, fiscal 1968 was a banner year for Jim Walter Corporation. Every individual segment of the company increased sales and earnings!

With thirty-three manufacturing plants in the United States and Canada, the company's sales of building materials increased from $103 million in 1967 to a new high of $188 million in 1968. Home building and mortgage financing rose from $48 million to a record $58 million in 1968 and another record $71 million in 1969. Mid-State Homes now carried 52,995 individual home mortgages valued at $331 million!

With the easing of the money supply and record housing starts, Brentwood Savings and Loan turned a $600,000 loss in 1967 into a profit of $400,000 in 1968, and doubled those earnings the next year.

Even the weather cooperated, and without hurricanes the South Coast sugar company had one of the best years in its history, producing a bumper 1968 crop worth $34 million. Everything was going so well that on October 4, 1968, the company declared a very special dividend for its shareholders: a three-for-one stock split. Financial analysts began paying more attention to the phenomenal growth of this young company. In 1969, JWC stock on the Big Board rose from $18 to $67 a share.

And Jim Walter, having prepared beforehand, knew what he wanted to do next. He went on a swift buying spree. He bought a roofing company, a paper company, a marble company, a carpet company, and a giant pipe and foundry establishment. And when he was done, he had more than doubled the size of Jim Walter Corporation.

CHAPTER 8

— *Building for Diversity* —

HEALTHY CORPORATIONS GROW in two fundamental ways. One way is to expand from within, providing needed or desirable products or services at attractive prices, and as sales increase, productivity is expanded to satisfy increased demand. The other, quicker way is to buy an already-established business and add it to your own. The extra dividend in this process is the normal savings in overhead expenses when two independent companies are able to share corporate staffs.

Jim Walter Corporation flourished in both directions. It had become the undisputed leader as the world's largest builder of shell and partially finished homes, selling about eight thousand homes each year. Celotex, while prospering and growing under the JWC aegis, was still not large enough to challenge its competitors when it came to setting standards for the industry.

The late 1960s and early 1970s was a momentous era of growth for virtually all of American industry, a turbulent time of mergers and acquisitions. Men like Tex Thornton of Litton Industries, James Ling of LTV, Harold Geneen of ITT, and Charles Bluhdorn of Gulf & Western created and implemented the new concept of the conglomerate. They built business empires by gobbling up companies as if they were jelly beans.

The word on Wall Street was synergism, the combining of two or more similar businesses to make one centralized company that would be more cost-effective, more productive, and more profitable than its separate parts. The concept of conglomerates went one step further: businesses being merged and combined did not need to be similar in product lines or services; diverse businesses under one roof could spread the risk of cyclical economic downturns and also be cost-effective under modern management. But under whatever concept and for whatever reasons, there were always buyers and sellers in the marketplace of American businesses. It is the bringing together of the right buyer and the right seller that makes the right business deal.

Having been tagged as a buyer after the well-publicized acquisition of Celotex, JWC received a steady stream of unsolicited offers and proposals of companies for sale. Walter, Cordell, and their staff could pick and choose. There must have been thirty or more proposals coming into their offices for every one they would consider in depth, much less buy. For them to even look at a proposed acquisition, some kind of synergism had to exist; the company also had to be already profitable, not a high risk, turnaround situation; and, last but not least, the price, whether paid in cash or stock, had to enhance rather than dilute JWC's earnings per share. These were the criteria Walter and Cordell, working closely together, had adopted by trial and error in looking over hundreds of proposals. Of course, in an imperfect world, it is mighty difficult to find a perfect business deal.

JWC's first big acquisition since Celotex in 1962 came as close to perfection as anyone could possibly hope for: the Barrett Building Materials Division of the giant Allied Chemical and Dye Corporation. The Allied Chemical subsidiary was a profitable company virtually the same size as Celotex and producing the same products. It would be a beautiful fit. The synergism was definitely there. Merging the two operations would double the productivity and sales of Celotex while cutting in half the overhead expenses of the combined operations.

John Loeb, who sat on the board of directors of Allied Chemical, brought the proposal to Jim Walter, saying that for strategic reasons of its own, primarily to concentrate its resources upon its flourishing chemical business, Allied Chemical had decided to divest itself of substantially all of its humdrum building-materials business contained in its Barrett Division. Barrett had been one of the five chemical companies that banded together in 1920 to create Allied.

Barrett had started out as a roofing company more than a hundred years before in Chicago. Actually, it was 1854 when Samuel E. Barrett, at age twenty, began installing roofs made of felt paper and tar. Chicago at the time had a population of 30,000 and the most popular song of the day was *Deal Gently with the Motherless*. When Mrs. O'Leary's cow kicked over that lantern in the barn on October 8, 1871, setting off the great Chicago fire, more than 17,400 buildings were destroyed, and that set the stage for a prosperous roofing and reroofing business for Samuel E. Barrett.

Down through the years this enterprising businessman merged and acquired other roofing companies, expanded into chemical by-products of coal-tar, and at the turn of the century introduced the Barrett brand-named "Tarvia" for paving roads, which literally took the newly developed automobile out of the mud and gave it some place to go.

His company, head and shoulders above the competition, set the standards for the roofing industry, standards that are with us today. To guard against unscrupulous roofers who were giving the business a bad name even back then, in 1906, Barrett introduced the "Specification Roof," which prescribed the number of layers of felt, the spacing between them and the amount and type of pitch tar, and just about everything else that went into constructing a roof. The company also started an organization which listed "approved roofers" who could be trusted, and followed that in 1916 with the first guarantees of work and material. Barrett "Specification Roofs" were bonded against repair and maintenance for varying periods up to twenty years.

In more recent years, the chemical operations of Barrett, largely in distilling and refining coal-tar chemicals, had vastly outdistanced its roofing and building materials business. In fact, Barrett had become the largest manufacturer of coal-tar chemicals in the United States when Allied Chemical decided to sell off Barrett's building materials division in 1967.

The deal John Loeb brought to Jim Walter was the best of its kind: both Allied Chemical and JWC would get what they wanted, both would benefit, and neither would lose anything in the process. The proposition was that JWC would purchase the entire Barrett Division of Allied Chemical, consisting of thirteen major plants and facilities, for essentially their book value of $49 million. Barrett had annual revenues of about $60 million, and the fit was beautiful. To Celotex's heavy production facilities in insulating fiberboard and its single roofing plant in Los Angeles, the Barrett acquisition would bring six large roofing plants in the eastern half of the country, two fiberboard plants in Iowa and Pennsylvania, a felt factory in Iowa, and a large hardboard facility in upstate New York. Moreover, the synergism of doubling the size of Celotex would more than double its presence, recognition, and impact in the construction industry.

John Loeb brought the deal to JWC, but it was Gene Woodfin who handled the detailed negotiations, and when all was said and done, JWC paid $20 million in cash and 731,607 shares of newly created convertible preferred JWC stock (at $40 per) for Barrett. Essentially it was an exchange of assets. Barrett operations would be absorbed within Celotex and their sales and earnings consolidated, adding to the earnings per share of JWC. It was so much easier, physically and mentally, than the acquisition of Celotex and those three years of backbreaking work in Chicago.

When the final legal papers were signed on August 1, 1967, Walter and Woodfin, now fast friends, celebrated the new acquisition with a splendid lunch at one of New York's finest and most expensive French restaurants. Indulging in superb French cuisine and an exquisite vintage wine, Woodfin wistfully remarked that among the finer things in life he always wanted but did not feel justified in buying was a Rolls Royce. Walter, exhilarated over the day's events, taunted the investment banker with a deal he knew he would find hard to refuse.

"I'll make you a proposition: We'll buy a Rolls together, half and half; when I'm in town, the car is mine—and, you know, I'm not here that often—and when I'm not in New York, the car is yours." Woodfin snapped up the offer.

The two men strolled the few blocks to the Rolls Royce showroom on Second Avenue, happily selected a maroon sedan, made arrangements for it to be ready by 5 p.m., and went out shopping on Fifth Avenue to bide their time. When the time came to pick up the car, Woodfin rubbed his hands in delight, saying, "I can't wait to go out tonight in that Rolls."

"Gene, you forgot our deal," remonstrated Walter. "I'm in town tonight. Tonight the Rolls is mine."

Playing one-upsmanship, Woodfin tried to negotiate the use of the Rolls for that first night. Walter refused. Back and forth they went on the dilemma: Both wanted the luxury automobile that first night. They settled the dispute so that neither man was denied by agreeing to buy another maroon Rolls.

The dealer was delighted with the prospect of selling two instead of one, but then at the last moment was dismayed and apologetic that Walter could not have his Rolls that same day; he would have to wait two days for preparation and delivery.

"Oh, that's all right," rejoined Walter, pausing for words that Woodfin would never forget. "I really don't need a car for tonight; I just want to make this cheap son-of-a-bitch buy a Rolls for himself." It rained that night, and both men used taxicabs.

The fun and games of big business is in the buying and selling of companies. It has all the elements, albeit on a much larger scale, of the ordinary man or woman buying a house, an automobile or, if one is that fortunate, a yacht. You have to pick and choose and bargain over price and decide whether to buy this one or wait until something better, cheaper, or better and cheaper comes along. You have to use all your past experiences and your judgment and your instincts. You have to have the courage to take risks. There is never a sure thing. If you make a mistake, you have to pay for it, and if you make a big mistake, you can lose all the marbles. Of course, if you are a wise buyer most of the time, you try to make sure you have a back door by which you can escape. When you buy a house, a car, or a company, it is wise to calculate how much and how quickly you can sell it, if and when you are forced to bail out. That's why, if your figures are right, a bargain is a bargain is a bargain.

JWC's next significant purchase, in February of 1968, was the Marquette Paper Corporation of Chicago, which, with its wholly owned subsidiary, the Nackie Paper Company of Milwaukee, was a wholesaler of fine printing papers. It bought paper in bulk from various mills and sold it in smaller quantities to book publishers and printers. Where was the connection, the synergism, with JWC's building materials or shell homes? There was none. Did it come highly recom-

Jim Walter, 23, at the beginning *(left)*.

The young businessman with his own car, 1946 *(right)*.

Humble beginnings: Walter Construction Co. *(below)*.

The entire office staff celebrating the first anniversary of Jim Walter Corporation as a public company in 1956. Jim Walter, center, cutting the cake; Buddy Alston at his side; Arnold Saraw between them in back row; Kendall Baker at the far right.

The original $895 Jim Walter home, repurchased and moved onto headquarters property in 1966, with original partners, Buddy Alston, Jim Walter and Arnold Saraw.

A typical Jim Walter home of the 1950s, the "Meadowbrook," for $2,495 (without the Studebaker in the carport).

A typical turnout for the opening of a new JWH display park, 1950s.

One of two JWH "Band Wagons" that played bluegrass music and loudspeaker announcements for Jim Walter homes, touring Georgia, Virginia, and the Carolinas in the 1960s. Note house prices.

Two Jim Walter Homes
newspaper advertisements
from the late 1950s.

The first two-story corporate
headquarters in 1956.

Jim Walter Corporation
listed on the New York
Stock Exchange on March
9, 1964. Jim Walter and
Buddy Alston bought 100
shares each of JWC.
G. Keith Funston, president
of the Exchange, on the
left; William M. Meehan,
a specialist in the stock,
on the right.

Jim Walter Homes:
home construction and
financing, 1946–present

The Celotex Corp.:
insulation board, interior
wallboard and various
building products, 1962–88

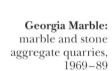

**U.S. Pipe and
Foundry Company:**
ductile iron water pipe
and related products,
1969–present

Georgia Marble:
marble and stone
aggregate quarries,
1969–89

Jim Walter Resources: deep underground coal mining and methane gas production, 1972–present

Sloss Industries: coke, coke by-products, and chemicals, 1969–present

Jim Walter Papers: paper products distribution, 1968–88

JW Aluminum: aluminum sheet and foil products, 1979–present

Jim Walter with Joe Cordell at his side in 1980; happy days before being hit by economic "stagflation."

Corporate headquarters as it appears today. The first tower was built in 1965, the second with connecting sky bridge in 1976. In Tampa, it is a landmark.

JIM WALTER HOMES TODAY

The American
3 bedrooms, 2 baths
984 sq. ft.

The Madison
4 bedrooms, 2 baths
1,441 sq. ft.

The Ridgemont
3 bedrooms, 2 baths
1,144 sq. ft.

The Victorian
3 bedrooms, 2 ½ baths
1,583 sq. ft.

Kenneth Matlock, a long-time CFO, with Joe B. Cordell, who became president and COO of the company in 1974.

With the opening of the new Celotex Thermax plant in Texarkana, Arkansas in 1978, a street there is named for Jim Walter.

The national media begin to take notice of Jim Walter in 1960. Here, *Business Week* features him in a cover story in its June 4 issue.

Thirty years later, *Builder* Magazine profiles Jim Walter as a "legend" in the industry.

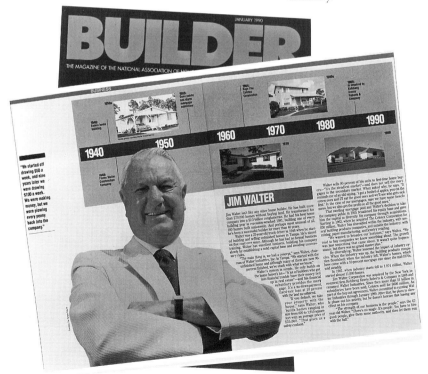

Part of the JWC senior management team in 1986, when the company achieved record sales and earnings. From left to right, Armando Flores, VP and group executive; Kenneth Hyatt, executive VP and COO; Joe B. Cordell, president and CEO; James Kynes, corporate counsel and senior VP *(standing)*; William Temple, VP and group executive; Dennis Ross, VP public affairs.

Joe B. Cordell,
president and CEO,
1983–91

G. Robert Durham,
president and CEO,
1991–present

Jim Walter greeting stockholders at the corporation's
annual meeting in 1971.

Well-known stockholder
advocate and annual meet-
ing "gadfly" John Gilbert
with Jim Walter and Joe B.
Cordell prior to the annual
stockholders meeting in
Tampa, December 14, 1979.

A typical Jim Walter Homes
display park of today.

Jim Walter *(center)* in 1982, suited
up for a trip underground at
Blue Creek #3 mine in Alabama,
with Buck Piper, Jr., VP operations *(on left)*, and Red Robbins,
mine manager.

Henry R. Kravis

George R. Roberts

Michael T. Tokarz

Perry Golkin

Fifty years of building—from
the simple to the sublime.

mended from an investment banker you could trust. No, not really. But it was a bargain. And a bargain is a bargain.

Celotex's vice chairman and former president, Henry Collins, had a next-door neighbor named Peter Halligan who owned and operated Marquette Paper for many years and for estate reasons now wanted to sell his company. Collins brought Peter Halligan and his proposal to Jim Walter.

Walter and Cordell listened to Halligan and learned just how good the paper business could be. Marquette had virtually no fixed assets or overhead, and consisted of cash, receivables (cash owed), and inventory. Almost all of its work was done on the telephone, taking orders from publishers and printers, and informing the mills where and when to send the paper, extracting a modest commission on each order. Small inventories were stored in rented warehouses in Chicago and Milwaukee. The company employed only ninety people, half of them salesmen, handling sales ranging from $35 to $42 million a year. Earnings were on the low side, only about 1.5 percent of sales, but they were steady year in and year out. The price? $6 million—not in cash, but in subordinated debentures maturing over the five to ten years. With some judicious prodding, salesmanship, and a little bit of luck, Cordell figured the company could easily earn its own price, if not more, over that time period. Even not knowing the paper business, this was an offer they could not refuse. They bought.

Walter and Cordell liked the simplicity and stability of the paper business so well that later that year they bought the Knight Paper Company of Jacksonville, Florida. A much larger operation, Knight not only wholesaled paper, it also converted paper bought from the mills into envelopes and tablets and notebooks of various sizes, which it then sold wholesale. And that worked out well, too. Down through the years, when the price was right, JWC continued to buy various paper converting and wholesaling companies. In time, with acquisitions and modernization from within, a new JWC subsidiary called Jim Walter Papers formed in 1974, with headquarters in Jacksonville, and became one of ten leading companies of its kind in the United States. What started out as a casual purchase of Marquette Paper grew into a subsidiary that marketed more than 30,000 different products through thirty-three distribution centers serving more than 25,000 customers with a sales volume of more than $300 million a year.

In 1968, JWC ventured into the carpet business, which was highly recommended by outside strategy consultants. The first step along these lines was Celotex's purchase of Majestic Carpet Mills, of Cartersville, Georgia, which manufactured and sold nylon-, acrylic- and polyester-tufted carpeting. The company was merged into Celotex. As the years went on, several smaller carpet companies were acquired in an attempt to capture a significant share of that highly diversified and competitive industry. Majestic was a particularly attractive purchase because it had had a bad previous year, suffering a net loss of $388,000 on sales of $3.7 million and could be bought for a modest multiple at $13.5 million. It seemed like an excellent fit, highly recommended by consultants. In theory, the consultants said, carpeting could be considered another building material for a finished house. A popular concept at that time was known as "interior landscaping" by which a company would sell or try to sell as many products as possible that went into a home or commercial building. Rather than show one product at a time, a Celotex salesman, without much added effort or expense, could try to sell a customer a complete line of ceiling tiles, wall paneling, lighting fixtures, and carpeting. JWC expanded Majestic's warehouses and distribution points to Los Angeles and Chicago, transforming the company into a national organization. The next year JWC entered the lighting field, acquiring Luminous Ceilings, a leading manufacturer in Chicago and Los Angeles of fluorescent lighting fixtures and integrated ceiling systems which handled lighting, air-conditioning ducts, and wiring behind grids or dropped ceilings. Anything having to do with "interior landscaping" of homes and commercial buildings was of interest to Jim Walter.

In mid-1968, one of the more intriguing buying opportunities to reach JWC offices came directly from the chairman and chief executive officer of The Georgia Marble Company of Atlanta. John Dent, the chairman who was approaching retirement, explained that the directors of this closely held, hundred-year-old company, which was traded in the over-the-counter market, had decided with his concurrence to sell rather than pour in more money for needed expansion. On sales of $26.2 million the previous year, the company had earned a meager $1.4 million producing marble, limestone, soapstone, serpentine, and granite. Without the leadership of the company's largest shareholder, James Douglas Robinson, chairman of Atlanta's First National Bank, who had recently died, the other directors, representing the eight or ten largest shareholders, had put Georgia Marble on the block. Was Jim Walter Corporation interested in buying? John Dent wanted to know.

Yes, marble was nature's most beautiful natural resource used as a building material, primarily as structural facing for important buildings and as a prized material for statues and monuments. The marble quarried by Georgia Marble in the foothills of the Appalachian Mountains in northern Georgia was not only hard, dense, and durable, but its crystalline structure made it sparkle and gleam in the sunlight like no other marble in the world. The revered Lincoln Memorial in

Washington, D.C., was carved by Daniel Chester French of twenty-eight separate pieces of white Georgia marble, some of them weighing more than forty tons each. The Library of Congress, the Folger Shakespearean Library, the Corcoran Art Gallery, the Supreme Court Building, the House of Representatives, the East Front of the U.S. Capitol—all the landmarks in Washington—were built with Georgia marble, as were the New York Stock Exchange, the Museum of Modern Art in New York, the U.S. Naval Academy at Annapolis, the U.S. Air Force Academy in Colorado Springs, Emory University in Atlanta; the list goes on and on.

The Georgia Marble Company, the largest of its kind in the United States, was founded in 1884 to extract marble from Long Swamp Valley in north Georgia, but the history of Georgia marble itself goes much further back—say about six hundred million years, give or take a few million. It was about then, according to archaeologists, that the shells and bones of trillions of tiny sea animals sank to the ocean floor and gradually formed a huge reef of calcium carbonate. Nature and time did the rest.

Not until 1842 was that calcium carbonate, in the form of marble, discovered by a very drunk, very lucky Irish stone cutter named Henry T. Fitzsimmons. Legend has it that Fitzsimmons was thrown off a stagecoach for imbibing too freely from a jug of "white lightning" on a public vehicle, and he landed in a place called Long Swamp Valley. Scratching the earth beneath him, Fitzsimmons discovered an outcropping of beautiful white marble. An itinerant but not ignorant stone cutter, he knew enough when to stop traveling. He set up his own mill right there in Long Swamp Valley and lived out the rest of his life carving marble monuments. What he did not know was that he had set up shop atop the greatest source of marble in the United States, estimated to last for at least thirty centuries, even at modern production levels.

Another fortunate young man in the 1840s, named Sam Tate, opened a general store in Pickens County and began acquiring thousand of acres of land, unaware that his land contained an enormous vein of the finest structural grade marble in the United States—a solid block of gorgeous Georgia marble three-eighths of a mile wide, four miles long, and two hundred feet to half a mile deep.

Over forty years later, two businessmen, Henry C. Clement and Frank H. Siddall, seeking a way to quarry, sell, and distribute this "white gold of Georgia," incorporated The Georgia Marble Company in 1884. They struggled with the business until 1905 when they sold out to "Colonel" Sam Tate who was running the general store that his grandfather had started in the town named for him. Colonel Sam, as he was known, ran Georgia Marble for the next thirty-three years until his death at age seventy-eight. He was the patriarch of Tate, Georgia, a legendary father figure, running the company and the company town with a kindly, iron hand. When he died in 1938, Georgia Marble was the one and only marble company in Georgia with facilities in Alabama, Tennessee, and elsewhere.

To Jim Walter and Joe Cordell, looking through Georgia Marble's financial statements some thirty years later, it seemed like a feast-or-famine business. When economic times were good, people bought marble for their buildings and their family tombstones; when times were bad, there were cheaper ways to go. And yet, it was a good, steady business, quarrying and crafting a limitless natural resource, with skilled craftsmen and loyal employees going back two and three generations. While the company did not earn much money, it had never lost any either. What was it worth to JWC?

Digging more deeply for firsthand information, Cordell made the rounds of Georgia Marble plants, presenting himself as a financial security analyst, asking questions about the company and its products. In the past ten years, he learned, the company had acquired other, smaller marble companies in Vermont, Tennessee, and Alabama, and through stock mergers and outright cash purchases had also picked up several limestone, granite, and other stone companies. He learned how rough blocks of dimensional marble were quarried and cut out of the mountain mass with air drills and channeling machines. The blocks, cut into ten-ton blocks, were then moved to various company fabricating plants for sawing into slabs of varying thicknesses, then cut by huge diamond saws to the precise size of job requirements, and then finished by machine or sometimes by hand to provide the final surface finish and shape. The marble, of course, comes in varying colors ranging from translucent white pinks to dark greens to black.

Toward the end of his tour, Cordell struck paydirt at the company's crushed marble plant in Sylacauga, Alabama. The opportunity for growth and the exciting part of The Georgia Marble Company, he learned from the Sylacauga plant manager, was not in the beautiful translucent white marble for which the company was famous; the growth of this company, if it were to grow at all, would come from the by-products of crushed and ground marble which could be used as extenders and fillers for all sorts of basic, everyday products. The technology involved in using powdered marble as a filler in other products was still in its infancy and the company was just beginning to recognize the potentialities.

Cordell was impressed with this information and also with the young man imparting it. Beneath the deceptive country boy charm, Cordell recognized a sharp, energetic, informed budding businessman in this plant manager named Kenneth Hyatt, whose father had recently retired as executive vice president of the company. Hyatt, who held degrees in civil engineering and industrial management from Georgia Institute of Technology, would go far, Cordell surmised, as he listened intently to Hyatt's description of the crushed marble operations.

The company, which used to dispose of its marble waste to another company, only in recent years had built facilities to crush and grind marble for industrial uses. If you broke up the marble into small sizes, it could be used as the crushed rock beneath concrete highways; if you chopped it into small bits, it could be used as the colored chips in terrazzo floors. If you ground it into a fine powder, it could then be used as a cheap filler or extender in the manufacture of paints, plastics, rubber products, and hundreds of other items, including the matting and backing of carpets, an important industry in Georgia. The marble quarried in north Georgia was an almost pure, white, crystalline calcium carbonate and it added strength, durability, and bulk to hundreds of industrial products without diminishing the characteristics of the original product. It could even be used in food as a calcium supplement. The extra fine powder sprinkled on every stick of chewing gum to keep it dry was calcium carbonate, or, in other words, marble. And, best of all, Hyatt explained, marble was basically a rock, cheaper than just about anything else, and the company had lots and lots of it. In time, Hyatt predicted, crushed and ground marble would account for more sales and revenues than all other divisions of the company combined.

An excited Cordell telephoned Jim Walter from the Sylacauga plant, recounted the potentialities of crushed and powdered marble and said straight out, "I like everything about this company, Jim, and I think we should we buy it be-

fore someone else does." With that kind of strong recommendation from his usually cautious colleague, Walter had
no misgivings about moving forward swiftly. The two men
had worked together so closely and smoothly for so many
years by this point that each knew the other's thought
processes. Given the same facts and choices they almost always reached the same conclusion.

JWC and Georgia Marble quickly reached an agreement
in principle and the acquisition was consummated on February 21, 1969, in an exchange of Georgia Marble stock for a
new issue of JWC convertible preferred stock valued at about
$23 million. It would turn out to be one of the happiest, most
pleasing of all of Jim Walter's acquisitions. With capital infusion from JWC, Georgia Marble's production of crushed and
ground marble increased progressively year after year. Much
as Ken Hyatt had predicted, in time there would be a complete reversal in the focus of Georgia Marble's business. At
the time of the acquisition, calcium carbonate and crushed
marble products accounted for only 15 or 20 percent of
sales. As the years went by, those industrial-use products rose
to more than 80 percent of sales, while dimensional and
structural marble fell to less than 20 percent of production
and sales.

It was during the amiable negotiations to acquire Georgia
Marble in the fall of 1968 that the possibility, call it opportunity, arose to play the part of a white knight and to rescue a
Big Board company from the grasp of an unwanted suitor.
Once again, all the pertinent facts were in the public domain
as the financial press played story after story about the all-
out battle for survival of United States Pipe and Foundry
Company of Birmingham, Alabama, a company five times
larger than Georgia Marble.

Founded in New Jersey in 1899 and with plants and
foundries across the country, U.S. Pipe had long been a stal-

wart of traditional heavy American industry. It was and still is the largest domestic producer of ductile iron pressure pipe, used principally to carry water and sewage in cities across the nation. Three of its original pipe foundries—in Bessemer, Alabama, in Chattanooga, Tennessee, and in Burlington, New Jersey—are still in operation today. Even more remarkably, since its founding in 1899, the company has had only fourteen presidents. And its products last even longer. More than one hundred cities in the United States have cast-iron pipe that has been in service for more than one hundred years, and it has been estimated that of all the cast-iron pipe installed throughout recorded history, more than 90 percent is still in service. The famous fountains of Versailles Palace hold the record, still using cast-iron pipelines laid in 1664.

U.S. Pipe's success dated back to 1921 when it acquired the U.S. rights to a revolutionary new process of manufacturing cast iron pipe by a centrifugal casting method invented by a French engineer named Dimitri Sensaud DeLavaud. Pouring molten iron into a rapidly rotating mold produced a smooth, high quality iron pipe at a significantly lower cost than had ever been known before. Today practically all iron pressure pipe is cast using the DeLavaud process. U.S. Pipe stayed in the forefront of pipe technology and through the years acquired and merged with companies making it one of the leaders in producing concrete pipe, soil pipe, irrigation piping, specialized tooling, valves, fire hydrants, and gas pipes. Moreover, it became completely integrated, mining its own coal which it converted in huge ovens to coke, which was used to make pig iron, which was then used to make cast-iron pipe. Its two huge blast furnaces, located since the late 19th century in the center of downtown Birmingham, are landmarks symbolic of American heavy industry and thought to be the most photographed blast furnaces in the country.

It was this venerable behemoth of American industry that found itself suddenly vulnerable to a hostile takeover by a company not more than five years old, the Automatic Sprinkler Corporation of America. Behind the corporate names, it was a battle between a soft-spoken Southern gentleman named Robert E. Garrett, chairman of U.S. Pipe, and a rough and tough empire builder out of Cleveland named Harry E. Figgie, Jr., chairman of Automatic Sprinkler.

Figgie, who acquired the privately owned Automatic Sprinkler in 1963, went public with it two years later and then in the next thirty months rapidly acquired seventeen more companies, building Automatic Sprinkler into a growth complex with revenues of $250 million a year, ten times what it had been before the offering. His stock was hot on Wall Street, selling at thirty-seven times earnings. In February of 1968, he announced to the world that he had acquired 10 percent of U.S. Pipe stock, accumulating it quietly over the past year, and that he intended to make a tender offer for control of the company.

Figgie's reputation as a ruthless, bare-knuckles fighter, albeit a brilliant and successful one, was well known in the business world. He himself made no secret of it. Some thought his crude abrasiveness was not real, for he was, after all, a lawyer, a Harvard Business School graduate and he held two degrees in engineering. But others who had worked with him said it was real enough. Soon after announcing his intentions for U.S. Pipe, he demanded a meeting with its top management, and there in Garrett's office, the heavy-set six-footer, who weighed more than 230 pounds, was blunt and brutal. "I'm going to get control of this company, and I want your help," he told them. "If you don't help me get that control, you're going to find yourself out on the street the day after I take over. That's the way the game is played. You understand?"

They understood all right. Bob Garrett, who had worked his way up from the coal mines through the ranks, wanted no part of Harry Figgie. Despite his red hair and Irish ancestry, he controlled his temper and waited out the Figgie onslaught. When Figgie left, Garrett and some of his top managers spent ten days consulting with the company's biggest shareholders: Did they want to fight or succumb? They decided to fight.

First, Garrett sent a letter to his shareholders, advising them not to heed Figgie's blandishments. His lawyers filed suit in federal court for an injunction to stop Figgie from buying any more U.S. Pipe stock on the grounds that a combination of the two companies would violate antitrust laws because both companies manufactured hydraulic equipment and fluid controls. Then Garrett sold off some $3 million in land and timber for ready cash so that U.S. Pipe could go on a buying spree of its own. His executive vice president Ben Harrison led the battle to acquire a series of smaller companies, primarily for newly issued U.S. Pipe stock. The strategy was that U.S. Pipe would issue new stock in making acquisitions as quickly as Figgie bought U.S. Pipe stock so that Figgie's percentage of ownership would not increase. Harrison bought all kinds of companies—a cement company, a barge company, a retail jewelry store chain, a mobile home manufacturer—just so long as they added to U.S. Pipe's total sales and revenues. They did just that, adding $23 million in sales and $3 million in profits, raising U.S. Pipe's earnings per share from $1.79 to $2.59.

Figgie countered in the fall of 1968 by getting his shareholders to approve a new issue of Automatic Sprinkler stock and debentures worth $100 million. Now, he announced, he had more than enough to buy U.S. Pipe. He had already acquired more than 20 percent of the company's stock and had more than another 20 percent in "friendly" hands, he stated.

It looked to most impartial observers that the battle was just about over—unless a white knight galloped on the scene.

Looking over U.S. Pipe's annual reports and balance sheets, Jim Walter was intrigued with the possibilities. With its own coal, coke, pig iron, and foundries, U.S. Pipe was a fully integrated pipe manufacturing company, an important segment of the construction industry, of which JWC was a part. It had $152 million in annual sales, bountiful physical assets, and low debt, making it an attractive addition to JWC's position in the building and construction industry. Furthermore, U.S. Pipe had a capital structure with substantial unused borrowing power, and, much like Celotex, it had substantial physical assets carried on its books at the original prices paid. Its coal mines, for instance, were listed as containing a reserve of some 160 million tons with a value of a mere $4 million, which was the price paid for them in the 1880s.

Walter discussed the figures, details, and potentialities with Gene Woodfin at Loeb Rhoades, and then telephoned the embattled chairman of U.S. Pipe, introduced himself, and asked if he could drop in to see him. Armed with his own company's annual reports and SEC documents, Jim Walter explained his mission.

"Mr. Garrett, we don't own one share of stock in U.S. Pipe and I'm not going to buy a share without your total approval. But I've looked at your company just from the annual reports and one thing and another, and, you know, I think it makes sense maybe for us to try to get our two companies together."

Explaining a bit about the history of JWC, Walter urged the U.S. Pipe chairman to contact Henry Collins and ask him about the friendly and successful Celotex association and the mutual advantages to be gained by joining forces. Garrett was very gracious. "Well, that's very nice, Jim, I appreciate what you're saying, but we very much prefer to go it on our own."

"I can certainly understand that," Walter replied, adding, "but if you ever change your mind, please call me. We would be interested in talking it over, but only if you want it. Unless it is friendly and with your cooperation, as with Henry Collins, we would have no interest." Walter left his annual reports for Garrett to peruse.

Walter did not hope, nor did he despair; the ball was in the other man's court. And he knew that Henry Collins would be JWC's best salesman when it came to future acquisitions.

A month or so later, the federal court denied U.S. Pipe's bid for an injunction against Figgie and he was free to make his move. Garrett then made his move: he telephoned Jim Walter.

"Jim, I think we ought to talk."

"Fine."

"Well, I don't necessarily want you to come to Birmingham, so why don't we meet somewhere private in Atlanta? It will be easier for you to get to, and it'd be better for us."

At the Holiday Inn of the Atlanta airport, Walter and Cordell met with Garrett and Harrison, and in short order they reached a verbal agreement on the broad outline of an affiliation of their two companies through an exchange of stock. JWC would issue $145-150 million of its preferred convertible for all the outstanding shares of U.S. Pipe. Later, that figure was scaled down to $135 million, which still was higher than Figgie's $100 million offer. It was the quickest (and biggest) deal Walter had ever made. The approval of his board of directors came *after* the verbal agreement. The only obstacle to a smooth transaction would be the handling of Harry Figgie.

Characteristically, Figgie fought back with letters to the shareholders of U.S. Pipe and with stronger press statements. Walter responded with a formal tender offer at the end of December, which was warmly endorsed by U.S. Pipe's management. Negotiations to buy out Figgie were carried on at arm's length through intermediaries of their respective investment bankers and, finally, in April of 1969, it was established that it would take $31.5 million cash to buy out Figgie's 24 percent holdings in U.S. Pipe, roughly $36 a share for 876,000 shares.

Expressing some misgivings over the amount of cash needed, Walter complained to John Loeb, "Well, I don't know about that much cash. I just don't know where I can lay my hands on $30 million quickly enough."

"Why don't you try getting some of the banks here in New York to give it to you as a separate line of credit?" queried Loeb.

"I don't have a lot of time," said Walter.

"I'll tell you what," Loeb suggested softly. "I'll take $10 million of it personally. Tell the banks that and see what influence that has." Then he added with a smile, "I'll be your bell cow."

John Loeb was a very good leader in the financial canyons of New York City. Within forty-eight hours, visiting favorite banks in the Big Apple, Jim Walter gathered loan commitments of some $60 million. He only needed half that amount and John Loeb ended up taking only $2.5 million personally. Once Figgie's shares were bought out for cash in June, the remaining shares were acquired by an exchange of stock and the acquisition of U.S. Pipe was finalized on August 30, the day before JWC's fiscal year of 1969 ended.

In one swift swoop, JWC had added to its balance sheet its single largest asset, one bigger than Celotex. U.S. Pipe provided more than $179 million in sales and $12.5 million in earnings for 1969. Not only was it the largest producer of cast-iron pressure pipe and fittings in the United States, the company also manufactured a wide range of pipes, valves, hydrants, and other related products used in general construction. Through one of its subsidiaries, operating nine plants across the country, it also was a leading manufacturer of mammoth concrete pipes used for city water supply lines, sewer lines, culverts, and irrigation projects. In its final year of independence, fighting off the hostile takeover attempts of Harry Figgie, this staid, old company had acquired, among others, a prestressed concrete company, a barge company, a mobile home manufacturer, a plastic pipe plant, a shopping mall in Birmingham, and the aforementioned retail jewelry store chain. It would be up to Jim Walter and his colleagues now to straighten out that mess of acquisitions.

Rapid growth brings along with it a whole host of new problems, and that was to be expected. In little more than two years, Jim Walter Corporation had come a long, long way, farther than anyone in its management had ever dreamed ten years earlier. Jim Walter Corporation for fiscal 1969 generated earnings of $23.5 million on total sales of $623.5 million, with Georgia Marble, U.S. Pipe, and the paper and carpeting companies now added to the Homes Division, Celotex, and the sugar operations in Louisiana. The company and its subsidiaries now employed more than 20,000 people in offices, plants, and factories across the nation. That's real growth. In fact, JWC was now one of the fastest-growing companies in the nation, the 287th largest industrial company among the Fortune 500.

CHAPTER 9

— *Building Internally* —

L ESS THAN THREE MONTHS after acquiring U.S. Pipe, Jim Walter was negotiating with the "professional manager" he would hire to become the new president and chief operating officer of Jim Walter Corporation. "I may not be smart enough to run a $600 million company, but I'm smart enough to hire someone who can," Walter told him. "This can be a $1 billion company, a $2 billion company, maybe more."

With all its far-flung operations—U.S. Pipe out of Birmingham, Georgia Marble out of Atlanta, the Brentwood Savings and Loan in Los Angeles, and the scattered divisions and facilities of Celotex across the nation—it became abundantly clear that JWC could not longer be run by seat-of-the-pants decisions. The company had grown too big for the luxury of its casual, ad hoc, country boy style of management. It now had thirty-nine subsidiaries, seven major product groups organized into twenty-five divisions, and turned out products ranging from building materials to paper, chemicals, heavy piping, marble, iron ore, and coal. Decision by instinct no longer was good enough. The old saying around the office that "rules are made when brains run out," would have to give way to the new disciplines of modern management.

Walter himself was the first to admit that he may well have gotten in over his head with the rapid pace of acquisitions over the past two or three years. Nothing had gone wrong with the company—yet. But he was aware of the dangers inherent in too rapid growth. He had read plenty of stories about young companies hurtling down the road of success and not knowing they were out of control until they crashed. A realist to his core, Walter had no problems with his ego or image in agreeing with his board of directors that he needed help from beyond the ranks of his own current management.

Working with the outside members of his board, Walter delineated the kind of professional manager the company would need. Primarily because both Celotex and U.S. Pipe were such large, diverse manufacturing companies, JWC required someone with a broad industrial background, a professional manager who was experienced and skilled in handling production, labor, and man-hour costs, inventory control, budgeting, and all the organizational concepts of modern management. JWC had no one in its ranks of management with that kind of know-how and experience, he had to admit.

Walter discussed the decision candidly with Alston, Saraw, and Cordell. Buddy and Arnold presented no problem. Neither of them wanted to run the company. Arnold was happy where he was, and Buddy wanted no part of the company beyond its home building operation. From the very start he had objected and been outvoted on every acquisition dating back to Celotex in 1962. He believed and never ceased to argue that the company would have fewer headaches and be better off financially if it had stuck to home building. Even as company president he had eschewed the executive offices on the eighth floor and chosen to remain in his original office in the old two-story building adjacent to the tower.

Joe Cordell was disappointed but took the news with equanimity, acknowledging that at this stage of his career he did not have the necessary industrial management skills required for the job. Eugene Katz, who had moved up from his small screen company to become president of Celotex three years earlier, clearly was not qualified, and Robert Garrett, who headed U.S. Pipe, was nearing retirement.

Jim Walter did what other chief executives do in similar situations. He turned to an executive search firm, Heidrick & Struggles, and hired Gardner Heidrick, a top professional headhunter, to find him the best professional, corporate manager available.

Heidrick screened several candidates and in November 1969, shortly before Thanksgiving, brought him Frank J. Pizzitola, an MBA from Harvard, who at forty-six and just ten months younger than Walter, had eighteen years of corporate experience in several large and diverse chemical companies. As one of three executive vice presidents of Celanese Corporation, he had been in charge of half the company's $600-million-a-year operations in chemicals, plastics, and petroleum. Before Celanese, he had held operating and administrative positions at Monsanto Company and at Olin Corporation, leaving them when he felt he had not progressed fast enough up the executive ladder. He was good and he was ambitious, and he made no secret of his being on the fast track.

What Jim Walter saw before him at their first meeting in the company's New York apartment on East 56th Street was the epitome of the professional manager, mentally sharp and decisive. Pizzitola had thoroughly done his homework for this first meeting. Having read and absorbed the most recent JWC annual report, he was prepared to discuss the company's return on assets, return on investments, and allocation of resources. Displaying a firsthand knowledge that Walter lacked in intricate corporate planning and financial controls in multidivision companies, Pizzitola impressed Walter as just the kind of professional manager JWC needed. The man was remarkable, too, for his tremendous self-discipline, control, and self-confidence. The more he told Jim Walter about himself, the more the self-made Walter liked him.

Beneath the surface image of a hard-driving, successful New Yorker in a hand-tailored, black business suit was a man who had paid for his own schooling by digging ditches, working on road gangs, running a drill press, driving a cab. "I was a whiz at patching hot asphalt," he recounted with a smile. Pizzitola told the story of his childhood, his near-poverty upbringing, his study of Spanish literature in a small New England college, and how he got into Harvard's Business School through perseverance when that august institution had turned him down for graduate study in the romance languages. Because of the need to work his way through school and his service in World War II, Pizzitola had a late start in his business career, earning his MBA at twenty-eight, and, eager to catch up, he had put himself on the fast track ever since. Walter saw before him a self-made man.

Along with his accomplishments, Pizzitola was equally candid about his faults. He was, he told Walter, often perceived as being too aggressive, even abrasive, in getting what he wanted. But, he explained, he was as "objective oriented" in his personal life as he was in business. If he came to JWC, he would be there to succeed at his task. "I do what I think is right for the company, and I don't give a damn what people think of me," he said. "I'll earn their respect, and whether or not they give me their friendship is entirely up to them."

Pizzitola made no secret of his personal objective in coming to JWC as president and chief operating officer. He wanted to be more than a well-paid corporate executive. It was time in his career for him to become financially independent, he said, and that translated into what he described as his "overwhelming desire" to be a millionaire. He asked for JWC stock options that would earn him $1 million, if he succeeded in bringing to JWC what he called "more bang for the buck."

Walter had some misgivings over introducing this hard-nosed MBA into the ranks of JWC's Southern-styled, country boy management, but he liked the open, straightforward cut of the man. With his "back door" escape route in mind, he invited Pizzitola to Tampa to meet the other executives, proposing that if everything worked out, he would hire Pizzitola as JWC's executive vice president. His first priority would be overseeing the management of U.S. Pipe, the company's newest acquisition. Then, if that worked out, at the end of the year, he would make Pizzitola president of the corporation. At any time during the year, either man could call it quits, with no hard feelings. He warned Pizzitola of potential difficulties in fitting into the JWC culture. "How tough are you?" he asked. "They're going to try to pull your hat down over your eyes."

"I'm as tough as I need to be," Pizzitola replied, before he even figured out the reference to the ancient school yard trick.

Even sartorially, with his severe black suit, starched white shirt, black hair, and deep set dark eyes, he clashed with the shirt-sleeved executives in Tampa who delighted in ragging and taunting each other. At his very first get-acquainted meeting, Bud Alston put him to the test. With a straight face, the feisty shell home builder greeted him, saying, "I'm pleased to meet you, and I want you to know right away I've got nothing against Italians. The fellow I buy my liquor from is an Italian, and so is my barber." Taken aback, Pizzitola retorted, "Who's Italian? What the hell are you talking about? My family's been American for generations!"

Jim Walter was delighted with that exchange when Pizzitola described to him his day at the company headquarters. Walter offered him the job of executive vice president with the promise of the presidency. Pizzitola shook hands on it, subject to their working out a satisfactory option agreement. He had quickly learned that there were some twelve JWC executives in the headquarters building that had become millionaires holding company stock, and he figured there was room enough for one more.

Pizzitola had no illusions about the lifestyle changes that lay ahead for him and his family. His wife, Betty, was distressed over the move, but she agreed, as she had many times before, to go whither he would go for the sake of his career. They would be leaving their fourteen-room home with its three-car garage in Scarsdale, one of the poshest suburbs of New York. They would have to sell their new Lincoln Continental because it was bigger than the one his new boss drove. Their friends, their country club, their favorite New York restaurants and Broadway shows would have to be sacrificed for his career's sake. But they both understood, as their New York friends would, that relocation was often the price paid for a significant move up the corporate ladder.

The one impediment to taking the job was Pizzitola's demand for options on 50,000 shares of JWC stock. The company's executive stock option plan cut off at 20,000 shares. Pizzitola hired a top law firm to find a way around the company's by-laws. The arithmetic in his head went like this: 50,000 shares at roughly $30 each (its then current price) was $1.5 million. If he could double the price of JWC stock, which was not at all unlikely considering the under-utilized assets in U.S. Pipe and elsewhere, he would then have a gain of $1.5 million and be able to pay for the stock held for him. It took three months to devise a plan under which Jim Walter agreed to lend Pizzitola out of his own personal holdings options on 30,000 additional shares of stock. If the new executive could double JWC earnings, Walter thought, he would be justifiable earning his $1 million. To be fair to the men who had helped build the company before Pizzitola's arrival, Walter offered the same options to his other top executives. This offer hardly pleased Pizzitola because he had paid out considerable legal fees to get this new executive perk.

In February 1970, Pizzitola came to work at JWC and that turned out to be the first month in the company's history that total revenues showed a net decline from the previous year. The housing cycle had hit a trough, home starts were down, building materials were not moving, and sales of pipe were abysmal. Those first few months on the job, Pizzitola stuck out like a sore thumb. His coworkers in the executive corridors did not know what to make of him, and he did not change his ways to fit in with his new Tampa environment. Every day he wore his impeccably tailored black suit, white shirt, usually with a black and white striped tie. His colleagues surmised that he must have bought six identical black suits. The nickname they chose for him was "the undertaker." Pizzitola never minded being different. He wanted to be noticed without being overbearing. He wanted people to react to him, rather than the other way around. He took a special delight in starting his day by running up eight flights of stairs to the executive floor, ostensibly for exercise. Sharp and demanding in all his dealings with coworkers and subordinates, he kept his thoughts to himself.

As the new executive vice president, he felt he had the title but not the power. Nothing along those lines had been spelled out. He felt he was on trial for the year because he had no real assurance he would get the job. He could hardly make demands on the top executives because so many of them had become wealthy on JWC stock and could tell him to go to hell. Nor were they the kind of men who would show much respect for a title. Gene Katz, for instance, who was then president of Celotex, introduced himself by handing

Pizzitola his special calling card, which read: Eugene R. Katz—Millionaire. And with a twinkle in his eye he added insult to injury by saying, "I hope you aren't going to do anything that makes me sell my stock in this company."

Long acquainted with office politics, Pizzitola believed there were two routes to power in a corporate hierarchy. You fought for it openly and fiercely, or you infiltrated quietly, planned and prepared, waited to be asked, and then you pounced with your well-prepared answers to the problems at hand, thereby demonstrating your ability. Pizzitola, who felt that the company valued friendships more than performance, spent a good deal of his time quietly planning and preparing.

With responsibility over U.S. Pipe, Pizzitola went to the Birmingham headquarters and toured the plants with Robert Garrett, the chairman. He found so much pipe stacked up in all the plant yards that there was no room to get the fork lifts in. The figures showed that U.S. Pipe had the biggest inventory of unsold pipe in the nation and that the manufacturing division was turning out pipe as fast as it could, in utter disregard of the housing slump and poor sales of pipe.

"Bob, you're going to have to shut down," he told Garrett.

"We can't do that," Garret protested. "We're the second-biggest employer in Birmingham. Think what it would do to our reputation in the city."

"Well then," Pizzitola said facetiously, "We'll just have to go the board of directors and ask them to buy more land to stack all your pipe on."

There was nothing facetious, however, in his order to stop producing pipe they could not sell, to get the receivables down, and to start coordinating the rate of manufacturing with the volume of sales. Before he left Birmingham, he unveiled a detailed plan that he had worked out for improving

U.S. Pipe's return on assets, a neglected management tool up to then.

"Frank, I understand what you're trying to do, and you're going to need someone younger and more vigorous than I am to carry this through," Garrett said. "I'm going to step out."

Pizzitola asked for recommendations for someone to succeed him and Garrett proposed two men, one a "nice guy" and the other a noted "hard nose" manager. The "hard nose" was exactly what Pizzitola was looking for, and with Walter's approval, Ben F. Harrison was promoted to president of U.S. Pipe. Walter prevailed upon Bob Garrett to remain as chairman of Pipe and a director of JWC.

Meanwhile, with the help of a personnel executive, Pizzitola reviewed dozens of employee folders and met face to face with those he thought had skills as yet unused. Similarly, he went through all the company operations seeking assets that were unused or underused, and he drew up one of his detailed, watertight plans for improving profitability. And then, with unusual patience for so tense a man, he sat back and waited to be asked.

In April, three months after he had come aboard, Walter strolled into his office and pointedly asked, "Frank, what are you doing?"

"Nothing," Pizzitola replied, tongue in cheek.

Momentarily surprised, Walter said somberly, "Frank, we better have a talk."

"Yes, let's go somewhere where we can talk for several hours," he proposed.

When they got together, Pizzitola laid a fistful of documents in front of Walter, charts, columns of figures, written proposals and then, with cold logic, he compared the company's lack of organization with a table of organization he had prepared that would give JWC a discernable structure of executive management. He showed Walter a three-year plan to utilize more effectively the assets that the company already possessed. And lastly he proposed a tough austerity plan, labeled the Profit Improvement Program, to pull in the corporate belt, cut fat, and make better use of assets. The belt-tightening went all the way from freezing corporate salaries and selling off more U.S. Pipe assets to such attention-getting actions as sharing secretaries (because most JWC executives were on the road half the time), removing excess telephones, buying smaller and cheaper company cars, and even eliminating free coffee in the company cafeteria. The millions of dollars salvaged by these actions, Pizzitola asserted, would go straight down to the bottom line, and could save JWC from a losing year.

Walter, who always believed in the bottom line, wholeheartedly embraced the Profit Improvement Program, offering to share his own secretary. Pizzitola wouldn't hear of it. "You're the boss and as long as your name is on the building, you are the exception—but the only exception."

When tearful secretaries, demoted from the executive floor, besieged him, Pizzitola stopped them cold by saying, "If you can show me where I'm not being fair, I'll listen to you. But if you just don't like it, please don't waste my time. All my life I've done things I did not like. This is for the good of the company."

Pizzitola went out to all the divisions of the company and preached the gospel of tight planning and budget controls. Using Joe Cordell's detailed financial analyses, he laid before the managing executives page after page of statistics backing up his crusade for a better return on assets used. Every uncollected bill, every piece of unsold product was an unused asset, he would point out, adding that since JWC lived on borrowed money, every dollar worth of assets not being used had to be replaced with a borrowed dollar, and interest had to paid on that dollar.

He did not just ask them to cut inventory and receivables. With Walter's unswerving support, he instituted a system that charged each division a percentage for each dollar of its assets, the percentage based on what it cost JWC to borrow money. Reduce the nonworking assets, he told the managers, and some of the money saved will show up in your bonus checks. Cutting costs and conserving assets became a challenge throughout the company, especially for the divisions that hoped to reach or surpass the profitability of the home builders. "Get Hip to PIP" was the slogan of the year.

At U.S. Pipe, Pizzitola's prime managing responsibility, two West Coast concrete plants were closed down when they failed to reach targeted returns. One of Pipe's blast furnaces in Birmingham was shut down as redundant. A Texas land development got the axe. Unused real estate holdings were sold off, along with a good many of the small companies Pipe had acquired in its fight to ward off a takeover by Automatic Sprinkler.

There was one small, oddball company that Pipe had acquired that did not fit in anywhere. However, they simply could not sell it off. The Lorch chain of small, credit-type retail jewelry stores was located in Birmingham and its environs. The stores were profitable but the offers to buy were so low, somewhere around fifty cents on every dollar of inventory, that Jim Walter refused to sell at such bargain basement prices. The Lorch chain stayed on the block for years, and each year, under the management of Pete Petro, who had gone to work for the first store in 1954, the jewelry stores earned more money than they had the year before. There was nothing wrong with the Lorch chain, except the difficulty in explaining to financial analysts what a shell home/

building supplies company was doing selling watches and gold link bracelets.

Working closely with Ben Harrison, the new chief executive of U.S. Pipe, Pizzitola drew up a new organizational structure which divided the company into three separate and distinct profit centers, making each one responsible for its own maximum utilization of its assets and its bottom-line profits. In the major overhaul of this giant subsidiary, not only were plants closed, jobs slashed, and overhead cut back sharply, but in some instances prices were raised. With the company's earnings at an all-time low in a down market, Pizzitola persuaded Pipe's management to raise the price of its pressure pipes from $105 to $156 a ton, and he turned out to be right. Pipe lost only a minuscule 1.6 percent of the market rather than the 15 percent feared by its management.

Pizzitola and Harrison also proposed a $6 million development program to step up its production of high-grade metallurgical coal, as part of its effort to maximize the use of its assets. Owning a coal reserve of some 160 million tons, U.S. Pipe was mining only enough for its own needs and some small outside sales. With the onset of an energy shortage and an increase in the price of coal, U.S. Pipe approved plans to more than triple the present output of coal over the next few years. By opening up deposits 1,200 to 2,000 feet deep, projected earnings from mining coal became more than attractive; they were mind-boggling.

So, the future looked rosy with the discovery of a new potential for significant earnings in the mining of coal; a housing shortage seen to be as great as that following World War II promised a boom in the sale of building materials, pipe, and general construction. But 1970 had been an anxious, if not terrible year for JWC's earnings. A tight money supply designed to stem inflation had cut housing starts and general construction severely. While JWC's sales increased 8.5 percent, a trifling amount compared to its 50 to 70 percent increases in the golden years, its net earnings in 1970 dropped from $30.5 million in 1969 to $22.9 in 1970. Net income dipped from $1.83 to $1.16 a share. Return on stockholder's equity, after all the acquisitions and increased revenues flowed through the company books, amounted to only 8.1 percent.

But Jim Walter could see behind those figures. He was pleased with the belt-tightening measures, the management disciplines, and the strategic planning that Pizzitola had introduced over the past half year. At the December board meeting, he formally proposed Pizzitola as president, with Alston moving into the new slot of vice chairman, and the board stamped its approval.

As president and chief operating officer and with the chairman's support behind him, Pizzitola now had all the clout he needed to impose his concept of modern management upon the company. Planning his every move, he was wise and cautious enough to sell his ideas to the vice presidents and managers of the company, rather than tell them what to do. His challenge was to impose planning controls over all the far-flung profit centers of the company without dampening the entrepreneurial spirit that had always sparked Jim Walter Corporation. He did not want to change a company that was so successful, but he wanted to impose a certain structure and order upon it. Jim Walter had allowed each of the subsidiary companies to operate with a great deal of autonomy, reporting results to the home office every month, making changes only if the subsidiaries got into trouble. That style of management worked well when JWC was still a relatively small company. As Walter explained it, "Frank taught us how to refine the controls we had as a small company and extend them to a multidivisional organization. Put simply, he made systematic the things we used to do instinctively."

Entrepreneurial spirit was emphasized in all of the company's profit centers, and once they learned to be responsible for their own spending, allocation of assets, as well as sales and profits, Pizzitola introduced a formal system of budgetary planning. To an extent unusual in most other companies, JWC plant and sales-office managers were asked to forecast their future sales and production needs and to set their own goals for the coming year, which were coordinated within each profit center. Each manager was responsible for developing a budgetary plan of needs and goals. These plans were reviewed by the corporate staff and then submitted to top management for further review and inclusion in the company's overall business plan for the coming year. No manager's budget was modified without his agreement, but once set, it was the manager's responsibility to meet the goals to which he had agreed.

Budgets and financial controls were reviewed by each profit center and by the home office each month. The managers who fulfilled their budget plan received bonuses at the end of the year, those who surpassed their goals received extra bonuses. Anyone who strayed from his budgetary goals heard from the home office in the form of a visit from either the financial or administrative staff from headquarters in an attempt to resolve the problem. "Silence from the home office was golden," divisional managers discovered.

While the rewards for performance were substantial, a manager who failed to meet his budget for an extended period was usually transferred to a less responsible job elsewhere in the company or he resigned or was fired. The system of profit centers, accountability, and budget reviews was augmented by a wholesale realignment of titles within the company so that each manager at whatever level would know to whom he reported and how to measure his own performance. It turned out to be a good system of communications within the management hierarchy of the company. And yet, while the structure and organization may have seemed similar to that of other large corporations, the free-swinging atmosphere of JWC prevailed over and beyond the organizational charts.

When it came to actually communicating with anyone in your own or in another division, you did not have to go through a chain of command. Anyone could pick up the phone and talk to the man who had the information needed. It was that fast and simple. If Matlock, who by this time had become controller of JWC, questioned an assistant controller or his assistant at U.S. Pipe, it was up to that man to inform his boss of the inquiry if he deemed it sufficiently important. At JWC the "classless society" endured, titles did not interfere with clear communications, and executives high and low kept their office doors open to indicate their ready availability. After all, they were not only managers, they were owners working at Jim Walter Corporation. Down to the level of plant managers, about 450 executives participated in stock options, growing richer as the company prospered. Employees of the company owned more than 14 percent of its outstanding stock, which was an unusually high percentage for corporate America.

Pizzitola next cast his business eye upon the company's need to modernize, refurbish, and reevaluate its older plants, factories, and facilities. He asked the divisional managers to submit three-year plans, estimating and justifying their monetary needs for modernizing or eliminating outmoded equipment. While the company cut costs on overhead, staff, and nonproductive facilities, it poured more than $30 million into an aggressive program of building new plants and facilities and also into updating, modernizing, and recharging its subsidiaries, particularly the larger ones like U.S. Pipe, Celotex, and Georgia Marble.

At Georgia Marble, millions were spent to open new quarries and to build new facilities to hasten the changeover from structural marble to crushed and ground marble for industrial uses. Millions went into research and development. At U.S. Pipe, perhaps more than in any other subsidiary, huge capital expenditures began to flow into new technology and facilities transforming the manufacture of pressure pipe. Where once the company had mined the coal, baked its own coke, and produced its own pig iron from which its "gray iron" pressure pipe was made, a new process was implemented by which a more flexible and durable "ductile iron" pipe could be produced by melting down used scrap steel as the raw material. It was a great deal less expensive, eliminating the need for blast furnaces and reducing the need for coke ovens, and thus increased the margin of profit. In similar fashion, a total refurbishing and modernization program that included new product lines developed at the company's modern research laboratories in St. Petersburg was installed throughout the various plants of Celotex, increasing its market shares and margins of profit. That year Celotex introduced a new system of installing, taping, and spray-finishing its gypsum wallboard in one-quarter the time it had previously taken, which would increase its gypsum sales significantly. It also started construction on an $8 million plant in Marion, South Carolina, which would double its production of the medium-density hardboard being used extensively as a substitute for wood in kitchen counters, cabinets, shelving, and a host of other building applications.

This plan was an investment in the future, for not only was some $30 million spent in 1972 for capital improvements, but plans were formulated for the expenditure of $65 million in new plants and facilities in 1973. It was one of the advantages of being a subsidiary; without the size and borrowing power of the parent Jim Walter Corporation, no single subsidiary could have afforded such large expenditures for future growth.

On the acquisition trail, the biggest and most significant move of 1972 was Celotex's purchase of the Panacon Corporation, which owned and operated Philip Carey, one of the three largest roofing companies in the United States. Combining that subsidiary with the Barrett roofing plants under the umbrella of Celotex made Celotex the leading roofing company in the United States at a time when housing starts (and each of them needed a roof) were at an all-time high.

Panacon was acquired from Meshulam Riklis, the well-known conglomerateur and chairman of Rapid American Corporation, who wanted to sell the company for needed cash. The purchase was done in two stages. In April of that year, Celotex bought 89 percent of the company's stock for $62 million cash from Riklis, and in June, bought out the remaining 11 percent of stock which was publicly held for another $11 million, merging Panacon, with all its assets, liabilities, and $180 million in annual sales, into Celotex.

In addition to the roofing facilities of Philip Carey, Panacon brought Miami Carey, which specialized in kitchen and bathroom accessories; Briggs Manufacturing Company, which produced a line of bathtubs and related products; and Carey Canadian Mines, Ltd., in Quebec, Canada, which mined and milled asbestos fibers, a very profitable product used in many facets of building construction. Asbestos was a world-renowned fire retarding material long used in virtually all commercial buildings and ships as protection against spreading fires. Carey Canadian was the third-largest asbestos producer on the North American continent.

In considering the advisability of the purchase, JWC staff

looked into all phases of Panacon's operations. Though the legal department warned that the government might step in to challenge the merger of the roofing companies under its anti-trust laws, no one paid any attention to a handful of lawsuits then pending which claimed that asbestos caused lung cancer. At JWC, they would long rue the day of that oversight.

However, when the fiscal year of 1972 ended on August 31 and they added up all the numbers for all the thirty-three profit centers, everyone rubbed his hands in glee. A glow of happiness and gratification suffused the company. Jim Walter Corporation had had the most successful year in its twenty-six year history. Sales and revenues reached $893 million, an increase of 20 percent over the previous year, and fast approaching the milestone of $1 billion. Net earnings topped $45 million, an increase of 30 percent, and the company's return on stockholders' equity rose from 7.5 percent in 1967 to 13.5 percent in 1972. For the past six years, 1967 through 1972, the compound annual growth rate in earnings per share exceeded 24 percent.

From Frank Pizzitola's viewpoint, everything he had done as a professional manager and president of JWC had worked out well and succeeded, except the one thing over which he had no control: the stock price of JWC. From his start in 1970, a down year, through fiscal 1972, he had helped the company earn an additional $22 million in profits, almost double that of the start, and his driving focus on return on assets had helped more than double JWC's earnings per share from $1.17 to $2.49. And yet the fickle stock market went the other way. The price of Jim Walter Corporation stock fell from around $29 and $30 a share when Pizzitola came aboard in 1970 to a range of $23 to $26 in early 1973. Pizzitola's stock options were worthless.

On a business trip to London early in 1973, Jim Walter put

his arm around Pizzitola and said, "Frank, you don't seem happy. What's the matter?"

"I'm not happy," Pizzitola replied, having waited as usual to be asked. "I wanted to be a millionaire and I'm no closer to that goal than when I joined the company. I've produced tens of millions in profits for this company, and I think I should be rewarded."

Walter posed the next obvious question, and his company president told him what he had in mind. It was a carefully worked out plan which was breathtaking in its audacity. Simply put, Pizzitola wanted Jim Walter Corporation to give him one million dollars in cash or in stock as a bonus and then lend him another million at low interest to shelter the taxes on the first million.

"What do I do about Joe?" Walter temporized, knowing that Pizzitola would understand that he could not give $1 million to one executive, even if he wanted to, and not to another executive on that level, not without disrupting the harmony of top management.

Pizzitola would have none of that. "Joe is not your problem. I am. I've performed. I want to make some dough. Either I'm going to be treated special because I am special, or I'm not. I want to be a bonus baby. I don't just want more salary."

Walter heard him out, and said he would think about it. When he thought about it, he could not believe Pizzitola had been serious. Certainly he never thought of it as a threat. No one in the history of corporate America—at least up to that time—had ever received such a package. It was five times larger than the man's annual salary. Besides, Walter was not even sure it would be legal. So he said nothing and did nothing.

Pizzitola did not ask again. From his perspective, he had

asked for what he thought he deserved, he did not get it, and so he would move on. A few months later, when the legendary financial wizard Andre Meyer, head of Lazard Frères, offered him a general partnership in the investment banking firm, Pizzitola accepted. He estimated that Lazard Frères offered him a faster, more direct path to the millionaire status he wanted so badly.

In mid-May, Pizzitola walked into Walter's office and announced a fait accompli: he was leaving June 1, and this was his two weeks' notice. Walter was dumbfounded, unbelieving, and then furious. He had supported Pizzitola through the trauma of coming in as a top executive from the outside, of forcing new ideas and yardsticks upon his managers, of the discords among his staff, and now, bang, Pizzitola was quitting, and on short notice, and without debate or any negotiations. It was an insult.

Two weeks later, Walter informed his board of directors and made the public announcement, with the usual disclaimers of any conflict. "Frank just had an opportunity that he couldn't say no to," Walter told the press. "We're friends and there is absolutely no animosity between us."

With considerable candor, Pizzitola announced, "I intend to keep my stock and let it make money for me. I have much confidence in this company. It was a basic reason of money. I'll be going from one very prestigious firm to another, but in the corporation, I am an employee, and at Lazard, I'll be a general partner."

In his final two weeks at JWC, Pizzitola worked as hard and as diligently as ever, getting his workload in the best shape possible for whoever took over, cleaning up the bits and pieces of unfinished business. And, as hard-nosed as ever, one of his last acts as president of the company was to abruptly fire an unsuspecting executive whom he himself had hired for an important position. "He was my worst mistake and I didn't want anyone else to have to clean up after me," he explained.

When Frank Pizzitola left, he had earned the respect of his fellow executives at Jim Walter Corporation, and to this day he is given credit for the formal structure and management controls he brought to the company, but, man for man on a personal level, there were no tears shed at his departing.

CHAPTER 10

— *Building Beyond a Billion* —

T HE YEAR FRANK PIZZITOLA resigned, leaving a gap-
ing hole in management behind him, turned out to
be a landmark year in the history of Jim Walter Corporation. The company, with its 115 plants and factories
across the nation, now marketing the broadest range of
products in the building materials industry, passed the $1
billion mark in annual sales. What's more, its net profits of
$54.1 million and its primary earnings per share of $3.01
were at an all-time high.

In achieving $1.1 billion in sales for fiscal 1973, the com-
pany joined the exclusive Billion-Dollar-A-Year Club, to
which only 140 industrial companies in the United States belonged. Incorporated in 1955, the company was a mere
twenty-seven years old. But even more remarkable was that
almost all of its phenomenal growth had come within the
past eleven years.

JWC had been a regional builder of shell homes with annual sales of $37 million in 1962 when it acquired Celotex,
with its $60 million in annual sales. That launched the com-
pany on its fast track to becoming a major force in the building materials and construction industry. Its year-by-year
internal expansion and outside acquisitions added up to one
of the most outstanding growth records in the history of
American industry. By broadening the base of products the
company produced and sold over the years, JWC was poised

as well as it could be to survive the tumultuous ups and downs of the housing industry, dependent as it was upon interest rates beyond its control. Its home-building and financing operation now amounted to only 8 percent of the company's total annual business. Building materials and products used for new residential construction, largely out of Celotex, comprised 20 percent; remodeling and reroofing contributed 16 percent; commercial and other nonresidential building products, from Georgia Marble and Celotex, accounted for 14 percent; and water and sewerage pipe and products from U.S. Pipe contributed 13 percent of the company's overall revenues. Thus, the spread was fairly even across the variety of products, and it also spanned the timing of the construction business. In any major construction development, for example, builders first had to install water and sewerage pipes before putting up buildings. Then when the buildings were near completion, they needed Celotex insulation fiberboard, Celotex gypsum wallboard, and a host of other materials manufactured and sold by the company.

All in all, 1973 was a very good year, a billion-dollar year, and, as the company's annual report noted:

> The long-range outlook for the construction industry continues to be excellent. . . . Commercial building and household formations are expected to increase dramatically over the next five years. . . . We continue to be optimistic about the short- and long-range future of the economy in general and the construction industry in particular. Each of our divisions has embarked on a long-range business planning program and the Jim Walter Research Corp. continues to develop products, systems, and processes for tomorrow's building needs.

Gazing out and forecasting the future, everything looked good, but the rosiest picture of all was deep underground: coal. With the quadrupling of oil prices in the early 1970s, the whole industrial world was plunged into an energy crisis. Arab oil production was arbitrarily rationed, oil prices soared, and gasoline became scarce. Coal was seen as a premier alternate supply of vitally needed energy, and its prices climbed rapidly to record heights. This price increase provided an incredible opportunity for U.S. Pipe to cash in on the hundreds of millions of tons of coal it owned.

Ben Harrison, president of U.S. Pipe, reported the good news to Jim Walter and the board of directors: U.S. Pipe owned land or the mining rights to land in Alabama that held a coal reserve of at least 160 million tons of the very best, high-grade coal available. It was the kind of coal most eagerly sought by steel companies and electric utilities because of its high metallurgical quality and its low sulphur content. All told, that coal had an estimated potential value of some $6 billion! And, JWC had bought it all for a mere $4 million, which was the original price U.S. Pipe had paid way back in the 1880s. Walter and Cordell had hardly given a second thought to the coal when they bid for U.S. Pipe, as it was considered to be too deep underground to be mined profitably. But that was in 1969 when coal was selling at $6 a ton. With the worldwide oil shortage, the price of metallurgical coal had risen to $19 a ton, and was still going up. Potential profits looked very fat, indeed.

Harrison reported the facts and figures to Jim Walter and then made a full presentation to the board of directors. He proposed the sinking of four mines over a period of three years on U.S. Pipe property along Alabama's Blue Creek coal seam, about twenty-five miles southwest of Birmingham. The cost would come to about $25 million per mine, he reported, and if JWC wanted to guarantee its earnings rather than gamble on fluctuations in the open market, it could sell half of the coal to the Alabama Power Company, and the other half to steel companies in Japan or Germany, under long-term contracts.

The first mine to be developed, 1,300 feet deep, would be U.S. Pipe's Blue Creek #3 mine in Adger, where #1 (Bessie) and #2 (Nebo) mines had been producing some 900,000 tons per year for U.S. Pipe's needs since the turn of the century. The new mine, Harrison told the board, could be completed in a year, would yield 500,000 tons of coal its first full year, and 1,750,000 tons of coal every year thereafter, starting in mid-1975. The next three mines had a potential yield of at least two millions tons a year each, so that by the 1980s, according to Harrison's projections, the company would become a major force in the coal industry, selling from eight to ten million tons of coal a year. If coal prices followed projections, the four mines would more than double JWC's total present earnings. It was almost too good to believe.

With the board's approval and the first $25 million appropriated for JWC's entry into the coal business, Harrison plunged into the enormous amount of work which had to be done in sinking exploration holes and shafts for the first mine, hiring miners, expanding land acquisition, mineral rights, and, of course, preparing for the sale of the product. Walter chose to pre-sell the coal even before it was out of the ground and to sell it on long-term agreements, rather than to encounter the ups and downs of the fluctuating spot market for metallurgical coal.

By February 1973, a month before the scheduled start of production from Blue Creek Mine #3, Harrison had signed up the Alabama Power Company for the purchase of a minimum of 1,250,000 tons of coal a year for the next fourteen years, beginning in April of the following year. At $20 a ton, that would yield JWC $250 million. The power company also agreed to buy the entire yield of a proposed second mine, Blue Creek #4, which, when completed, was expected to provide 250,000 tons in 1977, increasing to a peak production of two million tons a year by 1979.

In recognition of his added workload and expanded responsibilities, Ben Harrison was promoted to senior vice president of JWC in addition to his position of president of U.S. Pipe and a member of the board of directors. This promotion elevated the forty-eight-year-old Harrison, who had worked for U.S. Pipe the past fifteen years, to the higher echelons of the corporation, just under Jim Walter and Bud Alston, and on a titular level with Joe Cordell, who was chief financial officer and also a senior vice president of the corporation.

Five months later, in June, when Frank Pizzitola quit, Ben Harrison lost no time in putting in his bid to succeed him as president. It was not so much that he *deserved* to become the heir apparent, since he had been with JWC only four years, but he maintained to the chairman that his experience and ability made him the most capable amd qualified man for the job within the company.

Of course, one man who disagreed with that appraisal was Joe Cordell, who had been like a right arm to Jim Walter throughout the development of the company. He told Walter that while he had acquiesced when Pizzitola had been hired, he now believed he was ready, willing, and able to serve as president and chief operating officer of the corporation. Besides, having worked hand in glove with Jim through the acquisitions of Celotex, Barrett, Georgia Marble, and U.S. Pipe, as well as in all the intricate financial dealings of the company, he thought he *did* deserve the top spot next to Jim. In fact, if he did not get it, he thought he might have a tough time continuing to work for the company under a different man. Cordell did not say this to Walter in so many words, but then he did not have to.

The rivalry for the presidency, barely concealed, started immediately after Frank Pizzitola quit so abruptly. Despite all the kind words and smiling faces at the public announcement of Pizzitola's resignation, Jim Walter had been dismayed at first and then angry that Pizzitola had quit so abruptly, without a "by your leave," without a discussion or consultation, and after so short a time with the company. In informing his board of directors, Walter declared that his next president and chief operating officer would be chosen from within the ranks of the company. Loyalty was Jim Walter's middle name, an integral part of his nature. His company, as well as his own business and personal relationships, had been built on personal fidelity. Pizzitola's sudden departure hurt, and, he told himself, never again did he want this sort of thing to happen to him. In reassuring all the division heads and company presidents who had gathered at the annual managers' meetings, Walter announced that the company would continue on the same path as before, he would assume the title and responsibilities of president, as well as chairman, and he pledged to them: Never again would he go outside the organization for a president of the whole corporation.

That announcement immediately set up an intense rivalry between the two leading candidates for the job: Cordell and Harrison. It split the company into two camps: the Cordell men, the core employees who had been with the company the longest, such as the staff people at headquarters and the managers in Jim Walter Homes, and the Harrison faction, composed mainly of U.S. Pipe people. Other subsidiaries were split between the two men. Every two months when the board of directors met, the company came to a virtual standstill as managers waited with bated breath for an announcement of the decision. Every two months the guessing game and speculation became more intense: Which one would be chosen? Wives telephoned their husbands at the executive suites, divisional managers phoned their bosses at headquarters: Did they make a decision? Who got it?

For Walter it was an agonizing choice that he and he alone would have to make, and he did not want to be rushed or pushed into it. This time in choosing his own heir apparent he would take all the time he needed to reach a decision with which he would be comfortable.

In any large company with a depth of management, no decision is more difficult for a chief executive officer than choosing his own successor. The choice is usually highly complex with far-reaching ramifications, and few men ever have the occasion to face it more than once. Competence and managerial ability comprise just the baseline in selecting a man to lead an organization of other managers and leaders. In choosing a successor, a chief executive must give weight to a candidate's personality and integrity, his inner drive, his courage to take calculated risks, and his inherent stability and caution in eschewing ego-building ventures that could jeopardize the company. Then he must consider carefully the effect of each candidate's leadership on the key people in the company. Which ones will follow one leader and not another? How will the company be changed if one or the other man is put in charge? The factors to be considered are endless and there are no simple answers.

When Jim Walter had gone "outside" to find Pizzitola three years before, the selection had been relatively easy: He had needed a professional manager for a specific purpose. There had been no thought of Frank Pizzitola succeeding him. But now, choosing a man from within the company, Walter thought of the man he would select as his eventual successor, unless the man clearly flubbed the job in his early years, which Walter considered a remote possibility.

For Walter it was agonizing to have to choose between two good men, each of them capable and qualified to lead the company he had founded, and knowing that when he embraced one, he would lose the other. No way would the man not selected remain. Out of pride, if for no other reason, he would seek another job, or he would be offered one that he would accept. Jim Walter wanted to keep them both, and for a man accustomed to making swift and sharp decisions, having to choose between them was sheer torment. Each man had his attributes.

Ben Harrison, tall, good looking, and energetic at forty-eight, was a hardworking, domineering kind of business executive. He had shown himself to be dynamic, decisive, and forceful in transforming U.S. Pipe from a stodgy, tradition-bound bureaucracy into a more aggressive and profitable enterprise with an eye on the bottom line. With degrees in accounting and in law, he had first worked for the Internal Revenue Service, and then moved over to U.S. Pipe, where in the past fifteen years he had worked his way up from controller to president. Now every bit at home in industrial management as he was in finance, he was overseeing the company's most important new venture, entry into the coal-marketing business in so big a way that coal mining promised to surpass the earnings of all of the company's other subsidiaries combined. It was no surprise that he wanted to be the boss at JWC, under Jim Walter, of course.

While every bit as hard-nosed, hardworking and demanding as Pizzitola, Harrison was much better at fitting in with the casual, friendly company atmosphere. No black suits for him. He wore sports jackets and slacks, spoke softly and half-kidded his colleagues, urging them to call him "Sweet Old Ben." But he was hardly sweet to subordinates who failed him in any way. Some thought he was overly self-confident, inflexible and that he got his way by instilling fear in those who dared to oppose him. But no one denied that he was effective; he got things done.

Joe Cordell was much more like an old shoe, comfortable and easy to get along with, and still as sharp and hard-driving as any man in the company. He fit right in with every group and faction, for he knew the men, their problems, and their goals. Less outgoing than Harrison, perhaps, he was every bit as knowledgeable and capable and got things done in a more quiet way. Moreover, he was thoroughly accepted and respected by Homes, the soul of the company, where Pizzitola and Harrison never had been. Although he may have lacked Harrison's industrial experience, Harrison lacked Cordell's knowledge of banking and his recognition by bankers across the country.

Jim Walter weighed the capabilities of both men, testing them, observing them, evaluating them for a full year, and then in June 1974, two days before a scheduled meeting of the board of directors, he took Ben Harrison out to lunch at a local country club. It did not go unnoticed. Rumors flew swiftly through the eight floors of the office building, and betting men placed their wagers. Half of them were wrong, of course. At lunch, Jim Walter explained as diplomatically as he could why he was going to propose Joe Cordell to the board of directors as the next president and chief operating officer. He asked Ben Harrison to stay on, to move from U.S. Pipe to the company headquarters as JWC's new executive vice president with primary responsibility for the coal program, for U.S. Pipe, and for other subsidiaries, which would put almost half of the company's operations under his jurisdiction. He meant to tantalize Harrison with the increased challenge, as well as increased compensation, to carry on as part of a triumvirate leading the company to new heights.

Harrison accepted the offer. At the board meeting, Ken Mat-lock was promoted to treasurer and chief financial officer. Cordell, as president, did everything within his power to make Harrison comfortable in the executive suite, and the arrangement lasted a full year. In June 1975, Harrison left to join U.S. Homes as president and chief executive officer, a job he did not seek but could not in good conscience turn down. He had always wanted to be the number one man where he worked. After a year at U.S. Homes, he left to start up a business of his own, which he subsequently built into a successful miniconglomerate in Birmingham, Alabama. With Harrison's departure, Michael M. Marchich, a mining engineer and longtime general superintendent of mines who served as president of the coal, iron, and chemicals divi-sion, was promoted to corporate senior vice president and made a member of the board of directors.

Why did Jim Walter choose Joe over Ben? Asked that ques-tion a thousand times, by his own estimate, he never could point to any one reason. Such decisions ultimately are sub-jective. Balancing all the tangibles and intangibles of one man against the other, the scales finally tipped toward Joe Cordell. He chose the man he thought would better lead the company as he had, changing it the least and bolstering its entrepreneurial spirit, when the time came for him to step down.

Once the decision was made and Joe Cordell was named president, a great sigh of relief was felt throughout the company. The suspense and uncertainty which affected em-ployee relationships and everyday operations ended. Execu-tives knew now where they stood vis-à-vis top management; now they could get on with the business at hand. And, it was a very good year all around for the corporation. Despite a general economic downturn across the country and the most severe decline in total home construction since World War

II, Jim Walter Corporation for 1974 was showing increased sales and increased profits. Symbolic of the company's growth and progress, construction was begun that year for a $2 million twin tower to match the 1965 corporate headquarters building. A bridge, containing an elegant sixty-foot-long boardroom, connected the identical buildings at the eighth floor level.

But it was the new coal program that dominated the financial news reports on Jim Walter Corporation. Jim Walter was hailed far and wide as an aggressive, intrepid chief executive who was taking full advantage of his good fortune in finding so much scarce high-grade, metallurgical coal in land owned by U.S. Pipe. With the worldwide energy crisis, the spot market prices for oil and for coal were rising exponentially, and Jim Walter Corporation, with its millions of tons of coal for which it had paid virtually nothing, was sitting in the catbird seat. *Forbes* magazine, for example, reported that Jim Walter "has watched a long-ignored asset (coal) turn almost overnight into some big bucks."

Early in 1974, JWC signed another contract with Alabama Power Company to provide the electric utility with an additional two million tons of high-quality coal per year over a twenty-one year period beginning in 1976. That coal would come out of Blue Creek Mine #4, then under development. All told, Alabama Power was buying virtually the full production of JWC's two new mines at Blue Creek, a total of more than three million tons a year at a cost of close to $2 billion! Thus, the coal was presold before it even was out of the ground. And the prices, based on a complex formula covering costs of production and market prices, were virtually guaranteed. By mid-1974, Jim Walter announced he had begun exploratory talks with steel manufacturers in Japan to sell them the production of two more mines scheduled for development at Blue Creek.

The coal bonanza so overshadowed everything else the company was doing in 1974 that Jim Walter felt obliged to reassure his stockholders with a letter, saying, "Important as the coal program is, we want to assure our stockholders that Jim Walter Corporation management will also continue to focus its attention on the growth and expansion of product and service capabilities for the overall construction industry. The coal program in no way detracts or suggests a departure from our overall corporate growth strategies." Fiscal 1974 would, in fact, turn out to be the most successful year in the company's twenty-eight-year history. Sales and revenues would reach a record $1.3 billion, 21 percent above the previous year; net income of $63.3 million was 17 percent higher than in 1973, and return on stockholders' equity hit a record 17 percent, one of the highest returns in U.S. industry.

Nevertheless, it was the coal program and every facet of coal development that fascinated Wall Street investors, and it was at a quarterly meeting of securities analysts that Jim Walter, with a chuckle and a smile on his face, explained, "To succeed in business, you have to be smart and lucky." He then paused and drawled, "But if I had to choose, I'd rather be lucky."

It was a very good year for Joe Cordell, too. Whether it was skill or luck or a combination of both, in that summer of 1974, after ten years of trying, Joe Cordell, fishing from his forty-one-foot boat, hauled in a 445-pound blue marlin, which he proudly mounted on the wall of his new president's office.

In the spring of 1975, after lengthy negotiations, an ebullient Jim Walter returned from Japan with a signed contract in his briefcase worth $2.2 billion over the next fifteen years. Six giant Japanese steelmakers, led by Nippon Steel, had happily contracted to purchase a minimum of three million tons of coal a year for fifteen years, starting in 1978 when the third and fourth JWC mines were scheduled to start production. So eager were the Japanese steelmakers for scarce metallurgical coal that they also agreed to lend JWC $40 million toward the development of the two new mines. It was by far the largest single contract ever negotiated by Jim Walter, and it contained the added benefits of a long-term agreement, which guaranteed a level of earnings despite the uncertainties of future coal prices. At the time, metallurgical coal was selling on the spot market at $75 a ton, five times the price it was in 1972 when JWC started its coal development program, but no one could predict the future. The Japanese in this instance were paying in the range of $50 to $70, depending upon market prices, and they were getting in return a guaranteed source of essential coal for their steel mills.

With the Japanese contract signed and sealed, JWC announced its projected coal earnings from the Japanese firms and Alabama Power. In 1975, when full production would begin on the first mine, coal sales would amount to $25.8 million and a profit of some $14.6 million. Those figures would rise steadily each year, so that in 1981 sales of eight million tons of coal would bring in $217 million, yielding a profit of $117 million, or about $71 million after taxes. Those income figures, the company was careful to point out, did not include the cost of borrowing the money needed to develop the four mines. The capital investment for developing the four mines was estimated at $184 million, not the original $100 million, and, according to earnings projections, all of capital investment would be recouped by 1980.

After that, it would all be gravy.

What could possibly go wrong?

When the date for reaching full production at the first new mine rolled around in mid-1975, a report came in from the Birmingham office that Mine #3 was running at a production level of 300,000 tons a year. That was nowhere near the

1,750,000 tons projected to fulfill the contract with Alabama Power. What happened? demanded Cordell. Why were they so far behind?

Along with a whole bunch of other reasons, they had hit rock. They had to drill through the rock to reach the coal seam.

How much rock? When would they get through the rock? They couldn't say. No way of knowing.

All that summer, they drilled through rock in southwest Alabama, while in Tampa, Joe Cordell and Jim Walter sweated. There is nothing harder in Mother Earth than solid rock; some days they drilled as little as four feet. It chewed up the drilling equipment, and it was expensive. Increased costs were eating the company alive. They drilled through five hundred feet of solid rock all that summer before they reached coal, and the seam they found on the other side was only about a foot wide, and they hit rock again. Catastrophe loomed.

How could that happen? It seems that the exploratory bores drilled to locate the path of the coal seam had been too few and too far apart so that the first two mine shafts had been sunk in positively the worst places possible, between bores that showed coal, but in a location where, apparently, a fault in the earth had shifted the coal seam to one side. They continued drilling and this time, fortunately, they hit a major coal seam in a few days.

Walter and Cordell flew up to the mine to see for themselves what was going on. Mike Marchich, the man in charge, tried to explain that hitting rock had been bad luck, and that there always were uncertainties and delays in starting up a brand-new operation. On the other hand, he pointed out, they had the most modern, automatic continuous mining equipment used in the United States. He reassured them that the mine would be in full production in a few more weeks, and, with added work shifts, they should be able to catch up with projected production levels.

In reviewing the entire operation at the home office in Birmingham, Walter and Cordell were astounded to discover that the land they intended to mine formed an irregular checkerboard pattern and they would have to buy up or lease more properties in order to have a contiguous stretch of land between #3 and the other mines still on the drawing boards. That substantially increased the company's capital investment in coal, but it also doubled the coal reserve from 160 million to an estimated 340 million tons. With the energy crisis expected to last indefinitely, coal still was almost as good as gold. Oil and coal prices, the economists predicted, would never again be as low as they had been before.

Cordell, a stickler on promises, marked his calendar when he returned to Tampa, and three weeks later he flew up to Alabama again to ask in person, "Are we in production now?"

No, replied an embarrassed Marchich. Blue Creek #3 would not be in production until the following June, almost a year away, he admitted. What had happened in the past three weeks to change his opinion so drastically? Marchich tried to explain, and Cordell listened to him, suspecting that the real reason was that the man simply did not like to give bad news to his boss. Dismayed by the latest forecast and unfamiliar with coal mining himself, Cordell nosed around, soliciting opinions from various mining engineers on the site. He was nonplussed when one or two of them frankly expressed the opinion that they would never get into full production in the new mines.

Sick to his stomach over what he had learned, Cordell reported back to Jim Walter that, to put it mildly, their whole coal development program was in deep trouble. He had reached the conclusion that while the men in charge were good enough to mine coal from the old #1 and #2 mines, which were not deep mines, they were over their heads in modern, deep-shaft mining. Cordell proposed that they seek outside consultants to inform and advise them. Checking around among his banking friends, Cordell took the recommendation of Citibank's coal expert: The top coal management consultant in this country was Paul Weir and Associates in Chicago. After conferring on his problem, he hired the Weir firm and it sent a team of three mining experts to the Jim Walter mines under the guise of doing some work for one of the banks lending JWC money for its coal program. Cordell nervously awaited their report and recommendations. He waited from October until February of 1976 and heard nothing. Attending a coal convention in Detroit that month in the hope of learning something about mining, he ran into the Weir group and invited them to a private breakfast meeting the next morning. At 7 a.m., before they had their orange juice, he lit into them: "You guys have been up there stumbling around, and after four months I haven't heard pea turkey from you about what's going on, what you've accomplished, what you think, right, wrong, or indifferent, and I want to hear it right now!"

"I'm sorry, but we're not ready to write our final report quite yet, and it'll probably be another couple of months," the leader of the group, a tall and lean Englishman named William Carr, replied in a broad English accent.

"I don't need a final report," Cordell insisted. "I just want a preliminary report."

The British mining expert took a deep breath and told him the worst: "First of all, it is going to be a minimum of three years before you will be in full production, and it will probably be closer to four."

Cordell exploded with an expletive. After a pause, the expert consultant continued, "Furthermore, you're not going to be able to mine this coal with your continuous miners.

You're going to have to change your whole method of mining." Cordell did not want to believe what he was hearing, but he surmised he was hearing the truth. For an hour he listened to Carr describe the problems he found at the mines and his proposed solution of switching to a new method of deep mining, called "longwall," which although not well known in America was used extensively in England and in Germany. Longwall equipment was much more expensive, Carr declared, but it represented the most advanced mining technology in the world, and it was quicker, cleaner, safer, and produced three to four times as much coal as continuous mining methods.

"I want your written report on this in three weeks, not three months," Cordell demanded, adding, "You'll hear from me then."

Back in his hotel room, alone, Cordell reviewed what the mining engineer had told him, and the more he thought about it, the sicker he felt. It meant that JWC could not possibly live up to its contract with Alabama Power, and the electric utility would sue them, and the Japanese would probably sue them, too, and the company would lose even more money because of the delay, and they would need to borrow more capital to develop longwall mining, and the banks would look askance, and all of the corporation's borrowing power might be put in jeopardy . . . and there was no end to the disastrous ramifications he envisioned.

"What do you think we ought to do about it?" asked Walter when he heard the unnerving scenario.

"Well, I think we just have to go out and hire somebody who knows deep-shaft mining, someone who can run that whole operation the way it should be run. I don't know anything really about mining, and neither do you," said Cordell.

Cordell recommended Carr. He had been impressed with the man and his command of the subject. Carr came from a

family of coal miners in Newcastle, England. A third-generation miner and a licensed mining engineer, Carr had worked
for the National Coal Board in England, which ran the whole
country's socialized coal mines. Obviously, the Weir firm
thought highly of him because they had brought him to
America just five months earlier as their in-house expert on
the state-of-the-art mining technology.

With Walter's go-ahead, Cordell flew to Chicago to talk
with Jack Weir, one of the heads of the firm, and rather than
go around the firm's back, he explained JWC's desperate
need to hire one of Weir's consultants to run the mines.
When he mentioned Carr's name, he thought Weir was
going to have a heart attack. "I'd rather you not talk to him,"
he sputtered. "I was sure you'd prefer that," Cordell replied.
"But I want to be in your good graces when I do talk with
him, and I assure you that if Carr accepts my offer, I'll make
all the arrangements necessary to compensate you for the
expenses of bringing him over from England."

It was not easy but, as Cordell put it, he "baited" the mining expert "with the coin of the realm," and Carr agreed to
head the JWC Mining Division and to implement the very
same recommendations he had made as a consultant. He
considered the job a worthy challenge. He would be somewhat of a pioneer in introducing the efficacy of longwall mining in America. In Cordell's estimation, Carr was still an
unknown quantity. He did not doubt his expertise, but there
was no way to foretell how good he was in practicing what he
preached. Cordell also harbored some misgivings over introducing a very British boss to a bunch of headstrong Alabama
coal miners, backed up by the powerful United Mine Workers Union. On the other hand, the tall, well-built Carr, despite his white hair, rimless spectacles, and British accent,
would never be considered a wimp. He had been the heavy-

weight boxing champion of all English universities when at college.

Carr impressed the JWC board of directors with his presentation on the intricacies of ultradeep coal mining and the necessity to introduce the longwall mining methods used in Europe. He convinced them, as he had Cordell and Walter, that while it would take all of three years to reach peak productivity using the more costly longwall mining equipment, in the long run the Jim Walter mines would prove to be very profitable indeed. With the board's blessing, Carr set about his task, while Walter and Cordell prepared to inform Alabama Power and the securities analysts who followed the fortunes of JWC the bad news about the coal development program.

It took Alabama Power about six months to respond formally, and then they slapped a $600 million lawsuit on JWC for nonfulfillment of contract. As bad luck would have it, a meeting of the New York Society of Security Analysts had been long scheduled for the week in which JWC announced the three-year delay in coal production. It did not take long for the financial analysts to pounce upon bad news.

Joe Cordell, as president, faced more than two hundred analysts and stock market seers at a meeting which usually attracted only thirty or forty. For the better part of two hours they threw at JWC's new president factual and speculative questions about deep coal mining, geological faults, cost overruns, and the effect of all of this upon the future well-being of the company. Cordell considered it the worst grilling of his life. "They ate me up like a pork chop, licking their lips all the time," he told colleagues back at the office.

The same securities analysts who had hailed and praised the daring of Jim Walter and his company for launching its coal program in a time of desperate energy needs, now chastised the management for embarking so precipitously in trying to develop four deep coal mines all at once. Many wrote of "a credibility gap," and hard times ahead, plus a dangerous degree of uncertainty about future earnings and possible losses. JWC stock was downgraded from the "buy" recommendations, and the stock promptly plummeted from $42 a share to the low $30s, giving up all of its gain since it announced its coal program in 1972.

At the Blue Creek mining site in west-central Alabama between Birmingham and Tuscaloosa, Bill Carr just about had to reinvent the wheel. No one there had ever seen longwall mining equipment, much less used it. Nor did one simply go out and buy the equipment from one manufacturer. The configuration of the Blue Creek mines required custom-crafted equipment and the various components were bought from the best manufacturers, who happened to be in Germany and England. The first longwall mining machine to reach the mine site was used as a demonstration model. The one-hundred-foot piece of equipment had to be assembled and started above ground so the miners and engineers could become familiar with it, then it had to be torn down, moved piecemeal some thirteen hundred feet below the surface, reassembled, and put to work.

The longwall machine consists of huge drum-shaped cutting heads, called shearers, which travel the length of the coal seam face, grind out coal, and dump it on a flexible steel conveyor belt that hauls it to the outside. The miners work under a protective roof of steel plates, called shields, which are supported by powerful hydraulic jacks. As the shearers complete a pass, which was about five hundred feet in length, grinding coal off the face of the wall, the longwall equipment—shearers, overhead shields, and conveyor belt—is moved forward and the roof behind it caves in. To prepare the way for this massive equipment, the roadway areas must be dug out and developed beforehand by other mining methods, usually by the continuous mining machine which grinds coals from the face, and dumps it into shuttle cars to be carried outside.

As important as this new longwall equipment was, more time and more effort was put into preparing the people involved in using it. Everyone even remotely connected with the new venture had to be informed of what was to be done, why it was to be done, and then persuaded that it was the best thing to do, and, finally, that it would work. This was no easy task. To train the first crew of miners and mining engineers, Carr recruited nine longwall mining engineers from England. Then he selected the best available trainees, who would become the "pioneers" of longwall mining, and who, in turn, would later train others. Eventually, a $2 million training facility with four underground mining laboratories would be set up for a regular five-month course of training in the various aspects of deep-shaft mining. Plans were laid out for developing four deep mines using eleven longwall mining systems, costing anywhere from $5 million to $11 million each, and employing more than four thousand miners and support staff.

As the corporate management of JWC so painfully learned, mining coal is always fraught with problems—the possibility of roof cave-ins, explosions, poisonous gases, government regulations and inspections, union troubles and strikes, and ever increasing operating and labor costs. While the Blue Creek mines, with the latest in safety techniques, were spared the disasters, they had their share of troubles. In 1977, the mining operations lost $7 million; in 1978, they lost $10 million. Those operating losses were over and above the $125 million spent in developing the mines and the additional

$250 million earmarked for future development costs. The losses were normal in developing major coal mines, although the development costs exceeded the company's expectations.

The good news was that at the end of 1978, after twenty-one months of negotiations, the Alabama Power lawsuit was settled amicably out of court. The electric utility company agreed to take substantially less coal during the first few years while the mines were being developed, and JWC guaranteed to supply the same total amount of steam coal over the life of the contract. Alabama Power even acceded to price escalations in the contract to cover the increased costs of mining.

On February 28, 1979, just under the three years predicted by Bill Carr, the first longwall mining production began in Blue Creek #3. For the first three days, testing the equipment in place, they ran the machines one eight-hour shift, then two shifts per day for the next three days, and after that round-the-clock for three shifts a day. Carr was determined to catch up. The coal was presold. It was his job to get it up out of the ground, and as fast as he safely could. Optimism returned to the corporate corridors of JWC in Tampa. The coal program was commercially under way. Projections of future earnings still held true, even if it would take another six years to reach full production. Carr estimated a yield of 2.7 million tons of coal in fiscal 1980, 4.4 million tons in 1981, and increased tonnage each year to a peak production level of 8 million tons a year, starting in mid-1985. The financial beauty of mining coal, when all is said and done, is that once construction expenditures are completed, operating costs become constant, and the mines become cash cows, producing a steady, rich cash flow year after year.

The most important coal program projection was Bill Carr's estimate that the coal mines would turn profitable in fiscal 1981. The Mining Division's business plan for 1981 called for a profit of about $6 million. This was most welcome news because coal had not earned a penny in the nine years that JWC had poured some $125 million into the deep mines. Carr's forecast came at a time in 1980 when housing construction had hit one of its worst cyclical troughs in the past twenty years, interest rates were soaring, and the company was hurting. The news of the Mining Division going, at long last, into the black was disseminated to the financial community, and many of the financial analysts who followed Jim Walter Corporation were recommending the stock, at its depressed price, on the assumption that the company's fortunes would soon turn around.

So, it came as a complete suprise when just in time for the December, 1980 meeting of the board of directors, the Mining Division reported to Tampa headquarters that, no, they were not going to show a $6 million profit for fiscal 1981, which ended the following August; no, they now expected a $16 million loss for the year.

That, to put it mildly, attracted Joe Cordell's attention. He had no idea the mines were being operated at a loss. It was bad enough to lose another $16 million on coal when a $6 million profit was expected, but it was far worse to lose the credibility of the financial community. The company's name and reputation were at stake. Financial analysts, told that the company's coal program would turn profitable that year, would now logically conclude that JWC management either lied or exaggerated, or were in more trouble than they admitted, or simply did not know what was going on in their own company. Cordell, not liking any of those imagined scenarios, stormed into Jim Walter's office, and proposed that he take five or six auditors with him to Alabama and "find out what the hell is going on."

Cordell and his auditing team spent the better part of every week that January at the Alabama mines, going over the books to trace purchases, cash flow, capital expenditures and, finally, to find out where the money went. He visited the mines, particularly #3 in production and the others in various stages of development. It took awhile before he reached a spine tingling conclusion: Bill Carr was a fine mining engineer, but as a businessman, he had a lot to learn. In his focus upon coal production, he had been following a go-like-hell-and-damn-the-expenses policy. In setting up a completely new mining operation, Carr had been buying sophisticated engineering equipment to experiment with new approaches to various facets of mining. He was venturing into high-technology mining and it was expensive. Labor costs had sky-rocketed. His expenses seemed extraordinarily high. It was not any one thing that was wrong; it was a little bit of everything. Costs were continuing to rise and the mines still were showing no profits. Furthermore, when Cordell went over the books, he calculated that the coal mines would not lose $16 million that year. They would lose at least $25 million. He shook his head in wonderment. A coal mine is a black hole into which you throw huge sums of money. That's the businessman's definition of a coal mine, and Cordell concurred.

At the end of the month he sat down with Jim Walter and tried to explain the multitude of small things that added up to a big problem. He even took three days to collect his thoughts and to write a rare memorandum on the subject. When it came to the final point of what they could do about it, Cordell leaned across Walter's desk, and said ominously, "Jim, we just can't correct this problem from Tampa. One of us has to go to Birmingham to turn that operation around."

Walter leaned back in his chair and drawled, "When can you leave, Joe?"

CHAPTER 11

Beware Building Up Interest Rates

IN RETROSPECT, IT WOULD be difficult to imagine any man more suitable to the awesome task of making the failing coal mines at Blue Creek, Alabama, efficient and profitable than Joe B. Cordell. By profession, he was a numbers cruncher, a CPA, trained and refined by Price Waterhouse, and by experience he was a rough-and-tumble man's man who could match his personal machismo with any building construction boss or coal miner. Born and raised in a small Southern-style town in Florida, he had acquired big-city sophistication, and had developed the sensitivity to know where the other fellow was coming from and how to deal with him. It made no difference whether the man was a banker, a pencil pusher, a production manager, or a mining engineer, Cordell could empathize with a man's fears and ambitions, making him particularly adept at befriending and motivating those with whom he worked. Since most management problems involve people, Cordell had been singularly successful as chief operating officer of JWC. For all of his bonhomie, he was a thoughtful man, a worrier who planned ahead, and he prepared his campaign for the coal mines before he packed a couple of bags and hopped a plane for Birmingham, Alabama, in January 1981.

The news that the president of the company was coming to the mines to take over, to shake things up, and turn the operations around would send shock waves through the ranks of management at Blue Creek. Cordell knew that. Relishing the anticipation which would greet his arrival, he telephoned Bill Carr on a Wednesday to inform him that he would be at the mines on Friday "for as long as it takes." Setting the tone of a tough boss not to be fooled with, he directed Carr to fire a vice president of the Mining Division because of the man's negative attitude as much as his ineptitude. "I don't care how you do it, but I want that man gone and his desk cleaned out by the time I get there on Friday." That would send a message to the troops.

He also asked Carr to summon all company supervisory personnel as well as union officers at the mines for a meeting with him at 8 o'clock on Saturday morning. He wanted to talk to all of them right away. There was a certain tone for the future he wanted to establish on his first full day there.

Arriving at the mine headquarters on Friday, Cordell adroitly made his peace with the English mining engineer. Behind closed doors, he pledged the embattled Carr his full support.

"Bill, it's only natural that people here are going to think that I've come here to run the coal company. I want you to know that that's not true. I'm not going to run it; you are. I'm not a miner, and I don't want to become one. I'm not going to go around here giving orders. I'm not going to tell anyone here to do anything. But I *will* tell you what I think should be done from a businessman's point of view. I'm here to help you, and together we're going to make good things happen.

"Now, I know you're an Englishman and you've got self-discipline, an iron will, and all that, but you're going to find out, Bill, that I'm the same way. Sometimes we'll do things your way and sometimes my way. But together we are going to clean up this situation. And I want you to remember, no

THE JIM WALTER STORY 215

matter what, we're here to do two things: to mine coal and to make money." Cordell declined the Englishman's offer of his own big office, and chose instead to set up shop in a smaller, vacant one.

At the Mine Training Center early the next morning, Cordell laid it out in the plainest language for the seventy-five or eighty supervisors, managers, and union leaders gathered to get the word directly from the big boss from Tampa. Cordell, however, wanted to come across to these men not as a big corporate president but as a Southern boy who had hunted and fished all his life and spoke with a slow drawl, just like they did. He also wanted to make it clear that while Carr and his team of English mining engineers spoke and acted so differently from their American counterparts, they had his full and complete support.

"I've heard all this crap about Bill Carr and his twelve Englishmen, but I don't care where a guy is from, what color his skin is, or what his name is, he's going to do his job for us, and if you ain't satisfied with it, you can just pack your little ditty bag and get out now.

"And, if there's any of you out there that ain't willing to put your shoulder to the wheel and work, inside of two months I'll know who you are, and you ain't going to have a choice then. So save yourself and me the time and trouble.

"We're all here to mine coal and to make money. These coal mines have lost $75 million or more [actually it was close to $90 million], but I want you to know that Jim Walter and our board of directors are still solidly behind this operation, and we're going to continue to support it. But, I can tell you this, this operation is going to make money, or none of our little asses are going to be around much longer. And, you better believe it."

He spent the rest of that Saturday and part of Sunday visiting each of the four mines at Blue Creek and the two older

mines closer to Birmingham, wanting to see and be seen, re-
alizing that he had a lot to learn about coal mining before
he could make rational decisions, and the mining engineers
there had a lot to learn about how to run a business. He
knew he would be in Alabama for the long haul. Time and
hands-on management were needed to change things big
and small and to get the coal company managed efficiently
along the lines of good, solid business practices. It would not
be unlike the task he and Jim Walter had performed in turning around Celotex more than eighteen years before, except
it would be much more difficult. At Celotex, it had been
someone else's management mess; at Blue Creek, it was their
very own. He would begin with the numbers. The quickest
way to increase profits is to cut costs, and you start that by
finding out where the money is being spent.

He conferred with Jim Walter by telephone almost every
day, discussing problems at the home office as often as difficulties at the mines. In the middle of his third week at the
coal mines, Cordell was asked why he had not returned
home the previous weekend. "I got too much work up here
to go home weekends," he replied.

"No, no, I think you should come back to Tampa on weekends from now on," Walter suggested.

"Why? I'm up to my eyeballs with things to do here."

"I want you here on weekends," Walter persisted. "I don't
want people to begin thinking how really bad it is up there."

* * *

Jim Walter did not like to spread bad news, and there was no
hiding how severely adverse economic conditions had struck
virtually every segment of the company. With Cordell away
at the mines, Walter had taken over the day-to-day responsibilities of chief operating officer and was receiving the daily
flow of reports and problems that ordinarily came to

Cordell's desk. All of management was hard pressed to cope. Historically high interest rates and a tight money supply had put a virtual stop to the construction industry. After nine years of consecutive record-high earnings, even through the recession of 1974-75, the company in late 1979 found itself caught in a tight money squeeze of ever higher costs for capital improvements, particularly the coal mine development, and rapidly shrinking income from virtually all its operations. The company did not suffer alone. The entire country was flung headlong into a severe recession in 1980 that would grow worse before it got better. Before 1981 was over, economists were speculating aloud on when to call the economic situation a depression.

When interest rates, the bellwether of the construction industry, began to rise in mid-1979, alarms went off in the minds of JWC management. They could see what was coming, but not how bad it would turn out to be. Walter, Cordell, Matlock, and their group vice presidents sat down and worked out a comprehensive and stringent cost-reduction program which was sent out to every profit center in the company: Freeze all hiring, reduce staff to the minimum required to get the job done; cut costs of production, cut travel, cut expense accounts, increase cash flow, reach out and collect receivables. Every profit center was instructed to develop its own individual program for reducing costs and saving money. They were further instructed to report monthly to headquarters on specific actions taken and results achieved.

The first cost reduction program went to the heads of all the profit centers in July 1979. Nine months later, on April 14, 1980, Cordell as president of the company enclosed in every paycheck a personal letter appealing to employees "to sharpen and redouble efforts to develop methods for reducing costs and expenses." Noting all-time high interest rates, the scarcity of mortgage money, and runaway inflation,

Cordell warned: "We believe business conditions could get much worse in the months ahead."

To the head of each profit center this time, Cordell sent a much more stringent program for cutting costs: Personally examine and reduce all inventories; order supplies only as needed; collect on all outstanding bills; close unprofitable facilities and plants; reduce capital expenditures; cut advertising budgets; reduce the number of company cars used and use them longer; buy cheaper gasoline—do everything you can think of to reduce cash outflow. Each profit center was supplied with report forms for itemizing cost reductions, which were to be submitted each month to James Jurgens, the company's assistant controller, who would correlate all the reports for review by top management.

As chief executive officer of the company, Walter wanted it understood that everything that was being asked of the company's outlying profit centers was also being imposed upon top management and headquarters staff. Salaries were frozen, bonuses were eliminated, personnel were cut to a minimum. Walter and Cordell together did a surgical operation on executives and senior personnel, getting quite a few people to take early retirement, moving others around, shifting responsibilities, and firing those people who had to be fired. Offices emptied out were left empty. It was painful. As best they could, they tried to trim fat and not cut into the muscle of the company. Both men reassured themselves that what they were doing was right. In making reductions they tried to keep their focus on the reason behind all of this: It was better to sacrifice a few of the pieces than risk losing the whole company.

In the effort to save money, nothing was considered too small or insignificant to be overlooked. The company's two private planes, a Gulfstream II and a Falcon 20, were put up on blocks and all but two of the pilots were let go. The only reason the planes were not sold was that in hard times no one wanted to buy them. For the next two years, the company's top management, including the company founder, would fly on commercial aircraft at tourist rates. The most symbolic step taken in cost reduction, in the minds of many, was the turning off of the floodlights which illuminated the white brick of the company headquarters in Tampa. In the dark of night the twin buildings looked as somber as some of the executives' moods.

The cost reduction program was deemed a tremendous accomplishment. Overhead and waste were trimmed, not slashed, throughout the company. No single cutback came to more than $500,000, most of them were below $100,000, and many of those were below $50,000, but altogether they added up to more than $52 million in annual cash savings. It left surviving operations lean and much more efficient. Down through the ranks, employees would remember this period as unique in the history of this ebullient company. In sharp contrast to the optimistic, expansionist years of before, this was a blood bath, with plant closings, the reduction of about 10 percent of the workforce, and cutbacks and personal uncertainty everywhere.

Later on, when it was all over, JWC would rank as the lowest-cost producer in the building supplies industry. But from 1980 well into 1982, no cost reduction program could hold back the force of an oncoming tidal wave of rampant inflation and soaring interest rates.

At any given moment, no one can ever know with any degree of certainty the future direction of interest rates. At best, astute businessmen, financiers, and economists make educated guesses, and it was at the worst of times in the summer of 1980 that Jim Walter and his financial advisers made a serious mistake in judgment. From its inception JWC had been a highly leveraged company with an insatiable appetite to borrow money on a short-term basis to support long-term mortgages on its shell homes. Over and above the mortgages, the company's expansion programs required large capital investments. During the previous five years, $340 million had been spent on the coal development program and another $400 million for capital improvements throughout the rest of the company. Traditionally, the company borrowed from banks at the going prime rate of interest, which fluctuated, sometimes wildly, in relationship to the availability of money. When the timing was most favorable, the company would issue bonds at a long-term fixed rate of interest and pay off the short-term bank loans.

As interest rates rose by almost 50 percent from 8 or 9 percent in the 1970s to around 12 percent in 1980, Jim Walter and his financial advisers in the company waited for the opportune moment to convert their bank debt into bonds. The company's total floating rate debt, which had to be turned over and was at risk every ninety days, had ballooned to a worrisome $900 million. The interest paid on that much debt was chewing voraciously into the company's earnings. Each time the prime rate went up 1 percent it cost JWC another $4 million a year in interest expenses. Of course, when the prime went down, JWC would save that much money.

What everyone had been waiting for occurred in the summer of 1980. Interest rates dropped a half point, housing starts appeared to be on an upward swing, and Jim Walter consulted with three separate investment banking firms on the advisability of issuing bonds to pay off a big chunk of its bank debt. Each of them advised JWC to wait for the rates to decline further. Walter decided to wait. To his horror, he saw his window of opportunity slam shut in his face. Interest rates did not go down; they went up and up. From September to December of 1980, the prime climbed steadily from 11.5 percent to 21.5 percent, and it hovered there through 1981.

It cost JWC dearly. Even at those record-high levels of interest, the company had to keep borrowing more money to sustain its capital expansion program already under way. The company paid $79 million in interest in fiscal 1979, $103 million the next year, and $157 million in fiscal 1981. That hurt across the board, especially as it affected earnings. In fiscal 1979, for instance, the company hit its all-time high in earnings of $98 million. In fiscal 1980 (from August to August), earnings dropped to $75 million. In fiscal 1981, when sales and revenues topped $2 billion for the first time, no one celebrated. The company's earnings had sunk that year to a pitiful $19 million. Even worse, if those dollars were adjusted for inflation, it would show the company lost $48 million dollars in 1981.

For Jim Walter personally it was a bitter lesson in the vicissitudes of high finance, the worst year in his business career. Everything seemed to go wrong at once and, as a man accustomed to take quick, decisive action, he did not know what to do or what he could do. Kenneth Matlock, respected by securities analysts as the best chief financial officer in the building industry, was confounded by circumstances beyond his control. Essentially there was nothing they or anyone else could do. They simply would have to ride it out. Economists coined a new word to describe the malaise that had descended upon the nation's economy. They called it "stagflation," a combination of inflation and a stagnant, unmoving economy. That combination had never happened before, they said. It was not supposed to happen that way. But the economy and marketplace do not necessarily heed the theories of economists.

If economic conditions were bad in 1980, they became far worse through 1981. By February, housing starts had begun a downward slide to their third-lowest level in thirty years. All of JWC's building materials operations suffered, especially roofing, which was Celotex's largest product line. In the past when new construction was down, renovations and reroofing were usually up as people mended and improved their old homes, and that had always helped JWC through the down housing cycles. But in the stagflation of 1981, when the cost of asphalt roof shingles rose 35 percent and the company was building new plants to make fiberglass shingles, home owners shied away from reroofing, too, and the fierce competition for declining sales sent prices into a tailspin. The company's building materials group saw its earnings drop from $63 million in 1979 to $31 million in 1980 down to a net loss of $2.5 million in 1981. The Roofing Division of Celotex alone lost some $21 million in the last six months of the year. The coal mines, hit by a three-month strike, lost $21 million that year. Brentwood Savings and Loan, with all its subsidiary branches, took a beating from the high interest rates. Its income dropped from $6.7 million in 1979 to $1.9 million in 1980, to a loss of $4.7 million in 1981. Only the stalwart home-building group held its own, selling more than nine thousand homes in fiscal 1981 and contributing $55.8 million to JWC's earnings, and even that was slightly under its performance of the previous year.

By the end of that disastrous fiscal year, JWC's board of directors was obliged to cut the company's dividend almost in half, from $1.90 a year to $1 a year. The payout was not eliminated completely only because the board decided, after considerable discussion, that as long as the company earned any money, its owners, the shareholders, deserved a portion of those earnings. Nevertheless, cutting the dividend was a bitter first in the history of Jim Walter Corporation. The price of JWC stock promptly fell accordingly from $36.37 on August 31, 1980, to $18.37 on August 31, 1981. In one year, the company had lost half of its market value. In 1978, before the deluge, its stock price had been $42.86.

As if to seal JWC's fate, Moody's Investors Service and Standard and Poors reduced the company's financial rating from investment quality to speculative quality. In one fell swoop that reduction made it much more difficult and expensive, if not impossible, for JWC to sell long-term bonds or commercial paper to pay off its mounting bank debt. The company in effect was helpless and at the mercy of the 150 banks from which it had borrowed money, loans that had to be turned over every ninety days at the current prime rate of interest. Any one bank or all of them could decline to renew its loan and request immediate repayment.

Walter began to have nights when he did not sleep well. He swore that if and when the company got out of this tight hole, never again would he allow it to go so far out on a limb for short-term debt. He wanted to find a long-term, fixed rate on the company's borrowing, no matter how high. With a fixed rate, management would know what the annual interest was going to cost, and could plan accordingly. Furthermore, with fixed costs, they could sleep better at night.

At the mines, Cordell did not have to tell anyone how bad things were; they all knew. The four new mines were still in varying stages of development, but ironically, it seemed the more coal they mined, the more money they were losing. As Cordell told them, that was no way to run a coal mine. His task, he repeatedly reminded himself, was to make these mining engineers aware of the bottom line which reflected costs and profits, to show them that the more you decreased costs the more you increased profits. What he meant to bring to the management of the mines was the broad, overall picture of what had to be done to mine the coal profitably.

Going over the books with Carr, he came upon item after item of costly, esoteric equipment ordered by the mining engineers and together, sometimes arguing long and hard, they slashed the purchase orders. Many costly items were can-

celed. Equipment not immediately needed was put on a de-
layed-delivery schedule so that each piece would arrive and
be paid for only when needed and not before. Cordell
brought to the coal operation a businessman's common
sense, cutting through what he called "the engineer's dream
world at Blue Creek mines." It was not that the mining engineers were consciously extravagant or wasteful, but as engineers they were not particularly mindful of the costs involved
in trying out their rather inventive ideas. As Cordell digested
the fundamentals of coal production, Carr and his management team learned how to pinch pennies and cut costs.

Beyond the numbers, however, hands-on management
meant going down into the mines and learning firsthand
how coal is extracted from beneath the earth. Cordell made
a point of going underground from time to time to see and
hear what was going on. Along with the miners, he went
through the laborious process of changing out of his street
clothes into coveralls for the descent into the mine. On his
head he wore the miner's cap with its attached lamp. In Mine
#3 he descended some thirteen hundred feet straight down
a shaft and then rode a small railway car to one or another
site of operations. In Mine #4 he went down more than
twenty-one hundred feet into one of the deepest mines in
the country where ventilation fans sometimes drove winds
up to forty miles per hour. Timing his arrival at the mines
when the shifts changed, he made it a practice to talk with
the men and women miners coming up and those going
down. He wanted to see the mines and the miners and be
seen at the same time.

On one occasion he watched a man operate a continuous
miner grinding along a roof above a coal seam that looked
like rock. When the man shut down the cacophonous machine, Cordell inquired, "Why are we cutting that rock up
there?"

"It makes it easier to walk," was the quick, obvious answer.

"I thought we were in the coal mining business, not the rock grinding business," retorted Cordell. He went back to the central office that afternoon, and asked Carr, "Do you know the men are cutting through rock to make it easier to walk down there?" The miners were following a practice of cutting large, uniform, airy passageways and when the coal seam grew narrow, they cut through rock so the men could walk upright. "That costs money," Cordell insisted, "Let them bend over a little bit; it won't hurt them." Grinding rock for the sake of comfort was halted, and that alone increased productivity.

In mid-March, when Cordell had been there a little over two months, the United Mine Workers called a nationwide strike. It lasted into mid-June and cost JWC about $9 million in halted production. Nevertheless, on a certain level it was a blessing in disguise. Until they got the costs down, Cordell figured they were saving money by *not* mining coal. It also gave Cordell an opportunity to get better acquainted with the mine's supervisory personnel and gave all of them time to stop and reflect on all the operations. Cordell and Carr delved deeply into the cost-effectiveness of each and every activity. Putting his mind and calculator to the work shifts, Cordell questioned whether it might be more cost-efficient to operate the mines on two eight-hour shifts per day, leaving the other eight hours for needed maintenance of the equipment. The practice had been to use the mining machinery around the clock on three eight-hour shifts, leaving maintenance to the weekends. But that cost time-and-a-half on Saturdays and double-time on Sundays. Carr and his staff went to work on revising shift schedules. When the strike ended, they found the new schedule to be more productive than the old one and at a tremendous savings. Simply cleaning up all the odds and ends of equipment abandoned in the various nooks and crannies of the mines and bringing them up to the surface and back into inventory saved more than $3 million in usable supplies and apparatus. The application of common sense saved tons of money.

One day Cordell spent two hours in #3 mine observing the operation of a continuous miner, which dug coal to carve out a passageway for the much larger longwall mining machine. The continuous miner extracted the coal and dumped it on one of two shuttle cars for transportation to a conveyor belt, which carried the coal to the production shaft from where it was lifted to the surface. The continuous miner was not continuous at all. It was shut down waiting for the return of one of the shuttle cars about 50 percent of the time. Cordell asked questions. He had them try three shuttle cars. Then he learned that the shuttles had a long run because the coal pillars, separating the mine into rooms, were from 225 to 300 feet wide. Why were they so thick? To hold up the roof. Who determined the dimensions? No one quite knew. So, Cordell hired the foremost expert on coal pillars, brought him to Alabama from London, and within ten days had an expert opinion that the pillars needed to be only 125 feet wide. Now the shuttle cars could keep up with the continuous miner because their run to the conveyor belt had been reduced by half. The savings? About 30 percent in increased coal production.

Then there was the night when Cordell came upon a front-end loader, which was a huge truck used to load coal onto trucks, parked at a small commissary about a quarter of a mile from the "loadout" where it should have been. Cordell sought out the evening shift supervisor.

"Dick, what's that pay loader doing in front of the commissary?" he asked.

"Oh, he probably went down there to get a Coke."

"Do you have any idea what it costs to drive that big son of a bitch? I guarantee you it's $500 to get there and back."

"It won't happen anymore," the supervisor promised sheepishly.

"I'm gonna count on it," said Cordell.

Converting a clear and distinct liability into a profit-producing asset is always one of the peak experiences in a businessman's life. Mine #4 provided that kind of pleasure for Joe Cordell. While every coal mine naturally produces an off-shoot of highly volatile methane gas, Mine #4 had a gas build-up of such magnitude the engineers began to doubt their ability to de-gas the mine sufficiently to bring coal out safely. A team of experts was hired from a subsidiary of Kaneb Services, of Houston, Texas, and for six months they surveyed, drilled, computed, and then presented Cordell and Carr with a plan for the Mining Division to drill approximately seven hundred wells to capture and sell the methane. Kaneb would manage the program. JWC's investment would come to some $50 million over the next ten years but the company would reap substantial profits over the years. Cordell sent the Kaneb experts back to their drawing boards. Come up with another, better plan, he told them, because JWC was not about to sink that amount of money in any new development program. A month later, Kaneb proposed their taking over the whole program, including the capital investment needed, and paying JWC a royalty for the privilege. Cordell was impressed. He negotiated a fifty-fifty joint venture, which to this day has been highly successful and profitable. JWC's half-share in the fully developed degassification program earns the company about $11 million a year. More than incidentally, it also made Mine #4 a completely safe, degassed mine by the time its first longwall mining equipment was put to work there.

Little by little and day by day, the attitudes of the miners began to change. They began to take pride in being more productive. Carr instituted regular joint meetings of all the foremen, supervisors, and mine managers so that they could review together what was going on in the different mines. Some of them could not believe what the others were doing. It did not take long to introduce the element of competition based upon a man's pride that he could match or beat any other man's ability to mine coal. Just as Bud Alston had done with his shell home branch managers, Cordell and Carr pitted one mine against another. They bought and handed out baseball caps for the miners, embroidered with his mine's name and number. Production levels per mine, per shift, per man were measured and reported daily for all to know. Cordell introduced what came to be known as the Cordell Award, a small gold pin with a crossed pick and shovel on it, to be worn on the shirt, where no one could fail to see it. The mine manager whose mine produced the most coal each month received the pin for his accomplishment. When a man won three months' honors, he was rewarded with a new gold pin with a tiny diamond embedded beneath the gold pick and shovel. Those gold pins and tiny diamonds worked like a charm.

Cordell took a special delight in those unique pins because he had them designed and made up for next to nothing by another JWC subsidiary called Wedlo, which had been the old Lorch chain of jewelry stores inherited along with the coal mines themselves when U.S. Pipe was acquired in 1969. The jewelry stores had been like an adorable stepchild in the family of hard hat businesses. When JWC could not sell the Lorch chain after two years of trying, the founder was gracefully retired. Peter Petro, his chief assistant, was promoted to president and told to run the stores "like a business," closing the ones that did not make money and instituting some better inventory controls, pricing practices, and credit checks at the surviving stores. Seventy-eight stores were pared down to about forty, located mostly in shopping malls and downtown areas in Alabama, and then one or two stores a year were added judiciously.

When he had demonstrated his business acumen, Petro suggested that they were missing "the cream of the business." Instead of merely selling retail, he proposed that they get into the wholesale and manufacturing end of the jewelry business. That's where the high markups were.

Integrating backward, under Petro's direction, JWC acquired Everwed corporation, which bought diamonds directly from sources in New York City's 47th Street jewelry district or from Antwerp, Belgium, and sold them wholesale throughout the United States. Then JWC bought Perfect Polishers, a small New York firm which crafted gold wedding bands and the settings for diamond engagement rings. When they put all that together, JWC had a highly profitable, integrated business of manufacturing diamond and gold jewelry which they could distribute wholesale and sell retail through the Lorch chain of small jewelry shops. They called the new business Wedlo. Pete Petro was only too happy to supply the president of JWC with gold and diamond pins for deserving JWC coal miners. He sold the pins to Cordell "at cost," and still made a profit because, as only he could explain, he always bought "below cost."

The moods, attitudes, and morale of the miners underwent a palpable change toward the end of 1981 as Mine #3 reached full production with three huge longwall systems and eleven continuous miners operating at peak capacity. There was that undeniable sense of accomplishment. Blue Creek #3 had at long last turned profitable. Smiling faces, laughter, and in-house teasing became the norm as miners washed coal dust off in the end-of-shift showers every day.

There was a camaraderie that had not been there before, extending particularly to the relationship between the English mine managers and the Alabama miners. They had come to know one another and to acknowledge that they could, indeed, work together over the long haul.

After fourteen months at the mines, Cordell had good reason to feel a personal sense of accomplishment. He had not turned around the mines by himself. No one could do that alone. But he felt the satisfaction of a job well done. There was nothing more that he could do that the mining men now could not do themselves. He knew approximately what the year-end figures would show. Cordell returned to Tampa in April 1982.

When the Mining Division final numbers for fiscal 1982 came in that August, even Cordell was surprised. Everyone was delighted. Coal production and daily productivity had exceeded the estimated levels anticipated when Cordell left the mines. Blue Creek Mines #3 and #4 along with the old mines Bessie and Nebo produced 4.1 million tons of coal and Blue Creek Mines #5 and #7, still under development, yielded an additional 1.2 million tons. That was an increase of three million tons over the previous year, a 70 percent increase in production.

On the bottom line, the $21 million estimated loss when Cordell had gone to the mines had been reduced to a loss of $15 million by the end of fiscal 1981. At the end of fiscal 1982, coal sales had jumped from $186.4 million to $270.7 million, and the loss of $15 million had been converted into a nice, tidy, first-time operating profit of $54.7 million. In that recession-plagued year, only the Homes Division made more money for the company than did coal.

CHAPTER 12

— *Building in Bad Times* —

T HE DEEP, PAINFUL ECONOMIC recession of 1980-82 proved to be a crucial turning point for Jim Walter Corporation. The men who managed the company began to change their thinking and attitudes on the ratio between risks and rewards. Hard times will do that. Jim Walter and his colleagues had had a grand fun-filled entrepreneurial run for almost thirty years. They built a small, simple, one-product company into a $2 billion conglomerate ranked among the leading industrial corporations of America. The recession of the early 1980s, the deepest in forty years, stopped them short in their tracks.

A black cloud of doubt and uncertainty affected them all—Jim Walter, Joe Cordell, Ken Matlock, Jimmy Kynes, the group vice presidents, the division presidents. They faced a muddy, low tide of faltering sales, shrinking income, and horrendous short-term debt. It all brought home to them the realization that they had not been, after all, infallible.

When they stopped and looked around, it became abundantly clear that it had been a mistake to embark on developing four deep-shaft coal mines all at the same time. If only they had paused long enough to check the original estimates, they easily would have discovered that deep-shaft coal mines would cost far more than $25 million each. If they had exercised ordinary caution, they should have developed one mine at a time and never have built up the huge debt which had jeopardized the whole company. Fortunately, Cordell and mining management had made the mines profitable just in time to save them all from economic disaster.

If they had not so eagerly rushed in to buy Panacon and its roofing factories, they would not now be seeing the flow of red ink through the corporate books because the bottom had suddenly fallen out of the roofing market. Acquiring Panacon had made Celotex the third-largest manufacturer of roofing products in the country, and it also made roofing the single largest product of the company. When Panacon was merged into Celotex in 1972, roofing had been very profitable, the fit was near perfect, the synergism of the combined roofing plants was all anyone could hope for. It was regarded as a great acquisition, a textbook example of how one company can grow, increase its market share, and double its profits by acquiring a similar company in the same industry. But times change. New technology produced fiberglass shingles which were cheaper and better than the old wood fiber product, and by 1982, with overproduction and a price war, the roofing business was in shambles. As it turned out, Celotex would have been far better off if it had not bought Panacon, or, at least, had divested itself of the acquisition when the Federal Trade Commission demanded just that in 1974.

Ironically, Panacon never would have been acquired if the sale had been offered five years later when the government had changed the rules on acquisitions and mergers, requiring a company to notify the FTC and Justice Department of its "intent" to make an acquisition before the purchase. If the FTC had advised JWC of its objections, the Celotex-Panacon merger probably never would have come about.

The irony goes much further. Celotex acquired Panacon for its roofing plants but with them it also acquired several other Panacon divisions and Canadian subsidiaries. Its biggest division was Philip Carey, with headquarters in Cin-

cinnati, which manufactured asbestos pipe insulation and other insulating products along with roofing shingles. Then there was Miami-Carey which made kitchen and bathroom fixtures in Monroe, Ohio; Briggs which made plumbing ware; and Republic Water Heater. The two Canadian subsidiaries were Miami-Carey Ltd. which manufactured bathroom, kitchen, and general home interior products, and Carey Canadian Mines, Ltd., an asbestos mining and milling operation located between Quebec City and Montreal.

In June 1972, Panacon and its divisions were merged with all their assets and ordinary liabilities, into Celotex, JWC's building materials manufacturing subsidiary. A year later, in August 1973, the Fifth Circuit Court of Appeals handed down a landmark opinion, upholding the first jury verdict in favor of a World War II shipyard worker who had inhaled asbestos dust and had died of an asbestos-related disease. Philip Carey was named as one of those asbestos manufacturers held strictly liable for not disclosing the existence of a "reasonably foreseeable risk" in the use of the product. Actually, Philip Carey stopped using asbestos in its primary insulating product in 1969, and Celotex had affixed a warning label to all asbestos products just one month after the acquisition in 1972, in accordance with a new government regulation. But that did not free Celotex of liability for Philip Carey's alleged failure to do so twenty or more years before the government requirement.

Over the next ten years some 25,000 lawsuits were brought against some thirty-two manufacturers of asbestos products. In the typical case, a shipyard worker would testify to remembering having worked with fifteen different brand-name asbestos products and those fifteen manufacturers would be sued as codefendants. Any liability found would have to be apportioned among the defendants. The avalanche of lawsuits, each of them complicated and different, raised all sorts of legal issues involving the asbestos product manufacturers, their insurance carriers, the companies that used asbestos in their products, the United States government that had specified that asbestos products be used to fireproof its ships, the Asbestos Workers Union, and the hundreds of tort lawyers who went about the union halls recruiting shipyard workers who might have contracted one of several asbestos-related diseases.

In JWC's consolidated financial statements, the product liability suits against Carey Canada, Philip Carey, or Celotex were described in footnotes to the annual reports under "Litigation and Other Matters," starting in 1979. Year by year the number of lawsuits rose from 7,100 in fiscal 1981 to 11,600 in 1982 to 15,600 by the end of August 1983. Some cases were settled out of court for small sums ranging from $6,000 to $7,500, most of them were still pending, and all of the settlements and legal costs were covered by insurance; as the annual report noted, the lawsuits did not materially affect the financial condition of the company. Nevertheless, it was the potential liability extending untold years into the future which threatened the financial status of all manufacturers of asbestos, as well as Celotex. There were estimates of some 21 million men and women who had worked with asbestos products, presumably inhaling its fibers, between 1940 and 1980 and that eight or ten thousand of them might die each year for the next twenty years from asbestos-related diseases. The potential liability against all asbestos producers was estimated in the billions of dollars; no one really knew.

It was this potential liability that caused the Manville Corporation (formerly Johns-Manville), the world's largest asbestos mining and manufacturing company, to file for voluntary bankruptcy (under Chapter 11 of the federal bankruptcy code) in August 1982. Despite assets of more than $2 billion and more than fifty-five factories and mines employing 25,000 people in the Unitd States, this otherwise prospering company declared it was "overwhelmed" by more than $2 billion in potential liability in tens of thousands of possible lawsuits which might be filed against it in the future. Manville certainly was not admitting how many, if any, of those cases it would or might lose. Nevertheless, the company was seeking the protection of the courts.

The Manville bankruptcy sent shock waves through the industry, through Wall Street, and through the country. At JWC, Jimmy Kynes, its general counsel, led a group of defendant companies in an attempt to develop with their insurance carriers a system for the out-of-court settlement of the asbestos cases. Two-thirds of all the money being spent went not to the victims of asbestos, but to lawyers and court costs. Kynes sought to bring some order to the legal chaos involved in the thousands of potential individual lawsuits.

Kynes long rued the day that Celotex decided to fight the FTC demand in 1974 for divestiture of all its Panacon operations. At that time, Panacon could have been sold off when there were eager buyers around. Instead, the legal battle with the FTC went on for ten years and then died of natural causes when neither Celotex nor an impartial referee could sell the Panacon roofing plants in dispute. Celotex shut down and wrote off four of the five plants for economic reasons. It could not, however, sell or write off the asbestos litigation.

* * *

As Jimmy Kynes was facing up to the asbestos lawsuits, Walter and Cordell, with the help of Matlock, Weldon, and others, faced up to the problems the recession had engendered at JWC. In a series of meetings, they reassessed the current position and likely direction of the company, and, biting the bullet, came to some hard, realistic decisions. The cost reduction program, good as it was, was not enough. The time had come for "restructuring," a buzzword meaning to slim down, retrench, and sell off the unprofitable, highly cyclical units of the company. None of them believed, however, in fire sales in the midst of a recession, but that was the new direction they decided to take.

While struggling to find a way to reduce the $1 billion in short-term and floating rate debt, the company faced the immediate problem of convincing the banks that held their short term notes not to call any one of them. If one bank demanded payment, it might set up an increasing run of the banks on JWC, and that would spell disaster. The company could have been forced into Chapter 11, voluntary and temporary bankruptcy, not because it was broke, but because it did not have the immediate cash to pay off a debt being called. It was that old bugaboo that had plagued Jim Walter and his company from the very start of the shell home business: cash flow.

In fact, no bank pulled the plug. One major New York City bank came awfully close, however. In the summer of 1982 that bank proposed that JWC consolidate all of its bank loans into one "revolver" loan, held in common by the more than one hundred different banks that had extended credit to the company. In that way, if JWC did go belly up, all the banks would be equally protected. In practical terms, it meant that Jim Walter Corporation would be thrown into a "bad risk" pool, and that was almost as bad for its reputation as bankruptcy itself.

Jim Walter fought back hard. A detailed, in-depth accounting and explanation of the company's finances was prepared, telephone calls were placed, appointments made, and Walter, Cordell, Matlock, and company treasurer Don Kurucz fanned out across the country visiting some twenty leading banks, explaining JWC's plans for cost reductions, divestitures, and paying off the short-term debt, in effect, pleading for the chance to "clean up our own mess." They did not want the company to have to go into a revolving, bad-risk debt agreement.

Twinged with doubt and bad nerves, the company's top officers were rather surprised at the warm reception they received from the banks with whom they had been doing business for so long. Every one of those twenty banks, whose decisions would be spread to the others, reassured the officers of JWC. None of them would even entertain the thought of not standing by Jim Walter. As one leading banker exclaimed: "My God, I could never look Jim in the eye again if I ever agreed to put him in a revolver loan!"

Walter's personal integrity, good will, and sense of fairness throughout his thirty-odd years of friendly associations with his bankers paid off when it was desperately needed. These bankers knew Jim Walter and the men around him personally, and that made the crucial difference. They had attended some, if not all, of JWC's long-weekend annual meetings over the years. They appreciated the man and the company and owed him and his company their personal loyalty. JWC had earned it. Walter had adhered to a policy of long-term business relations in which neither side would take unfair advantage of any economic change in the supply and demand business cycle. Steadfastly, the company had maintained lines of credit at prevailing rates with some 150 banks across the country, spreading its business among them far beyond what was normally required. It was done as a matter of loyalty. Now that Walter's back was up against the wall of ballooning debt and declining earnings, the banks stood behind him with their full faith and credit. The one bank that had questioned the company's solvency was in due course paid off and "written off" in Jim Walter's book of loyal friends. When the financial picture changed and the bank returned to JWC eager to renew its business with the company, Walter responded with a "Thanks, but no thanks." Never again would JWC do business with that institution.

For all the other banks that had extended unsecured lines of credit, JWC provided detailed business projections and plans, followed by quarterly reports on sales, income, debt, financial status, and the like, comparing actual operating results to projections. The company was not required to do this, but Jim Walter decided to treat his creditors as partners or investors in the company's fortunes. His going that one step further than legally required did not go unnoticed or unappreciated in the banking community.

In the summer of 1982 the decision was made to sell Brentwood Savings and Loan and all its subsidiaries. It was done with some reluctance. But Walter and his colleagues recognized that along with all the S&Ls in the country, Brentwood had been hemorrhaging cash during the recession. Its long-term mortgage loans on homes were bringing in interest at below 10 percent while the bank was forced to pay out interest rates of 15 to 20 percent for its money.

In October 1982, JWC managed to sell Brentwood to the California Federal Savings and Loan Association, one of the largest S&Ls in the country, for a form of debt, which later was converted to preferred stock when CalFed went public, with a face value of $44 million. However, because these securities would not pay cash dividends for the first ten years, they were valued at the time at $14 million. JWC took a bath on the sale, but it released the company from its most cyclical, volatile operation located some three thousand miles from the home office. Late that year, Mid-State sold off some $79 million worth of its shell home mortgages, raising much needed cash.

As that horrendous year came to an end, interest rates across the nation began to fall ever so gradually, like a blessed, long-awaited soft rain upon a drought-ridden earth. Economic forecasters hailed it as the beginning of the end of the worst economic recession of the past forty years. Wasting no time at all, Ken Matlock worked feverishly with investment bankers to devise an attractive, hard-to-refuse offer for long-term financing. JWC went to the bond market with $100 million worth of 9 percent bonds, which could be converted to JWC stock at 15 percent above the current low price of $17 a share.

Like the swish of a broom, the bond issue sold out in a matter of days. It was a good deal for both buyer and seller, demonstrating that the market had faith that JWC stock would once again rise to its former heights. For the company it meant replacing 20 percent bank debt with 9 percent money. In the next four months, the company sold another $250 million worth of long term bonds. These were nonconvertible bonds paying 12½ to 13 percent interest. Jim Walter swore he would not stop until the company had wiped out all, or almost all, of its short-term and floating-rate debt. Once and for all time, he wanted to put the company on the financial straight and narrow of long-term, fixed debt, backed up and supported by the steady income of the company's huge mortgage portfolio.

Since the early days of Karl Kreher and his eccentric capitalization plan, Jim Walter Corporation had always been a highly leveraged operation. Needing cash, it had always been burdened with a large assortment of different kinds of debt and equity instruments. There were various layers of convertible and nonconvertible bonds of different yields and durations, some subordinate to others, plus a variety of preferred stock and warrants that could be converted to common stock under varying circumstances. Fundamentally, it was the same old story of having to borrow cash to finance the construction of shell and partially finished houses upon which the company took back mortgages, or in effect lent money to buyers at long-term, fixed interest rates.

The company always carried a huge amount of debt on its books in relation to its assets because it consolidated the financial statements of its Mid-State mortgage subsidiary with the rest of the company. From the beginning, Jim Walter thought of the home construction and sales process as one operation, so sales and financing were reported in the same, consolidated financial statement along with the home building. But almost all other corporations that owned and operated loan payment subsidiaries, such as General Motors, Ford, and others, kept their finance operations as a separate entity for accounting purposes. Why? Because industrial companies needed at least an equivalent amount of capital as debt to be an "A" rated company. Financial institutions were considered equally sound if they maintained a debt-equity ratio of three-to-one because their debt was backed by money owed to them. Many mortgage companies employed six to eight times as much debt as equity. Thus, if JWC for accounting purposes "deconsolidated" its Mid-State mortgage company from the rest of JWC, the debt ratio on all the company's other operations would fall to as low as 10 or 11 percent of shareholders' equity. The company then would be viewed as a solid, stable enterprise. But it was difficult for outsiders to grasp this concept and the company's stock had always sold below the price/earnings ratio of the rest of the market. It was a concept that Ken Matlock took upon himself as chief financial officer to sell to the bond rating agencies and financial analysts.

As interest rates nosed downward during the first six months of 1983, the housing industry, ever sensitive to the cost of mortgage money, took off with a racing start toward prosperity. That is, of course, the nature of a cyclical industry. People who could not buy homes for the prior three years came out in force, eager for housing at interest rates they could afford. Housing starts increased 64 percent over the 946,000 of the year before. The housing industry, sick and near death for the past three years, now led the way out of the nation's recession. Well poised for the turnaround and sharing in the renewed good times was Jim Walter Corporation. Almost all of its subsidiaries showed dramatic gains and those that did not were anticipating increased sales and profits for the next year when housing completions, in which Celotex products were used, would follow the gains of housing starts.

By the end of fiscal 1983, sales and revenues topped the $2 billion mark. But it was the net earnings, more than anything else, that brought the bright smiles back to the faces of everyone working for JWC. Net income for the year leaped to $70.6 million, or $4.05 a share, in sharp contrast to $6.1 million, or 29 cents a share in 1982! In May of 1983 the board of directors hurried to say "thanks" to the shareholders who had remained faithful to the company; it increased the quarterly dividend by five cents, bringing it to thirty cents a quarter or $1.20 a year. The company was back on track again!

It was an appropriate time, Jim Walter thought, to do what he had been contemplating for some years: step down as chief executive officer of the company and let Joe Cordell have his chance at the helm. In August 1983, a month before he would turn sixty-one, the company founder outlined his thoughts to his board of directors. There was no doubt that Cordell, who had worked at his side for twenty-five years, was capable of running the company. Furthermore, it was time to demonstrate to the outside world that Jim Walter Corporation was not, never had been, a one-man show, as some believed. It would also prepare the way for Jim's eventual retirement, which he thought might come at age sixty-five.

He had no desire to overstay his welcome, a tendency he had noticed in other chief executives. He proposed to the board of directors that he would ease himself out of the picture so gradually that people would hardly notice his absence. For at least four more years he would continue as chairman of the board and be available when needed, but he would be taking longer weekends and longer vacations. When the time came for his retirement, he intended not to be missed at all. It was a measure of his confidence not only in Joe Cordell, but also in all the other officers of the company. None of this was any secret to Cordell. Walter had discussed his intentions thoroughly with him before approaching the board. On August 26, 1983, Cordell, who had been president and chief operating officer for the past nine years, was elected chief executive officer, the second in the twenty-eight-year history of the company.

It was Cordell's good fortune to preside over the company at the start of the biggest and longest housing and construction boom since the end of Word War II, when Jim Walter started building shell homes. By the end of fiscal 1984, sales had reached $2.287 billion with net income just under $97 million, $20 million more than the company earned the year before. It was $91 million more than it earned in disastrous 1982! Again the company rewarded its shareholders, this time with a 25 percent dividend in the form of a five-for-four stock split.

In fiscal 1985, the company did 15 percent better than in 1984. Earnings topped $111.7 million. Shareholders equity increased $85 million, or 10 percent, to a record $906 million. The company's return on equity reached 12.9 percent, compared with 12.4 percent in 1984, and far from the company's low of 3.8 percent in 1981.

As sales improved, the cost reduction program begun back in 1979 played its part in increasing the margin of profits.

JWC had become a leaner, smarter, more mature company. Between 1982 and 1985, Cordell presided over the divestiture of nine companies that were not keeping pace with the rest of JWC. They were relatively small units, acquired as incidentals with larger acquisitions, but together they added up to $250 million in annual sales, though their profit margins were not much to brag about. Miami Carey and Miami Carey of Canada, Jim Walter Doors, Jim Walter Plastics, Southeastern Bolt & Screw, Briggs (plumbing fixtures), and Hamer Lumber were sold. The sale of these companies and Brentwood Savings & Loan, plus the closing of several unprofitable plants, added up to a cumulative loss in annual sales of some $56.5 million. But it cleared the way to higher profits and a higher return on equity for the rest of the company.

The highest priority of business, as interest rates declined, was, of course, reducing and getting rid of the short-term debt that had threatened the company during the recession. By the end of 1983, the company had gone to the market four times with bond issues which raised $340 million, and followed that with a $125 million bond issue in 1985, and $225 million in 1986. Each successive issue was more easily sold than the previous one as interest rates fell, fears of recession receded, and the company itself was showing ever-improving profits. With bond issues totaling $690 million and the sale of $250 million worth of home mortgages between late 1982 and 1984, the company achieved one of the most remarkable financial recoveries in the business world. It was able to wipe out all of its short-term and floating-rate debt, almost $1 billion worth, within three years! Short-term debt of more than $500 million was reduced to zero and floating-rate long-term debt of about $350 million was replaced by fixed-rate bond issues. Its ratio of total debt to capitalization (equity plus debt) spiraled down from a high of

64.4 percent in 1982 to 43.5 percent in 1986, and if the debt associated with the mortgage portfolio was deconsolidated, as it is with other financial institutions, JWC's debt-to-capitalization ratio for the non-mortgage, industrial portion of the company would fall to a mere 5.4 percent. The company was not only solvent, it was prosperous, and hardly leveraged at all.

In 1985, for the first time in its history, Jim Walter Corporation was in a positive cash position! At the end of that fiscal year it had $61 million in cash to deposit, yes, to deposit, in the banks of its choice. It had taken thirty years. And it was cause for celebration. Also, for the first time in many years, the company's total debt—all of it fixed debt tied to and covered by its mortgage portfolio—was less than $1 billion. Actually it was $930.8 million, and that was another cause for celebration.

Fiscal 1986 was even brighter. The company's operations generated a positive cash flow of $251 million, another record. That cash was used to support $115 million in capital expenditures, including two new acquisitions, to fund the $66 million growth in its installment mortgage portfolio, to pay $35 million in cash dividends, and to reduce the company's debt to a record low of $873 million. The company entered 1987 with $172 million in the bank and $285 million in available bank lines of credit (which it did not need or use).

The Cinderella of the postrecession era was the least noticed, least heralded part of the company, the tucked-away realm of Arnold Saraw and William Kendall Baker: Mid-State Homes, the company's mortgage financing subsidiary. In fiscal 1983, for the first time in the company's history, Mid-State earned more money ($53 million) than Jim Walter Homes, the company's home-building subsidiary ($29 million). The tail was wagging the dog. The mortgage subsidiary, which had been treated as a stepchild by the proud, rambunctious home-building group for almost thirty years, had finally grown up and bloomed into the most profitable subsidiary of the company.

By the end of fiscal 1983, Mid-State held 62,000 individual mortgages on Jim Walter homes sold, totaling up to $2.4 billion in installment notes owed to the subsidiary. Earning more money on its mortgages than by actually building the homes was no accident. The steady flow of mortgage payments would continue into the foreseeable future. By 1986, with a mortgage portfolio of $3.1 billion, Mid-State would earn $92 million in mortgage interest. Projecting the numbers into 1990 the mortgage portfolio was estimated to reach $4.4 billion, throwing off cash of more than $123 million, far outstripping earnings on home building. Of course the home-building division would have to continue selling and building homes to feed the mortgage portfolio, but now, at long last, the ever-troublesome mortgage portfolio, over which Jim Walter had struggled for so many years, would soon be providing enough cash to cover, or nearly cover, all of the money needed to build future Jim Walter homes.

It was, indeed, the sweetest of rewards for those in the company who had struggled over bank loans for so many years to support that mortgage portfolio. The turnabout went unnoticed outside the company because few financial analysts had delved into how the mortgages worked. Jim Walter Homes mortgages were unique. Most mortgage companies take their interest (i.e., profits) up front in the first years of the loan. A home buyer pays almost all interest and little principal on the first five or so years of the mortgage; if he sells his home during that time, as many do, the bank or mortgage company has already pocketed its profits. JWC, on the other hand, needing cash flow more than earnings in its early years, chose a more conservative, straight-line "financial charge," which remains constant in each payment. Thus, as the mortgage ages, the proportion of capital owed decreases faster and the proportion of interest (i.e., profit) in each payment increases. For example, on a twenty-year mortgage at 10 percent annual interest for a $30,000 Jim Walter home, the owner pays $289.50 a month, of which $102.50 is principal and $187 is interest. That is true of payment number one and payment number 240. Thus, the yield to the company on the first payment is only 9.1 percent. But the yield increases on each subsequent payment as the principal is reduced, so that the final payment, has a yield of 2,189 percent. The company's straight-line method of financing also serves to keep losses at more reasonable levels when houses are repossessed.

This well-fed cash cow was made up of the best of mortgages, too. Defaults were less than 1 percent, and for good reason. Monthly payments on Jim Walter homes averaged about 16 percent of income, far less than the 20 to 30 percent in most other home mortgages. The company had more than 100,000 active mortgages on its books, 65,000 of which it still owned, while it serviced (for a fee) the 35,000 it had sold during the 1980-82 recession.

The mortgage portfolio also served as a counterbalance to the financial aspects of the home-building division. When sales and earnings of Jim Walter homes increased, the mortgage division had to borrow more money to finance those homes, which reduced its profits. But when fewer homes were sold, Mid-State borrowed less money and as loan payments flowed in from previously sold homes, its profits increased. Working in tandem, this combination took on the appearance of a well-oiled, perpetual motion, money-making machine. By the late 1980s, Mid-State was able to borrow money at 10 to 12 percent, while its mortgage portfolio, taken in its entirety, was yielding about 17 percent. That 5 percent spread was money in the bank. The mortgage portfolio, for good reason, came to be seen as the crown jewel in the company's treasure chest.

Together, Jim Walter Homes and Mid-State, from which the whole company had sprung, continued to be the biggest profit-makers in Jim Walter Corporation. When things were bad in 1982, the two in tandem produced 47 percent of the company's profits, setting a record of 10,267 houses built that year. Afterward, the company averaged six to seven thousand homes a year, and that, in 1986, made JWC the No. 1 builder of single family detached houses in America.

With 102 branches and model home centers in seventeen states, ready and able to build in twenty-nine states, Jim Walter Homes still did business in 1988 the same way it had from the beginning. The company offered twenty-six different models, ranging from a 640-square-foot shell home for $13,000 to an 1,800-square-foot luxury model 90 percent finished for $65,000. The average price paid for a 1986 Jim Walter home was roughly $32,000. With no down payment, service charges, or closing fees, but with the land site mortgaged along with the house, the average monthly mortgage payment was $323. The biggest change, however, was that in recent years buyers switched from doing it themselves to having the company do it for them. In 1986, only 28 percent of its customers bought basic, unfinished shell homes of varying sizes. Three out of every five houses sold were 90 percent complete, which left to the customer only such finishing touches as floor coverings, inside paint, and outside hookups of utilities. The remaining 12 percent of home buyers chose various stages of completion.

Obviously, with the more finished, higher-priced homes, the company earned more money on each house than it had in earlier years. But basic business policies and practices did not change. Not one piece of lumber was purchased before the customer signed a contract, his credit rating and financing were approved, and a title search found that his property was owned free and clear. The sales force had grown to 350 men and women. As in the early days of the company, they were paid a basic salary, were covered by the company's health benefits and profit-sharing plans, and their commission on each house sold was the same, regardless of its size or price. The company still guarded itself against selling more house than a customer could afford.

The old esprit de corps and regional competitiveness never changed. The Florida Gators went on challenging the Texas Longhorns or Georgia Bulldogs over which region would sell more homes in the next week or next month. The old teletype machines were gone, replaced with modern personal computers and modems so that every Saturday morning, just as in the early days, each of the branch offices of Jim Walter Homes would report in its sales, houses on order, and houses built for that week. The key people in all branches and all their superiors, from the president on down, would be on-line, comparing, commenting, and passing judgment. Prizes and awards went to the winners. The losers reported in last, hanging their heads in shame. The order of responding depended upon how well that sales office did the week before. The office that came in last had to stay on the line until the other 101 offices had reported in. The salesperson who sold seventy-five homes in one year was considered outstanding. He or she was rewarded with a trophy, a bonus check, and induction into the Jim Walter Homes "Hall of Fame." Seventy salesmen and ten saleswomen had their names on brass plaques in the home office by 1989. At last report, they were still vying to prove who was the best sales person at Jim Walter Homes, which was the best branch office, which the top earning region. The competition was still "all in the family." Tommy Hires, who replaced Bud Alston as president of Homes in 1973, retired in April 1984 and was replaced by *his* executive vice president and top assistant, Bob Michael, who had joined the company twenty years before at age twenty-two. Continuity of management was never broken.

By the end of 1986, Jim Walter Corporation was enjoying corporate nirvana, with record sales, record-high income, no outstanding short-term debt, a bountiful cash balance for the first time in its history, and a bright future ahead. Celotex, its first major acquisition, had been expanded from $60 million in annual sales of building materials in 1962 to well over $600 million in 1986. U.S. Pipe had increased its capacity by 40 percent in ten years to become the largest, lowest-cost producer of ductile-iron pressure pipe in the nation. Georgia Marble had grown from $39 million in annual sales to $120 million. The coal mines were on-line with projections of the highest production levels and lowest costs in the industry, mining eight million tons a year, with coal reserves of 284 million tons, good at that rate for another thirty-five years.

The company was doing so well since its restructuring in 1982 that Standard & Poor's raised its rating on JWC senior debt three notches from BBB- to A-. It was the first time in the company's thirty-two years that it had reached the A level, representing an especially sound investment for bondholders.

In business, however, there is always some danger in too much success. The company had become so successful by the

end of 1986, so cash rich, so full of potential, that it also became a prime candidate for a takeover by those wily money
men on Wall Street. As more securities analysts recommended the stock as an excellent buy, the rumor mill more
frequently came up with the name of Jim Walter Corporation as a company worth a lot more than it was selling for on
the open market. In other words, it was a bargain.

CHAPTER 13

— *Building in Good Times* —

THE FATEFUL TELEPHONE CALL came in soon after the beginning of 1987, not to Walter, the founder and chairman, nor to Cordell, the president and chief executive officer, but rather to Ken Matlock, the company's chief financial officer. The caller was an old business acquaintance, albeit a relatively young man still in his thirties, named Michael Tokarz, who as the head of the Miami and then New York office of Continental Illinois National Bank and Trust Co. had worked closely with Matlock in extending multimillion-dollar lines of credit to JWC as far back as 1979. Tokarz, a lean, trim, highly motivated and energetic banker, had abandoned a brilliant, upwardly mobile career at Continental in 1984 for an even more stellar position as a deal associate with Kohlberg Kravis Roberts & Co., the foremost leveraged buyout (LBO) firm in the country. Now, ever so delicately, he was asking: Would Jim Walter like to meet Henry Kravis and explore with him the possibility of a leveraged buyout?

As a longtime admirer of Jim Walter Corporation, Tokarz had recommended the company to Kravis, the senior partner of KKR. Tokarz thought JWC was little understood by most security analysts, little known by the public, and grossly undervalued in the marketplace. Most of its stock (about 70 percent) was held by institutions. Tokarz proposed that KKR might upon further investigation be interested in buying the company in partnership with the JWC management. A great deal of hidden value could be added by restructuring and taking the company private, Tokarz said.

The young financier imparted most of this to Matlock as an introduction to KKR's way of thinking. He had no need to explain the LBO firm itself to Matlock. Everyone in the business world was, or should have been, keenly aware of Kohlberg Kravis Roberts. It was the most remarkable, most successful, most highly regarded, and possibly one of the most powerful financial institutions in the country. Just the previous year, KKR had completed the largest leveraged corporate buyout in history: the Beatrice food conglomerate for $6.2 billion. Started in 1976, KKR had a track record of one success after another: the first LBO of a major New York Stock Exchange firm (Houdaille, in 1979); the first $1 billion buyout (Wometco, in 1984); the first large buyout financed through a public tender offer (Malone & Hyde, in 1984). In fact, Jerome Kohlberg and Henry Kravis and his cousin, George Roberts, who left the investment banking firm of Bear Stearns to start KKR in 1976, are credited with having devised the modern LBO through a technique of borrowing virtually all the money needed with bridge loans from banks, paying them off with high-yield bond issues, and financing all of this by using the company's own assets as collateral.

There were no strings attached to the get-acquainted meeting. Tokarz suggested that the two men, Walter and Kravis, ought to meet because something might come of it. If Walter, after hearing Kravis's ideas, had no interest in taking his company private, the entire matter would end there and remain confidential. KKR, he added, only pursued LBOs on a friendly, mutually beneficial basis, and only if a company's board of directors and management welcomed the change. Matlock cautiously promised to pass the word along.

Jim Walter was intrigued, even fascinated. The phone call had not been entirely unexpected. For nearly two years, JWC had been written and talked about as an attractive takeover target. Management's success since the 1982 recession in streamlining operations, eliminating short-term debt, cutting costs, and raising sales and earnings to record heights, had, ironically, made the company a bargain on Wall Street. Its stock was selling in the low $40s, only eleven times earnings or about half of the whole market's P/E ratio. No wonder that more and more security analysts were estimating "breakup value" of the company at closer to $60.

With "merger mania" sweeping Wall Street, more than two thousand companies a year were being bought, merged, or gobbled up in friendly, not so friendly, and in downright hostile takeovers. Thousands of others were fighting for their independent lives with such anti-takeover techniques as poison pills, golden parachutes, legal impediments, and near suicidal improvisions of the moment. The possibilities of a buyout, a merger, or a takeover of one kind or another were all topics thoroughly examined by JWC's board of directors. What should the company do if and when an offer, friendly or unfriendly, was made? Should the company seek a friendly buyout rather than wait and chance an unfriendly one? What are the ramifications of a management LBO on its own? How should they handle a hostile tender offer for the company? What if JWC inaugurated one or more anti-takeover maneuvers tried by other companies? At meetings with security analysts, Walter and Cordell were frequently asked what specific steps they were taking to ward off takeover attempts of one kind or another. The answer was: None. The company would not adopt specific defensive measures simply to thwart a takeover bid. Jim Walter and his board of directors agreed to wait and see and to review any and all offers that came in and only then to base their decisions solely on what would be best for the company and its shareholders. Despite all the talk and rumors, the approach from KKR was the first to materialize.

Waiting for that first meeting with KKR representatives, Jim Walter was assailed with doubts and mixed emotions. One could try to plan ahead, but venturing into an LBO was very much like entering a hospital for major surgery. It was an entirely new arena for him, and the possibilities were fathomless. It might make economic sense to sell the company for a price far higher than its stock market value, but on a personal level it was like selling the house you had built yourself, with your own hands, and lived in for thirty or forty years. The company was his life's achievement. He did not particularly want to sell.

Walter knew he had to face the reality of the situation: Given the fundamentals of price and value, his company most likely would be bought out by someone, hostile or friendly; if that had to happen, he much preferred to do it in a friendly transaction with a first-class firm like Kohlberg Kravis Roberts. The people at KKR had a reputation for capability, integrity, and fairness. The firm, with its financial strength and know-how, was simply the best in the business. Every one of their multimillion- and multibillion-dollar deals had succeeded beyond ordinary Wall Street standards, and they had accomplished it all with a finesse and acuity that impressed even their own competitors. KKR was known to structure deals that were eminently fair to the managements and employees of the companies they bought. Walter felt his own people would fare well, if anything came of these talks. Obviously, KKR would be expected to offer a substantial premium over the market price of JWC stock if it hoped to buy the company, and JWC employees, who owned more than 11 percent of the outstanding shares, stood to benefit substantially.

Just what KKR would offer for the company, Jim Walter did not know. Then again, if the offer was not enough, he could always turn it down. With raging ambivalent feelings, Walter decided that his best posture was to listen with an open mind to what Henry Kravis had to say and to what he had to offer. Decisions would come later.

The traumatic meeting—and there is nothing more traumatic than facing the sale of your own company—took place three weeks after the initial phone call, on a Friday afternoon, January 30. At the appointed hour, having flown from New York City, Henry Kravis and Mike Tokarz were shown into the chairman's office, where Walter rose from his desk to greet them. Tokarz presented his boss, and Walter introduced his associates: Cordell, Matlock, and Jimmy Kynes, general counsel and executive vice president.

For all of his reputed financial power, dynamic lifestyle, social elegance, and multimillion-dollar annual income, Henry Kravis was a rather genial man, in his early forties. His manner, like his attire, was meticulous, crisp, and urbane, and as he spoke he came across as unpretentious, warm, gracious and, one had to admit, likeable. What he was saying made plain, common sense.

"A leveraged buyout can be a thing of beauty," Kravis said with a warm smile. "It is one of the few times in life when you can have your cake and eat it, too. You can sell your company and still have it, too." That was the main, most appealing thrust of his explanation. He reassured the men in the room that KKR was not a speculator or a raider. His firm had no intention of buying a company merely to chop it up and sell the pieces for a quick profit. Nor did KKR want to run any company themselves. They were not managers. Pure and simple, KKR was a firm of investors, he explained, backed by large, well-known institutions who as limited partners contributed to separate pools of venture capital funds that had grown through the years from $100,000 to $1.8 billion. That seed money gave KKR the borrowing capability of $15 to $20 billion. The limited partners who invested in KKR were substantial, well-known institutional investors. The largest of them were state employee pension funds and some of the country's largest commercial banks, insurance companies, and university endowment funds. As the general partner with sole discretion over an equity pool which still had almost $2 billion, KKR had the financial wherewithal and borrowing capacity to buy JWC or any number of companies for at least ten times the equity it could or would invest. KKR had already bought some thirty companies for more than $30 billion.

Kravis explained that a leveraged buyout of Jim Walter Corporation was an attractive proposition because it made "economic sense for both sides." His firm would pursue the possibililty of an LBO only if Walter himself, his managers, and his board of directors agreed that it made economic sense for the company and its shareholders. If not, KKR would go about its business elsewhere, he said.

However, he added, according to Tokarz's initial research, the company met all the criteria that his firm had set for a successful LBO, and at KKR they examined anywhere from sixty to one hundred companies a year for every candidate they pursued. As Kravis ticked off the criteria his firm set for a successful LBO, he was singing the praises of JWC, and, of course, he knew it. Jim Walter Corporation was a big, solid, mature company that had an excellent team of managers in place who had run the company in good times and bad. Its products and services, while cyclical, were in basic industry and would always be needed. The company also had free-standing, separate profit centers which could be sold off, if necessary, to bring down the size of the debt incurred in the purchase. Its operations provided substantial cash flow, enough to handle interest payments on the contemplated debt.

Furthermore, Kravis said KKR's practice was to ask current management to stay on and run the new company. But, he added with emphasis, management's future with the new company would in no way be tied to any presale agreement, as that might entail a possible conflict of interest. Only after the sale was assured would KKR negotiate employment contracts with the management. While he could not and would not promise anything specific beforehand, he would be happy to send over public documents which described management plans worked out in previous LBOs for JWC's guidance. But whether or not anyone bought or did not buy into the new company would not affect the purchase price of the company.

Kravis carefully pointed out that at this stage they were only talking about possibilities. It was extremely difficult, if not impossible, he said, to determine the fair value of a company before KKR had access to the company's internal financial figures in a "due diligence" examination and assessment of what KKR would be buying, if it decided to buy.

Walter expressed his concern for the welfare of his employees in a newly constructed, private company, and Kravis reassured him that it was in KKR's interest to build up, not tear down, any company it owned. The real work in making an LBO successful began only *after* the sale and merger were completed. "Any fool can buy a company," he remarked with a smile. But it is after the sale and merger that KKR goes to work with the help of management in restructuring the new company so that not only is the debt paid down, but the company becomes more profitable and more valuable as time goes on. The new company, privately owned by KKR and its own management, would then concentrate on long-range goals, cash flow, and building equity value. Ultimately, somewhere down the road, perhaps in two, four, or six years, the company could be taken public again or even restructured with new debt to reflect its inherent greater value.

Walter asked if Kravis was aware of Celotex's product liability suits involving asbestos and the financial cloud it created over the subsidiary. "Yes, we are aware of it," he responded "and we'll be looking into it very carefully, as we will everything else." Discussing the problem frankly, Walter and Kynes reviewed the history of the lawsuits and how they had been handled. Walter was equally candid in describing the operational problems his company faced in the cyclical housing and construction business and the efforts made over the years to diversify and to spread the risks.

The meeting lasted for just about one hour with probing questions from both sides. What came out of that get-acquainted meeting, more than anything else, was a sense of mutual trust and confidence, an intuitive feeling that they could, indeed, work together and enjoy the experience. These were two self-made, self-confident men, each of whom knew where the other man was coming from. Neither of them would ever bend to unwarranted force. They met as equals. More important than any sequence of financial statistics, the "chemistry" between them was right. No commitments or favors were asked for or given. Kravis did not promise to buy the company and Walter did not promise to sell. But the process of a leveraged buyout had begun, and nothing really would be the same again at JWC. Intuitively, both men knew that at the end of that first day.

* * *

The painstaking work of due diligence that is essential in any leveraged buyout began early the following week. But even before that, both KKR and JWC engaged specialized lawyers to lead them through the arcane securities laws, governmental agency regulations, and the ever-present threat of civil law suits from litigious shareholders. One false step could bring on troubles of enormous dimensions. The day after his meeting with Jim Walter, Henry Kravis telephoned Richard I. Beattie, of Simpson Thacher & Bartlett, one of the most prominent legal firms specializing in mergers and acquisitions. He then called Gary L. Mead, of Deloitte Haskins & Sells, an accounting firm expert in leveraged buyouts, and hired both to guide KKR in the "possible acquisition" of Jim Walter Corporation.

For his part, Walter engaged the company's regular outside counsel, Warren Frazier, of Shackleford, Farrior, Stallings and Evans, of Tampa, to handle the matter until the company could hire a specialized law firm. A three-week search led to Richard D. Katcher, of Wachtell, Lipton, Rosen & Katz of New York. Wachtell Lipton was considered the best in defense of companies about to be acquired. Katcher had represented Beatrice, Owens-Illinois, Borg Warner, Uniroyal, Metromedia, and others, and, like Beattie of Simpson Thacher, he had more than twenty years experience in mergers and acquisitions. Called upon by Jimmy Kynes and Warren Frazier, Katcher agreed, barring a conflict of interest with other clients of his firm, to stand by and be ready to represent JWC if and when he was needed.

After the lawyers came the accountants. JWC had its own in-house staff, led by Ken Matlock, who knew the numbers perfectly from their beginnings, as well as Price Waterhouse which did the company audits.

All through the month of February lawyers spoke to lawyers, accountants met with accountants, KKR people made requests for information, JWC management complied, consultations between lawyers and clients were held, discussions between principals on the phone or in one another's office took place, and it all occurred in a nervous aura of confidentiality. If word leaked out, it would wreak havoc within the company and would set every corporate raider on the scent of a good deal in Tampa. At JWC, only a handful of people at the top corporate level were aware of what was going on. KKR people did not visit JWC offices again. Requests for financial data were filled by JWC's accountants who were not told and did not know the reasons for the data requested. Heavy briefcases of financial books, records, and compilations were lugged by car to meeting rooms in Tampa hotels.

Even straightforward, friendly negotiations of this magnitude can become very complex. At one meeting, for instance, more than eighteen lawyers and accountants for the principals conferred on the process to be followed in conducting a "due diligence" search into the assets of the company. From KKR there were three associates, three attorneys from Simpson Thacher, and four accountants from Deloitte Haskins. JWC sent six of its top officers: Cordell, Kynes, Matlock, Kenneth Hyatt (executive vice president), William Weldon (controller), Robert Emerton (associate general counsel), plus Warren Frazier (outside counsel) and one accountant from Price Waterhouse. When they had ironed out the procedures, guarantees, and rules of the game, the KKR people duly signed confidentiality agreements which allowed them to see the innermost, detailed financial data of JWC, in return for which they were bound for three years from disclosing or buying stock in JWC without the prior permission of the company.

All through February they gathered the numbers in Tampa and crunched them in New York. Mike Tokarz was the senior deal associate, like an account executive, who would see the deal through from beginning to end. Working closely with him was Perry Golkin, a deal associate, attorney, and CPA who had come to KKR in early 1986 from Simpson Thacher & Bartlett. The two of them analyzed the financial data on each and every profit center, unit, plant, and individual product lines. What was the company really worth? What would it be worth if they sold this division or changed this product line, or cut costs here or there? How would that change the value of the company? What if interest rates went up? Or housing starts went down? Or if oil and coal prices, now at a low ebb, soared? Or plunged even lower? What was the worst thing that could happen? How likely was that? What could they expect of the nation's economy? How would JWC be affected? In each of the scenarios, how would the company's cash flow be changed? How much cash flow was the minimum needed to cover the debt? What was the up side that could be hoped for? And the down side?

Nothing in business ever goes straight up, and like good managers everywhere, the KKR partners and associates devoted a great portion of their time trying to foresee and plan for any and all eventualities.

In structuring the buyout and the financial position of the new company, they tried to anticipate what could happen, what might happen, what was likely to happen, and to plan for each possibility so that the new company would be able to handle its future without encountering too much danger or too high a risk. "No surprises" was the goal of good planning within KKR. Henry Kravis's dictum was: "We never want to be in a situation where we have a gun to our heads, because that is when mistakes in judgment are made."

Flexibility was another byword and way of life in the midtown New York offices of KKR. It was such a small, tight organization that it needed no visible chain of command. The partners and associates worked in their shirtsleeves, albeit custom-made shirts with starched collars and French cuffs. They wandered about freely, poking a head into another's office to check a point or confer on a problem. It was not unlike the work atmosphere at JWC offices in Tampa, only

more elegant. KKR principals held meetings sometimes literally upon five minutes' notice. They conferred with San
Francisco colleagues by telephone either privately or by conference calls. There was an ease and grace, even under pressure, at their place of business. They made plans and
modified them when a change was called for; they adapted
new strategies, switched directions, and set new goals with
the ease of a close partnership. Everyone knew one another
very well. The firm had old-fashioned continuity because the
men who joined stayed there. For such a young organization
employing the most innovative financial techniques, KKR
had the aura of an old, meticulous, enduring British banking firm. Its offices have been described as "the best spread
in town," which is as high a compliment as anyone could pay,
given the many luxurious office suites in New York City. The
floors were marble and covered with brilliant Oriental rugs,
the walls mahogany with silk coverings, the furniture beautiful antiques, and the paintings 18th- and 19th-century British
and American landscapes. The ambience was a blend of old
English and contemporary design—comfortable, utilitarian,
and unostentatious.

The evaluations, analyses, and projections of what could
be done with JWC as a private company were conducted by
Tokarz and Golkin, aided by other financial experts at KKR,
and reviewed over and over again by all the partners and associates in New York and in San Francisco. The results of the
in-depth examination were very close to what Tokarz expected: Jim Walter Corporation appeared to be ideal for a
leveraged buyout. Operating income had risen from $155
million in 1982 to $293 million in 1986. Depreciation had
increased from $69.5 million to $104.4 million, giving JWC a
cash flow of almost $400 million a year. As a private entity
with a debt of around $2 billion, the new company would

have the cash flow to handle the interest costs and KKR would not be "under the gun" to sell JWC assets.

At the same time, a great many of JWC assets were independent profit centers that could be sold individually without hurting the new company. Tokarz prepared a list of high and low valuations of what each of these companies might bring, based upon projected sales and earnings. Any one or a number of them—U.S. Pipe, Georgia Marble, Celotex, and the smaller building-materials companies—could be sold or not sold as the occasion warranted. The core home-building and related financing group—Jim Walter Homes, Mid-State Homes, and the two home insurance companies—would certainly be retained, along with the mining operation, because of its built-in depreciation, steady sales, and promise for increased earnings.

Jim Walter Homes, which fluctuated between being the first- or second-largest builder of single-family detached homes in the United States, operated at a steady, high-profit rate year after year, and the mortgage portfolio of $3.3 billion, representing some 74,000 current homeowners, was for Tokarz the icing on the cake. It was a package of solid receivables, like money in the bank, a flowing stream of cash coming in every month, replenished by some six to seven thousand new Jim Walter homes being built each year. The current value of those mortgages, as carried on the company's balance sheet, was around $1.1 billion and that alone represented just under half of the total price which probably would be paid for the whole company. The coal mines were another gleam in Tokarz's eye. Sales had almost doubled from $207 million in 1982 to $367 million in 1986, and while prices and earnings from coal were down, the combined earnings and depreciation produced another $100 million in cash flow.

The confidential memorandum prepared by Tokarz and Golkin for the acquisition financing ran to ninety-nine pages of numbers and analyses and when Henry Kravis reviewed all the facts and figures, he aptly characterized Jim Walter Corporation as "a beautiful company with a wart on its nose."

The wart was, of course, the asbestos product-liability lawsuits still pending against Celotex. In the end, they could amount to very little or a whole lot, and while the financiers at KKR could quantify the economic possibilities of the business elements of JWC, it was impossible—or next to impossible—even after legal consultations, to quantify the possibilities involved in the highly varied and complex lawsuits. In short, asbestos lawsuits represented an unknown amount of risk, and as prudent investors they were adverse to taking unknown and unnecessary risks. On the other hand, JWC was financially a beautiful company to buy, to own, and to operate.

To test the waters, Kravis phoned Walter in early March and probed the possibility of JWC selling KKR certain parts of the company rather than the whole company. He hinted that KKR might not, after all, want to buy the whole company.

That same day, Walter, Cordell, Kynes, and Matlock were exploring the possibility of doing an LBO on their own and had invited in an investment banker from Merrill Lynch, Pierce, Fenner & Smith to examine the ramifications of a deal backed by Merrill Lynch. Merrill Lynch's proposal was reviewed by the JWC board of directors and by top management for the better part of a week, and ultimately rejected because it would have required too large a capital investment by the company's managers. Besides, Walter was approaching retirement age and the other old-timers were not far behind. Frankly, they felt that they already had as much control over the company as they wanted. No sooner had management reached its decision, when Henry Kravis telephoned and informed Walter that KKR had decided, after all, not to make an offer for the company.

It was with a sigh of relief that Jim Walter in mid-March told his most intimate colleagues that it was back to work as usual. KKR's interest in a buyout had been kept confidential, as promised, and the company had not been put into play. Until someone else came calling, JWC would continue as before, which in itself was not all that bad.

But JWC had been Mike Tokarz's own favorite deal and he took it upon himself to go over one more time all the financial figures, the tax benefits, the insurance issues, and the troublesome legal uncertainties concerning the asbestos-related law suits. Despite Celotex's troubles, to him Jim Walter Corporation was still an attractive candidate for a leveraged buyout. And by the last week in April, almost two months after merger talks had been broken off, Tokarz succeeded in allaying the concerns of others in his firm. The change of opinion was based upon Tokarz's reevaluation of JWC assets and upon the legal opinion of attorneys specializing in product liability that an LBO was viable because, essentially, all of the lawsuits had been directed against Celotex, a separate and independent company.

With a single telephone call, Kravis reopened discussions with Walter. Once Walter gave his go-ahead, Kravis moved fast to arrange for the financing needed to buy all the outstanding shares of the company. He contacted his friends at Manufacturers Hanover Trust and Bankers Trust, the two banks he usually used in such matters, and invited them to provide the bridge loans he would need. For the long-term financing he contacted Drexel Burnham Lambert, the investment banking firm that "invented" and still dominated the sale of high-yield, so-called junk bonds. They all were delighted to accommodate him, of course. The interest and fees on mergers and acquisitions far outpaced ordinary banking loans, and the high-yield bond market, driven by mergers and acquisitions, had made Drexel in a very short time one of the top investment banking/securities sales firms in the country. They were talking of loans and bonds in the neighborhood of $3 billion to buy the company's stock and pay off its old debt. That's a heap of money, and brings in big, big fees for the banks and investment firms.

Once again rounds of meetings took place in New York and in Tampa. Cordell and Matlock flew to KKR offices in New York to meet with representatives of the two banks and Drexel, plus their lawyers and accountants, and once again arrangements were made for representatives of the banks and Drexel to do due diligence in examining JWC finances and operations before committing their own money. For the next two weeks, they went through JWC books in Tampa, and then KKR negotiated terms for the financing. Each of the banks committed to $500 million and Drexel signed on for another $500 million. But the banks insisted on an extremely rapid amortization schedule to bring down the debt that would have forced KKR to sell off more JWC assets than they planned. Kravis would not accept those repayment terms. He did not intend to strip JWC of assets in order to do this deal, nor was he a man to be rushed into anything.

Toward the end of May, he and Tokarz put in a conference call to Jim Walter explaining their dissatisfaction with the financing offered. Once again KKR bowed out. Walter, in passing on the word to his colleagues and to the board of directors, declined to speculate whether or not KKR would be back again. They had been so close to an agreement that anticipations were high and it was hard to believe it would all come to nothing. But, as far as Jim Walter was concerned, it was the other fellow's decision to make, and he refused to worry about it.

Seven weeks later, on July 15, KKR came back. Would Mr.

Walter be available after lunch for an important telephone call from Mr. Kravis?

Walter summoned Joe Cordell, Jimmy Kynes, and Warren Frazier, the company's outside counsel, to his office to wait out the call. In New York, Henry Kravis made it a conference call. On the line with him were the two KKR associates who had worked so hard on this deal, Mike Tokarz and Perry Golkin, and three attorneys from Simpson Thacher, the law firm representing KKR. They were all now entering the area in which they had to be extra careful. All the legal *i*'s had to be dotted and the *t*'s crossed.

Even then, after the introductions of everyone on the telephone line, Kravis did not actually make an offer to buy the company. What he advised Walter was that KKR was "willing to make an offer to buy the company at $50 a share, if . . . "

If the board of directors was willing to consider that offer.

This condition was the ultimate gesture of good will. The tacit point was that even now, at this late stage with all the preliminary work done, KKR did not want to move in unless they were welcome. It was Jim Walter's and his board of directors' last chance to back out.

— *Building on a Buyout* —

REALISTICALLY, IT WAS Walter's decision to make. He had created the business, sold its first unfinished house in 1946, incorporated in 1955, built and nurtured the enterprise from $895 to $2 billion; he had hired the men who managed the company in his image; and he had chosen the outside directors who had become his friends as well as advisers. The board of directors was likely to follow his lead. It was a public company, yes, but underneath it all, it was his. And yet, with all that, he really had no choice.

The decision had been made by the circumstances of the situation, when Walter had observed other companies struggling and floundering in the sea of merger mania. That was not for him. He had decided then that he would not resist a legitimate offer for the company just for the sake of personal pride or to save management's jobs—if the offered price was right. Besides, he was sixty-four and had resolved long ago that when his time came, he would go quietly; he did not want to be dragged out of office, kicking and screaming, down the road to retirement. All this had been examined and discussed within the confidentiality of the board of directors' room.

Since Henry Kravis first came calling six months earlier, the board of directors had investigated and examined the alternatives available to them. As far as what would be best for the shareholders and the longtime employees of the company, the decision was clear. A leveraged buyout was going to happen, and among all possible suitors, KKR was the best investment firm to make it happen. Polling the directors was a formality. The $50-a-share price was a fair opening bid. It was about 10 percent above the previous day's closing price of $45.50, which was an all-time record high for the company, considering the five-for-four stock split distributed as a 25 percent dividend the previous week. What's more, Walter figured, if past KKR buyouts were any guide, its final price would likely be higher.

Later than evening, he called Kravis back to inform him that, yes, the board of directors had voted to "consider" KKR's offer.

The formal offer, a two-page letter, was faxed from KKR in New York to JWC in Tampa at 7 o'clock the next morning, July 16, and Walter, Cordell and Kynes were there, eager to read it:

We are hereby making an offer pursuant to which a new corporation ("Newco") to be formed by a group of investors to be organized by Kohlberg Kravis Roberts & Co. ("KKR") will acquire Jim Walter Corporation (the "Company") at a cash price of $50.00 per share of its common stock in a merger transaction.

We hope that certain key members of the Company's management will eventually purchase equity in Newco, but such purchases are not a condition to the consummation of the transaction . . . .

. . . Based upon discussions with commercial banks, we are confident that the necessary financing for the transaction can be obtained . . . .

We are hopeful of receiving your favorable response to our offer so that we can promptly execute a definitive merger agreement.

Henry Kravis

When David Townsend, the company's vice president for public relations, reached his office at 7:30, unaware of the previous day's events, he found a note taped to his chair, summoning him into the chairman's office. There Walter handed him the Kravis letter, saying, "Hey, you might want to read this; you're going to have a busy few weeks, my friend." While a public announcement was being formulated, Townsend phoned the New York Stock Exchange to postpone the opening of trading of the company's stock. That way everyone would receive the news on the wire at the same time and have an even playing field for buying and selling JWC shares. That was the theory. In reality the hour's delay in opening was a tip-off to the professionals who watched the tape assiduously. From a record high close of $45.50 a share the day before, JWC stock opened on July 16 nine and one-half points higher, at $55 a share, with 128,000 shares traded at the start of the day's action. The company was now "in play." It was for sale.

The market, led by the arbitrageurs who speculated on such situations, was clearly saying that Jim Walter Corporation was worth more than the KKR bid of $50. At the end of that tumultuous day, 4.4 million shares of JWC had been traded, in contrast to its average daily volume of 100,000 shares. It was the third most active stock of the day, and closed at $58 a share, up 12.5 points, for a gain of 27 percent in one day. Townsend had the most frenzied twelve-hour workday of his career, juggling more than 140 demanding phone calls from the news media, securities analysts, institutional investors, and arbitrageurs. Local television news teams set up shop in the lobby of the building. Magazines and newspapers requested interviews, press conferences, personality profiles, and background information, all of which could not be handled that day or that week. Company executives had more pressing things to do than to see the press.

At 9 o'clock, in the boardroom on the crosswalk between the two towers, Walter called to order a full meeting of the company's board of directors. The old-timers from management were seated at the long walnut table: Buddy Alston, Joe Cordell, Jimmy Kynes, Arnold Saraw, plus Thomas C. Mac-Donald, Jr., a partner in the company's local law firm of Shackleford, Farrior. The outside directors attended the meeting via a telephone conference call. They included Raymond H. Herzog, retired chairman and chief executive of 3M Company; John B. Carter, Jr., senior vice president, finance, of Pogo Producing Company of Houston; Franklin A. Cole, chairman of Croesus Corp. of Chicago and former head of the Walter Heller Company; James L. "Rocky" Johnson, president and chief operating officer of GTE; Robert F. Lanzillotti, dean emeritus of the College of Business Administration, University of Florida; David F. Miller, president of JC Penney Stores; and Gene Woodfin, former chairman and chief executive of Marathon Manufacturing Company of Houston. Only two directors could not be reached: Daniel C. Searle, former chairman of the pharmaceutical company that bears his name, and Anders Wall, chairman of a Swedish investment company in Stockholm.

The board started out with two essential actions. It appointed a special committee of all outside directors to review and decide upon the KKR offer and all alternatives to that offer, namely any other bids that might come in. This action effectively cut Walter, Cordell, Kynes, and all other management directors out of all decisions pertaining to the buyout to avoid any possible conflicts of interests. Because the company managers were expected to stay on with the new company, they could not be in a position of appearing to influence the takeover agreement for their own personal benefit. The outside directors would have no such conflicts; none of them would continue as directors beyond the buyout. Gene Woodfin, who of all the directors knew the company best, was elected chairman of the special committee. It was fitting that he should oversee the sale of the company, for it had been Woodfin who had led Jim Walter by the hand when JWC made its first major acquisition of Celotex twenty-five years before. It did not hurt that Woodfin, an investment banker for many years, also happened to be the most experienced board member in mergers and acquisitions.

Next, the special committee appointed a sub-committee to represent it in handling the preliminary responsibilities and activities of all the outside directors. From among themselves they chose one lawyer, Frank Cole, and two investment bankers by profession, Jack Carter and Woodfin.

The subcommittee's first action was to protect itself and all the outside directors from legal entanglements of the buyout process that might endanger them. With so much money at stake and so many litigious shareholders ready to pounce, the outside directors did not want to be sued any more than did the inside directors. Arrangements were made for Woodfin, Carter, and Cole to fly to New York the next day to select a law firm and an investment banking house to advise them. They would interview two of each so that no one could accuse them afterward of not doing some comparison shopping in the selection.

By the end of the next day they had chosen Richard Katcher of Wachtell Lipton as special counsel to the special committee, and Stephen Waters of Shearson Lehman Brothers to serve as their outside financial adviser. Both were by reputation top professionals in their fields.

Meanwhile, early that first morning, before word got out, Walter called a meeting of subsidiary presidents and key staff people in the headquarters building and reassured them as to the impact of the impending leveraged buyout. He told them as much as he could, at this early stage: all their rights would be protected—their pensions, bonuses, and other benefit plans—and while he could not promise anything at that point, he expected that all of present management would continue, the operations would continue, and if and when certain assets were sold, employees there would be fully protected. Pledging to keep all of them informed, he asked for their continued loyalty to the company. After the meeting, he and Cordell telephoned the presidents and key people in all the outlying divisions. They spent the better part of the day on the telephone.

The next day, Friday, the pace, tension, and stress increased. Joe Cordell was surprised by a telephone call from Joe Gaynor, an investment banker friend who had moved from Merrill Lynch to the brokerage firm of PaineWebber. Gaynor asked to meet with JWC management to discuss the possibility of PaineWebber doing its own leveraged buyout of the company. Later that day Citicorp Capital Investors, the venture capital department of Citicorp bank, made the same request. These were more than requests. Both demanded the right to conduct a "due diligence" search of JWC's finances and operations. They wanted what KKR got, a chance to examine the records and to make a bid for the company. Both were referred to the company's special committee and its newly-hired attorney, Dick Katcher.

At his law offices, the three-member subcommittee worked with Katcher, drawing up the ground rules for all would-be buyers. There was nothing better for driving up the price than an auction or bidding war. JWC management was instructed first to get signed confidentiality agreements and then to give each and every interested party full cooperation in their search for information about the company. Management was also instructed to forward all future inquiries on mergers or acquisitions to Stephen Waters of Shearson Lehman, who would be acting as the special committee's financial adviser. Finally, Waters was instructed to oversee the due diligence searches and to have a Shearson representative present whenever would-be buyers were examining the company's records.

Bright and early the next Monday morning, Gaynor telephoned Cordell and announced that he was in Tampa and ready to discuss PaineWebber's interest in buying the company. There was no turning him away. This time, Walter and Kynes walked across the hall to Cordell's office to meet with Gaynor, who brought Jack Perkowsky, the head of PaineWebber's investment group, into the conversation by telephone. In person and by telephone the two men made it abundantly clear that PaineWebber wanted to buy the company, that they had been considering and studying the acquisition for the past six months and that they hoped to make JWC the first major LBO in PaineWebber's entry into the lucrative merger and acquisition business. The next day PaineWebber signed a confidentiality agreement and their financiers, accountants, and lawyers arrived at the Tampa executive offices and went to work. Citicorp was not far behind.

Over the next two weeks there were seven more requests for due diligence privileges by other companies and investment firms. Each potential buyer was invited to Tampa to examine the company's internal books, financial records, budgets, and projected earnings. Some of the biggest names in the investment/merger business were represented, as accountants, lawyers, and bankers from New York swarmed over the executive offices of JWC. It was easy enough to spot the invaders from up north. They wore the dark, often pinstriped, business suits and wing-tipped black shoes of the big city, while the natives worked in shirt-sleeves. They came in groups of three or more, and each contingent was given the same stack of financial data as had been prepared earlier for KKR. The men in JWC's financial departments, especially controller Bill Weldon and Jim Jurgens, assistant vice president for planning, worked frenetically being "nice" to all the suitors who came calling. They answered the same questions, proffered the same documents, and made the same explanations over and over again through the month of July and into early August.

Among the would-be buyers were Lazard Frères, one of the oldest investment banking firms, this time representing Companie S. Gobain, that had bought out the Certainteed building materials company; Forstmann Little & Company, a leveraged buyout firm competing with KKR; Drummond Company, a large, private coal company that had also served as JWC's agent for coal sales in Japan and elsewhere; NV Ryan, a Netherlands investment firm; and Pacific Holdings and WesRay Capital Corp., two more LBO firms. Some came only for a look-see, but others came back to "kick the tires," to see some of the company plants, and to dig deeper into the numbers and the implications behind them. In addition to all these suitors, there were also investment bankers from Shearson Lehman doing their own due diligence evaluation of the company on behalf of the special committee. In the end, when bids were submitted, Shearson would be there to render its own impartial opinion on what the company was worth and on the fairness of all bids received.

The art in buying a company, or anything of value for that matter, lies in the subjective judgment of the value of what you are buying. KKR, PaineWebber, Citicorp, Drummond, and the others examined the same data, received the same answers to their questions, and were invited to inspect any part of the company they desired. In studying the financial profile of any one subsidiary, they saw its sales, earnings, inventories, receivables, order backlogs, budget, and business plans. From these same figures, each investment group would have to devise its own rationale in estimating the probable market value of that subsidiary, if it were to be sold. The values assigned to each profit center would differ depending upon whatever assumptions were made, and the sum total of those assumptions, projections, and evaluations would determine for each potential buyer at what price Jim Walter Corporation was worth buying.

The most ardent, most aggressive suitor, other than KKR, was PaineWebber, whose investment bankers returned again and again with questions and points to be ironed out. On July 31, two weeks after the public announcement and after they had done their due diligence, three of the top Paine-Webber deal makers came to Tampa to discuss the situation with Walter, Cordell, and Kynes. Don Nichelson, president and chief executive officer of PaineWebber, accompanied by Jack Perkowsky, who headed the investment department, and Kamal Mustafa, who was spearheading the deal, stated that PaineWebber, after doing its evaluation of the company, would definitely be making a bid. In fact, they indicated they were thinking of making an attractive, preemptive bid, perhaps as early as the following week. They would put a "short fuse" on it in which JWC's board of directors would have twenty-four hours to decide one way or another. That, in effect, would shut out KKR and all the other potential bidders, if the PaineWebber bid was accepted.

Walter responded simply that the matter was completely out of his hands. It was strictly up to the special committee of outside directors to handle all aspects of the buyout.

They also tried to sound out Walter on how much management would want to invest in the new company. The figure they suggested was $20 million, which Walter thought was far and away too high. But he carefully responded that he would not know that until after the details of the PaineWebber proposal and the terms of the financing had been developed. In short, it depended on how good the whole deal would be.

As soon as the PaineWebber men left, Walter phoned the special committee's lawyer to report on the meeting, and Katcher advised him to inform PaineWebber that the special committee "was not amenable to short circuiting" the bidding process and that the committee would meet the next week to set a date when all bids would be invited at the same time.

And so the preparations, evaluations, negotiations, and decision making went on, with flurries of phone calls and meetings between potential buyers and the seller, and, of course, their lawyers. Joseph Flom, one of the leading attorneys specializing in mergers and acquisitions as a partner with Skadden, Arps, Slate, Meagher & Flom, represented Paine-Webber; since he knew Dick Katcher well from previous deals, it was often Flom who tried to sound out Katcher on PaineWebber's proposals to JWC. At one point he suggested that Katcher and he could negotiate a buyout contract that would be complete in all respects, except for the price. PaineWebber could then fill in the price in a preemptive bid and if the JWC directors accepted, they could wrap up the deal in one day. Katcher declined.

What would the directors think of a merger agreement rather than a cash tender offer, asked Flom? What would the special committee think if PaineWebber's bid was not all cash, but consisted of some small portion of securities? Katcher reviewed the implications with Gene Woodfin and then called Flom back. The special committee certainly would consider any proposal submitted in seeking the best value for the shareholders, Katcher said, but the committee would generally prefer all cash to cash and securities. And it would prefer a straight tender offer over a merger agreement because it would be quicker and cleaner.

The buyout proceedings moved en masse to New York

City on Tuesday, August 4, as ten of the eleven outside directors of JWC gathered at Wachtell Lipton's midtown law offices to set the procedure for accepting all formal bids for the sale of the company on the following Friday. Earlier in the day, Walter, Cordell, and Kynes paid a call upon Paine-Webber for a discussion of the investment firm's ideas on how a new, private company would operate. They met in the office of Donald Marron, PaineWebber's chairman, who was backed up with his key players, Nichelson, Perkowsky, and Mustafa. Walter expressed his misgivings on two points in PaineWebber's projections. He did not believe, he said, his key management group could or would want to come up with $20 million to invest as its share in any buyout. It was just too much money. He also questioned his company's ability to reduce overhead expenses as much as PaineWebber had projected. The company already had gone through a cost reduction program of mammoth proportions, he explained, and he did not want PaineWebber in its planning to expect too much. Marron and Perkowsky thanked him for his candor and promised to go over their figures once again and take what he had said into consideration for their formal bid.

The meeting in the conference room of the Wachtell offices was like a war council to prepare the JWC troops for the battle of the buyout. The outside directors of JWC, plus Warren Frazier of Shackleford, joined forces with four attorneys from Wachtell Lipton and seven people from Shearson, plus consultants. Walter, the founder of the company, was stopped at the door and told bluntly by Katcher that he could not attend. Walter fumed. But Katcher insisted, saying, "You're not invited in, and someday you'll thank me for keeping you out."

So, Walter stood at a window in Katcher's private office, gazing at the New York skyline, hating the legalities that stymied him, and thinking about all the implications of his company going private. Inside the conference room, Shearson representatives reviewed for JWC's outside directors the status of the buyout discussions with the bidders. The investment firm gave its own analysis of the buyout value of JWC, and reviewed its draft of a merger agreement which all the parties could use in making their own proposals. The special committee set that Friday for receiving the formal bids and the following Monday, August 10, for considering the proposals and deciding the future course of Jim Walter's company. There were three remaining bidders for the company: Kohlberg Kravis Roberts, PaineWebber, and Drummond/Citicorp.

The next day Joe Flom, representing PaineWebber, objected to submitting a bid on Friday, which he said would allow JWC an extra two days over the weekend to shop around for a higher bid. PaineWebber, he insisted, would submit its bid on Monday, August 10. That necessitated an evening session between JWC's subcommittee, the Wachtell attorneys, and the Shearson bankers on how to handle the bidding so that no one could accuse them of being unfair. It was apparent that PaineWebber, battling against KKR's inside friendly track, wanted very much to top whatever bid KKR offered so that the outside directors would be obliged to choose PaineWebber. It was also apparent to all that the form and terms of the transaction, the structure of the financing, and the debt incurred would be of equal importance to the bid itself. The company's objective, of course, was to keep as many bidders as happy as possible while negotiating the highest price and the best terms possible for the company's shareholders. To that purpose the parties were informed that one of them would not submit its bid until Monday. Of course, they all then insisted on rescheduling the bidding to Monday, August 10.

On the day of reckoning, ten of the eleven outside directors (with then-retired Bud Alston among them as an outside director but Anders Wall unable to make the trip from Sweden) converged at the Wachtell Lipton offices on Park Avenue. They smiled and exchanged jokes, but anxiety was thick in the air. For this meeting, JWC's top management— Walter, Cordell, Kynes, Saraw, Matlock, and Weldon—were invited in. They were permitted to observe the presentations, ask questions, even state their opinions, but they would have no vote. Warren Frazier, the company's attorney from Shackleford was also there, as were four attorneys from Wachtell Lipton and four representatives of Shearson Lehman. PaineWebber made its presentation first: a merger agreement, not an immediate tender offer, which consisted of $60 per share in cash, a junior subordinated bond that would begin to accrue 15 percent per year interest only after five years, which was said to be worth $5 per share, plus $4 worth of shares in the new company, for a total of $69. And the offer expired at midnight. It was a complicated proposal containing many contingencies, but the special committee members zeroed in on the time and uncertainty involved in getting the required financing in place before a merger could be concluded and the shareholders would be paid. Suppose PaineWebber could not line up the financing required? Then the merger would be doomed. Again, the special committee indicated its preference for an all-cash tender offer up front.

KKR came next. It proposed an all-cash tender offer for all the outstanding JWC stock at $56 per share, up $6 from its original offer.

Drummond Company and Citicorp Capital Investors submitted a joint proposal, consisting of a tender offer of $50 in cash plus preferred stock in the new company worth about $5 a share, for a total of $55.

Negotiations went on well into the night. Shearson Lehman presented to the special committee, with Jim Walter and other management men out of the room, its analysis and evaluation of each of the bids submitted. The special committee then met with the parties again, reviewing the terms of the proposals, particularly expressing its reservations to PaineWebber as to whether its proposal could be financed. Finally, PaineWebber said it would review its offer and agreed to withdraw its deadline for acceptance. There would be a second round of bids.

* * *

At 7 o'clock the next morning five financiers from Shearson Lehman met with Mustafa and others at PaineWebber to go over several aspects of the PW proposal and the assumptions underlying the financial projections. The nuts and bolts session went on past lunch and into the early afternoon.

Meanwhile, at 9:15 a.m., the special committee reconvened to go over Shearson Lehman's latest evaluation of the proposals. They then met throughout the day with representatives of each bidder, and then with representatives of the various banks and other financial institutions that were expected to provide or underwrite the financing of the leveraged buyout. As the meetings wore on—with each side jockeying for position, not knowing what their rivals had bid—the level of anxiety grew. With Katcher advising him, Woodfin, a born deal maker, was determined to wrangle the best price possible for the company he had known since its infancy. Each extra dollar per share he negotiated would amount to more than $40 million.

To PaineWebber, Woodfin said in effect, "Come up with a cash tender offer so the shareholders will know up front what they are getting for their stock."

To KKR, he said, "Is that $56 the highest you can go?" Accompanied by Katcher and Waters (as the financial adviser), Woodfin took a taxicab the few blocks to KKR's offices. At the conference table were all the KKR heavyweights involved in the JWC buyout, except Henry Kravis who was out of the country at the time. Sitting there in repressed anticipation were George Roberts, the senior partner who was heading KKR's negotiations in Kravis's absence, Paul Raether, another KKR partner, Mike Tokarz and Perry Golkin, the associates who had worked so long and hard to bring about the deal, and Richard Beattie, KKR's attorney from Simpson Thacher.

Shaking his head ruefully, Woodfin asserted that in his own judgment of what was going on, he did not believe KKR would get Jim Walter Corporation for $56 a share. Could they improve their offer?

No higher bid was forthcoming, but there was a hint, just the slightest indication, or so Woodfin thought, that KKR just might go a little bit, just a little bit higher.

Walter was personally troubled with the amount of debt that would be incurred if the PaineWebber offer of $69 per share in cash and paper was accepted by the outside directors. Discussing the problem that night with Cordell, Kynes, and Matlock, they decided to seek Katcher's advice. He had far more experience than they in such matters.

All of the JWC people shared another problem. Having expected a one-day session in New York for the bidding, most of them had run out of socks and underwear for the third, crucial day of negotiations. It seemed as though they had been living and eating in Wachtell Lipton's conference room for a full week, when in reality it had been only two long days and nights. Director David Miller solved that problem easily. During a recess in the negotiations, Miller took their orders at the conference table and sent out to JC Penney for the shirts, socks, and underwear needed. He delivered the items personally during dinner that same night at their hotel. It was the least he could do as president of a department store chain.

Early the next morning, Walter met with Katcher and expressed his dilemma: On the one hand, he knew he was not supposed to take part in any of the negotiations. On the other hand, he, Cordell, Kynes, and Matlock had come to the conclusion that as presently structured they did not want to invest their own money in the PaineWebber deal. They thought the financial structure would be too risky. The question was: Should they inform PaineWebber? And, if so, when? What would their decision do to the negotiations and the PaineWebber bid? Surely, without management's own equity investment in the buyout, no bank would finance the deal and the refinancing bonds would be very difficult to sell. What was the right thing to do? Better sooner than later, the attorney advised them. If they informed PaineWebber of their position now, it would give the firm a chance to act on that information before it was too late.

Don Marron, chairman of the board of PaineWebber, was not at all pleased with what Walter, who was accompanied by Cordell, Kynes, and Matlock, had come to his office to tell him. It was very late in the game, the final day of bidding, and the management of the company PaineWebber wanted to acquire was not happy with the investment company's proposed capital structure and plans for the new company.

Walter tried to couch the bad news as gently as he could. "If you're the successful bidder, we will continue to work for the company, if you want us to, and we'll do everything we can to manage the new company successfully, and we'll go out on the road shows to help sell the debt financing. But, given the terms of your proposed merger, we won't invest our own money in the project. And I must say," Walter added, "if prospective investors on the road show asked (as certainly they would), we would have to tell them the truth: that we are not investing our own money in this."

It was stunning news for PaineWebber. Marron, ashen faced, turned to Cordell, as chief executive of JWC. "What are your views on this, Joe?" he asked.

"You just heard them," Cordell replied.

Marron said he and his colleagues would consider the matter and that the special committee would hear from them later in the day. PaineWebber had a choice: revise its bid or give up.

Meanwhile, at KKR uneasiness and doubt were setting in. Six months of analyzing the various pieces of the company, making all the crucial evaluations, reaching the decision to buy and what to pay gave all the men at KKR an emotional stake beyond the financial aspects in the outcome. While they felt they had the inside track with the JWC management, they also realized they might lose out at this final stage if, in fact, the PaineWebber offer, even if not structured as well as theirs, was substantially higher. With all their experience, the KKR people had not expected so much competition for the acquisition of the company. When KKR had structured an LBO for Owens-Illinois earlier in the year, the deal had gone straight through without a single competing bid. Now there was PaineWebber, a powerhouse in the retail brokerage business, eager to enter the lucrative LBO field with a big buy like JWC. Also there was the Drummond Company which apparently was determined to get the JWC coal mines and either sell off the other businesses or expand into larger fields. Emotions and concern ran high at KKR on the final day. George Roberts, leading the KKR negotiations, invited Steve Waters of Shearson Lehman, adviser to JWC, to drop over and discuss the situation. It would be Waters who would evaluate the bids and advise the JWC special committee which of the three was the best. Waters advised Roberts carefully, without revealing what other bids were in or expected and that he did not believe the current KKR proposal of $56 a share would be selected by the special committee.

Drummond, in a joint venture with Citicorp, upped its bid that afternoon. When the special committee reconvened after lunch, it heard from the Shearson people that Drummond and Citicorp had submitted a revised proposal. Instead of $50 in cash and $5 in securities, they were now offering $51 in cash, $5 in subordinated debt, and $4 more in preferred stock.

At 4:30 p.m., while the special committee was still evaluating and comparing the three different bids and their implications, a phone call came in from Garry Drummond, one of the owners of the Drummond coal company. There had been a change!

Drummond and PaineWebber had that afternoon formed a partnership and wanted to present a new, revised joint proposal to the special committee; they were invited over to the Wachtell Lipton offices. Citicorp had dropped out, they told the special committee. Because of the committee's expressed concerns over the delay and uncertainties involved in PaineWebber's first merger proposal, the joint PaineWebber/Drummond offer would be structured differently: $52 in a cash tender offer to be followed with a merger which would then issue junior subordinated debentures worth $10 a share, for a total of $62.

The discussion which followed this new offer was intense. PaineWebber now proposed to acquire only 84 percent of the JWC outstanding shares in the first step before a legal merger agreement was consummated with the remaining shares acquired at the time of the merger. They offered 15 percent of the equity in the new company to JWC management. Their new proposal still contained the disadvantage of delay on getting the full price. The shareholders would get $52 plus paper, and no one could be sure what the paper might be worth after the four to six months that the merger agreement would take. Would PaineWebber/Drummond go any higher on the $52 cash offer? No, said their representatives. Fifty-two dollars was the highest cash consideration they were prepared to offer, and, they added, that offer expired at midnight.

The special committee and their advisers explored the ramifications of the new PaineWebber/Drummond offer and the possibilities open to JWC. They were now down to two offers on the table.

KKR was proposing a straight cash tender offer of $56 per share. It was a clear, clean proposal and the stockholders would get their money up front and right away.

The PaineWebber proposal still contained considerable uncertainties. The shareholders would get only $52 a share right away upon tendering their stock. They would lose the time value of the money not received until after the merger. Furthermore, no one could really tell what the PaineWebber securities offered would be worth in another four or six months, and then there was always the risk of the whole deal going sour before it could be consummated. On the other hand, if everything went right, the PaineWebber/Drummond proposal would pay shareholders $62 a share—if everything went right—which was $6 a share more than KKR's offer.

What was the right thing to do? Which was the best offer to accept? After hours of examining of all the issues, the special committee reached an interim consensus: They preferred the clean-cut cash tender offer of KKR to the uncertainties of a two-step tender offer and merger with PaineWebber/ Drummond—but they wanted more money, if they could get it. So the directors and their advisers spent

a few more hours planning their negotiating strategy. Waters
of Shearson Lehman gave his best estimate of what they
should try to get out of KKR, and Katcher and Woodfin re-
hearsed scenarios. The directors then authorized its subcommittee of Woodfin, Carter, and Cole to try one more
time to get KKR's "final best proposal" which the committee
would compare with the PaineWebber/Drummond offer
and then, finally, make a decision.

To seek KKR's final best offer, the JWC negotiators needed
only to walk across New York's Park Avenue, from the
Wachtell Lipton law offices to the midtown offices of Simpson Thacher, where the KKR contingent were waiting for a
decision. It was nighttime after a long hard day of negotiating, and for those weary men Park Avenue was a sight to be-
hold: one of the most beautiful thoroughfares in the country
with its center strip of grass and trees between the skyscraper
office buildings and the lighted street globes and gold fili-
gree of the famous clock atop the old New York Central
building gleaming in the dark. At the Simpson Thacher
office, Woodfin, Carter, and Cole, accompanied by Dick
Katcher, their legal adviser, and Steve Waters, their financial
adviser from Shearson, sat across the table from George
Roberts and Mike Tokarz from KKR, Dick Beattie and
Richard Garvey from Simpson Thacher.

Katcher revealed that PaineWebber in a new joint venture
with Drummond had submitted a new bid and, while not
mentioning the amount, indicated that it was a higher offer
than KKR's. Was $56 their best price? Their final offer? Or
could they come up with a number that the subcommittee
could recommend to the full special committee?

They talked back and forth, with Woodfin and Katcher on
one side of the table, Roberts on the other, skirting the issue
of price with expert delicacy. Katcher said the special com-

mittee had compared the offers with Shearson's evaluation of the company and it thought a fair price for the company would be $61 a share, plus the payment of the company's upcoming October dividend of thirty cents a share. There it was, out on the table: JWC's price.

There was a noticeable pause, a palpable moment of silence, and then with finality Roberts said, "I can't do sixty-one."

"Well, that's that, and I'm sorry," said Katcher, pushing both palms down on the table and rising from his chair, starting to leave. "I appreciate your taking the time . . . " The others on his side of the table began to get up and follow him.

"But I can do sixty!" interjected Roberts.

They all sat down again, and Katcher said, "Okay, George, let's talk."

* * *

The company's directors, reconvening at 9:30 that night, were delighted with the all-cash $60 offer. KKR had increased its original $50 offer by fully 20 percent, and at $60 a share was paying top dollar—$2.43 billion to the holders of some 40.5 million shares of JWC stock, plus assuming the company's outstanding debt of about $840 million, for a grand total of some $3.3 billion. Paying the thirty-cent dividend was a going away present to JWC shareholders, a nice touch that Woodfin got from George Roberts, something extra that was not needed to clinch the deal.

KKR's offer brought a wave of emotional relief to the Wachtell Lipton conference room where the company directors had been confined for the past three days with time out only for sleeping. They were fatigued, short-tempered, with nerves on edge from the stress and tension of the negotiations as much as from the long hours and many sandwiches and cups of coffee in the conference room. Now it was all over, except for the formalities.

The directors listened to Shearson Lehman once again evaluate the competing bids and reach the decision they already knew: In the impartial, objective opinion of Shearson Lehman—so said Stephen Waters—the "final" KKR proposal of $60 per share cash tender offer, with the thirty-cent dividend, was "economically superior" to the PaineWebber/ Drummond of $52 cash up front with a later payment of $10 in junior subordinated discount debentures. Furthermore, Shearson Lehman was of the opinion that the final KKR proposal was "fair to the stockholders of the Company from a financial point of view."

With that said, the special committee recommended to the full board of directors the acceptance of the KKR offer, and the same men, now acting as the board of directors of the company, with the management members abstaining, voted to execute the merger with KKR and to recommend that all shareholders accept the tender offer and approve the merger.

While some directors stayed over at their hotels, the Florida contingent made haste to get out of New York and to sleep in their own beds in what remained of that night. Walter, Alston, Cordell, Saraw, Kynes, Matlock, Weldon, and others piled into rented limousines, raced out to Newark Airport, and rode the company jet back to Tampa, arriving close to 4 a.m., which gave them plenty of time to get to work that morning at 8 o'clock.

Five days later, with the alacrity of experience, KKR, representing its investor group and working through a new corporation legally set up for that purpose, made its public tender offer to buy JWC stock at $60 a share. Within a month, more than 95 percent of the outstanding shares were tendered and bought. This first step of the buyout went smoothly. Approximately 70 percent of the company shares were owned by professional, institutional investors, and they were happy to rake in a windfall capital gain. They knew a good deal when they saw one. And so it was that on September 18, 1987, the investment firm of Kohlberg Kravis Roberts bought Jim Walter Corporation for $2.4 billion, plus the assumption of $840 million of old JWC debt. And that day just happened to be Jim Walter's sixty-fifth birthday.

Bankers Trust and Manufacturers Hanover and a consortium of ten other banks wired $2.4 billion into an account which KKR used to mail checks to the shareholders who submitted their shares. The bank loans were backed by KKR's excellent loan record, plus a letter from the investment house of Drexel Burnham Lambert, stating that Drexel was "highly confident" it could sell the bonds necessary to repay the banks. The investment firm was putting its "guarantee" on the bank loans.

KKR's capital structure plan for the company was based upon leverage and, as that wise old sage said long ago, "Give me a fulcrum and a lever and I can move the world." Jim Walter's company had been built upon the power of leverage. Working class people, with no savings, could afford to buy Jim Walter unfinished houses by using the building site as a down payment worth as little as 5 percent of the purchase price. All the rest they would borrow and pay off over the years. That was leverage, the same leverage used by home buyers throughout the country. Very few can or do buy their homes for straight cash. Walter himself, after years of struggle, maintained lines of credit with more than two hundred different banks so that he would not run short of sources of borrowed money to support his company's growth. That was leverage. As he said, "The road to success is paved with borrowed money." KKR, masters at the game, advanced the basic technique to what may be its ultimate limit. It made a cash down payment of $150 million and borrowed $2.4 billion with which to buy one of the two hundred largest industrial companies in the United States! That amounts to 6 percent down, the fulcrum, and 94 percent leverage!

The second stage of financing an LBO is to reduce as quickly as possible the short-term, variable-rate bank debt used as bridge loans and replace them with fixed, long-term debentures or bonds. No company wants to live with the risk of unpredictable interests rates, especially not JWC's management which had been put through the wringer of soaring rates back in 1980-82. To convert the bank debt into the known quantity of various types of long-term bonds, KKR brought in the "masters" of this part of the game, the investment banking house of Drexel Burnham Lambert. That firm's in-house genius, Michael Milken, had discovered in the mid-1970s the inherent value of high-yield bonds to finance companies younger and more entrepreneurial than the large, established, investment-grade companies like IBM.

These bonds became known as junk bonds, which is probably the most egregious misnomer in the financial world. Milken and Drexel amply demonstrated that there was a market out there among big, professional, institutional investors, who knew what they were doing and who did not consider these bonds "junk." They were willing and sometimes eager to buy these bonds because their yield was so high and their risk not as high as many supposed. Jim Walter Corporation, for instance, was not a start-up company; it had an excellent track record over thirty years of providing at a profit such basic, needed products as housing, building materials, pipe, marble, and coal. It was not likely to go broke.

In anticipation of the KKR buyout, Drexel had completed its own due diligence survey of JWC finances and operations and had committed itself to KKR's plan to sell three tiers, or "tranches," of high-yield bonds with different rates of interest and maturity dates of seven to nine years, to bring in $1.1 billion, and another $1.2 billion or more of debt securities backed by Mid-State's home mortgages.

The bulk of the $1.1 billion debt, backed by JWC's assets other than its mortgages, was financed through the private placement of high-yield bonds. It was at the time the largest single private placement of high-yield bonds ever attempted. The selling of the bonds to large, institutional investors was done through "road shows," or "dog and pony shows" for which Drexel had become famous, or, depending upon one's stamina for such travel, infamous.

Led by Drexel, a team of sellers hop, skip, and jump around the country. In fast-paced, tightly scheduled meetings, the JWC bonds were presented by Drexel people who made the sales pitch, while two or more officers of Jim Walter Corporation were there to explain and answer questions about the operations and financial aspects of the company, and usually one or two from KKR to explain the intricacies of the LBO. Because time was of the essence in paying off the bank bridge loans, it was not unusual to have three meetings in one day: breakfast in Houston, lunch in Kansas City, and dinner in New York. The pace was exhausting: Fly into a city on the company plane, take a limousine to the meeting place, make the presentation to anywhere from one to thirty potential investors, devote one hour to the presentation and one hour for questions and answers, and then fly out to the next engagement. The officers of the company, from Jim Walter down, were obliged to cooperate in selling the bonds. On one two-day jaunt, Walter, Matlock, and others covered meetings in New York, Boston, Hartford, Minneapolis, and Chicago. Flying from London to Tokyo consumed twenty-three hours in the air, but they managed to meet with twenty-five different institutional investors in Japan in just two days.

The road shows were going very well, as expected, until one Monday afternoon in October when Tokarz was speaking to a luncheon group in Kansas City and a waitress interrupted him with a message from his office. He stopped to read it, blanched, and announced, "The stock market has just dropped dead." The Dow was down 300 points. By the end of that memorable day, October 19, 1987, the stock market, as measured by the Dow Jones average, had fallen 508 points in the worst panic-selling spree since 1929.

The financial world shuddered and came to a standstill while investors tried to fathom whether the 508-point drop was the needed "correction" in an inflated market, as expected by some, or the beginning of the worst economic depression since the "Black Tuesday" crash of 1929, as feared by others. JWC bonds, like all others, were put on hold. The remaining Drexel road shows were canceled. Until the financial air cleared, the KKR-led investor group was left suspended on a scary financial limb, owing their banks more than $2 billion. JWC management simply dangled there in disbelief and suspense.

KKR used the time to secure another linchpin in its LBO plan: Key managers at JWC would be given a real equity stake in the new company, making them partners who would be sharing with KKR investors in the rewards and risks of making the new company a success. Walter and Cordell drew up a list of fifty-one managers who would be instrumental in the success or failure of the new private company. KKR offered these managers the opportunity to buy up to $5 million of KKR's $150 million equity. On top of that, for every $5 share a manager bought, he or she would also receive options to buy approximately 3.3 more shares at the same price. That would give management approximately 13 percent of the new company. If and when the LBO debt was paid down (in two, five, or even seven years) and the company went public

or was restructured again, the managers had the opportunity of making many times their investment. For them that
would be real wealth, more money than they could possibly
accumulate as salaried executives. If the company failed . . .

The investment opportunity was thoroughly explored in a
meeting of the fifty-one invited managers in the company's
eighth-floor conference room. There Tokarz, Golkin,
Raether, and Simpson Thacher attorneys explained in great
detail the risks, benefits, and expectations of the new private
company. They warned the JWC managers, as did the KKR
forty-page prospectus, not to invest more than they could afford to lose. Jim Walter spoke warmly to the men and women
in the room whom he knew so well, and he, too, emphasized
the opportunity and the risk involved.

"I'm not going to kid you that this deal doesn't have its inherent risks," he said. "You could end up with a lot of money,
or nothing but a cold, limp handshake goodbye.

"I want you all to have the first crack at this deal," he told
them. "By that I mean if what you invest uses up the entire
five million and there's no room for me, that's fine. If there
is anything left over after you all buy in, I'll take it, and that's
fine with me, too."

The participating managers made their investments in private, one-on-one, in Cordell's office and, surprisingly, many
of them were eager to invest substantial sums and had to be
cautioned against "risking the family jewels." Most of the
managers were able to make their cash investments from the
proceeds of the sale of their personal JWC stock holdings.
Others used cash received from KKR's payout of the company's supplemental retirement and stock appreciation
plans. All the invited managers participated, and the portion
left for the company's founder came to a little more than
$900,000. As he said he would, he took it all.

The stock market plunge never really endangered the KKR

buyout because it had been well structured, but it did significantly increase the cost of financing the purchase. Actually, the shareholders of JWC could rejoice in how lucky they had been. They had sold their shares at a top price two months before the crash. If the buyout had come in late October rather than August, KKR probably could have bought the company for $40 rather than $60 a share. The road show was resumed in November and completed in mid-December, and only then, after the potential buyers had had a chance to study the offer, did Drexel set the interest rates on the different JWC bonds.

Fully half of the purchase price of the company was supposed to be financed with something entirely new in the world of finance: $1.2 billion in bonds backed by the mortgages on Jim Walter homes. It was the brainchild of Mike Tokarz and the financial executives at JWC. They figured that the JWC portfolio of 74,000 active home mortgages had a market value that exceeded the book value of $1.1 billion. Therefore, Tokarz thought, these mortgages could be used to refinance a significant portion of the indebtedness incurred in the leveraged buyout. Working closely with chief financial officer Matlock, controller Weldon, and treasurer Kurucz, Tokarz came up with another altogether new concept: As an option they thought they might hire Financial Security Assurance Company (FSA) to evaluate, establish, and guarantee the credit quality of the mortgages, and then they would be able to borrow the billion-plus they needed at very favorable terms because of the financial stability of those mortgages. It was original, creative thinking.

Physically, it was a humongous task. It took almost six months to handle the mechanics involved in checking on 74,000 individual home mortgages in thirty states, transferring them to a trustee, and establishing new procedures for collections and foreclosures. The paperwork filled two bound books nine inches thick.

Drexel did encounter considerable difficulty in placing the mortgage-backed bonds privately with its clients. Part of the trouble was the unsettled market conditions following the October stock market crash. Part of it appeared to be Drexel's and/or its clients' unfamiliarity with the financial ramifications of mortgage-backed bonds. For five agonizing months, tensions rose in the financial offices of JWC as the due date approached for paying down the bank bridge loans. Finally, after much soul-searching, the top officers of the company decided to transfer the lead responsibility for selling the mortgage-backed bonds from Drexel to Salomon Brothers. Just as Drexel was king of the junk bond market, Salomon Brothers ruled the mortgage-backed bond market. JWC opted to go with the best. While Drexel participated in the sale of these bonds, it was Salomon Brothers who decided to sell the Mid-State bonds in a public offering, backed and guaranteed by FSA.

The insurance company gave the mortgage-backed securities a value of $1.75 billion with the highest bond rating of Triple-A and it guaranteed payment. For that, FSA was paid a fee of $43 million, but its guarantee allowed $1.32 billion of its bank debt (at 11.5 percent) to be repaid with 9 percent bonds. The bonds had maturities up to fifteen years and were scaled to match the estimated cash collections from the mortgage portfolio. Another innovative feature of the bond issue was that it was designed to avoid the volatility that might be caused by early payoffs of the mortgages. It was such a sweet concept. Those Triple-A bonds were sold out in a single day. The concept was so new, so good, that it was voted by *Institutional Investor* magazine as one of the ten best bond deals of 1988. In one transaction, using Mid-State's mortgages, 43 percent of the purchase price for JWC had been financed with Triple-A debt.

But it was financing of the other half of the debt which caused so much trouble and concern to the planners at KKR and the company. The uneasiness and nagging fears which followed the stock market debacle had the effect of raising the rates on all bonds, particularly high-yield bonds. Investors perceived greater risks in the marketplace. Before the crash, Drexel had projected selling the bonds at interest rates of 12, 14, and 15 percent. After the crash, Drexel said its customers would buy JWC bonds only at yields almost 3 percent higher, namely 14, 16.5, and 17.75 percent. That increase would cost the new company an additional $22 million in interest every year. Then, at the very last minute, Drexel added a kicker. It changed the "reset clause" on the senior and junior subordinated bonds, placing a floor on the rates, so that the annual reset interest rates on these bonds could only be increased, but never lowered, to guarantee that the bonds would be redeemed at 101 percent of their face value.

KKR protested vehemently. Jim Walter cried foul. But Drexel insisted they needed that guaranteed reset provision to sell the bonds. They argued about it heatedly, cross-country, in a drawn-out, three-way conference call. With Drexel in Beverly Hills, KKR in New York, and JWC in Tampa, they quarreled over what interest rates were fair and appropriate. Jim Walter and his financial people were shocked with the new rates proposed by Drexel. They thought they were outrageously high given the strength of the company's operations and underlying asset values. Tokarz agreed and demanded lower rates. But after much wrangling, squabbling, and shouting, Drexel prevailed.

The investment company's final position was "take it or leave it." The others had to acquiesce. They knew that

Drexel and Drexel alone had the customers and the power to sell the bonds.

On January 7, 1988, almost a year after that first get-acquainted meeting between Henry Kravis and Jim Walter, all of the long-term, permanent financing of the new company was in place, all of the innumerable legal agreements and documentation had been drawn, and the merger was signed and sealed by all parties. Actually, the paperwork on the $1.45 billion mortgage-backed bonds would not be completed until April 1988, but "highly confident" letters were accepted as sufficient guarantees on the loans. The company was reorganized to facilitate the sale of assets under the umbrella of a new parent company called Hillsborough Holdings Corporation (Hillsborough being the county in which Tampa is located). Later, Hillsborough Holdings was renamed Walter Industries, as a stronger link to the company's origins. It signaled the start of a new life for the old Jim Walter Corporation.

CHAPTER 15

— *Building to Survive* —

LIFE GOES ON AFTER a leveraged buyout. The new owners of the old Jim Walter Corporation—KKR and the Walter company management—set forth on a new course: Sell off assets as needed, namely those stand-alone subsidiaries which were not part of the company's core business. Then use those funds to pay off the high-interest bonds as quickly as possible, without, of course, giving anything away.

By the end of the first year, Celotex had been sold to a management group backed by private investors; Celotex Ltd. had been sold to its own management group in London; Jim Walter Papers was bought by a large paper company at a premium price; and a number of smaller building materials companies had been sold without difficulty. Georgia Marble went for a good price in May 1989. U.S. Pipe was targeted for possible sale, when and if the right price was offered.

The remaining profit centers continued as before, actually increasing their sales and earnings. There were no cutbacks. Jim Walter Homes built and sold its shell and partially finished houses at the same rate as the year before: six thousand houses. The Alabama coal mines continued at full production: nine million tons per year. Everything was on track. The sale of the various subsidiaries reduced the company's annual overall revenues from $2.4 billion to roughly $1.3 billion, still large enough to retain a position in the nation's top three hundred industrial companies. The company enjoyed a high cash flow and substantial earnings which could be devoted entirely to reducing its debt. KKR itself went on to bigger and bolder leveraged buyouts. Later in 1988, after the JWC merger was in place, the premier LBO firm outbid all rivals and took under its wings the giant tobacco and food company RJR Nabisco. The astounding price was $25 billion. It was by far the largest leveraged corporate buyout in history, and likely to remain so. In essence, as Henry Kravis remarked, it was no different than the JWC buyout, with the same proportion of equity, assets, and cash flow behind the amount of debt incurred to finance the purchase. By the end of 1988, KKR and Henry Kravis stood on a pinnacle of investment audacity and achievement never before seen on Wall Street.

But in business, as in most human endeavors, you never have it made. As that wily Scotsman warned so many years ago, the best laid plans of mice and men "gang aft a-gley." What started out as a mere fly in the ointment and then mushroomed into a big, black, ugly cloud was an unexpected class action lawsuit filed in Beaumont, Texas, in mid-July 1989 on behalf of asbestos injury victims against Walter Industries, KKR, and Drexel. The lawsuit challenged KKR's leveraged buyout of the old Jim Walter Corporation as a fraudulent scheme designed to shield the company from mounting asbestos injury claims against its former subsidiary Celotex. It asked the court to hold Walter Industries, KKR, and Drexel, as well as the principals, including Henry Kravis, George Roberts, Mike Tokarz, Jim Walter, and Joe Cordell, liable for more than 80,000 claims alleging illnesses and death from the handling of asbestos products years and years before.

The lawsuit received wide publicity throughout the country, and especially in the financial community, largely because it named KKR and Henry Kravis personally as well as

Walter Industries, and the sum of all those 80,000 claims was put at more than $3 billion. Also, it was brought by one of the most prominent and aggressive lawyers in Texas, Steven D. Susman, of Houston, who had won several big damage awards for plaintiffs in antitrust cases and had defended some very high-profile clients, including former House Speaker Jim Wright against ethics charges in congressional hearings, and the Hunt brothers in their highly publicized battles with major bank lenders years before. Behind Susman were other highly contentious asbestos attorneys who had previously won large settlements in other asbestos cases. It promised to be a battle royal. Susman predicted that his lawsuit "will prove to be a landmark case."

What threatened to make it a landmark case was Susman's attempt to "pierce the corporate veil" that legally separates the liabilities of a company from its stockholders, whether a stockholder holds one share or all the shares of a company. Separated by a "corporate veil," a parent company cannot be held responsible for the actions of a subsidiary, just so long as it does not exercise "undue control" over its subsidiary's independent management. This massive, class action case was threatening to test just that.

Jim Walter, Henry Kravis, and their colleagues were aghast at the lawsuit out of Texas. Not only was it unexpected, it had virtually no basis in existing law. Most of the major New York law firms specializing in product liability had been consulted on this matter. Prior to the JWC buyout, Jim Walter, KKR, the other bidders, the investment bankers, the banks, and the big prospective bondholders involved had all sought legal opinions on the possible danger of the new company being held liable for the debts of Celotex, and none had been warned away. And yet, there is no certainty in the law, certainly not in the parochial jurisdiction of Texas state courts, which had in the past awarded astounding verdicts in favor of Texas claimants in civil suits, such as the $11 billion award to Penzoil against Texaco. Mike Tokarz, who had spearheaded the JWC buyout for KKR, was particularly incensed by the moral and ethical injustice of the lawsuit. For the past several years Celotex had been settling all the asbestos lawsuits brought against it, paying out more than $500 million, and it was continuing to settle such claims through its insurance and cash flow. Any claims against the Walter company had been routinely referred to Celotex or summarily dismissed in the past. Despite all that, the Texas lawyers had decided to go after KKR and Walter Industries. Why? Because they had deep pockets. That was where the money was. Even if the litigants ultimately lost in the courts, they stood a good chance of forcing Walter and KKR to settle in order to avoid protracted litigation, negative publicity, and sheer aggravation. Some would call it legal blackmail.

For a start, the Texas judge ruled that Walter Industries could not sell off any more assets without giving the asbestos litigants a fifteen-day notice period in which to object. That order effectively stopped the company from selling off more of its subsidiaries and put an initial crimp in the company's drive to pay off its expensive bonds.

Then the bottom seemed to fall out of the whole high-yield bond market. Several companies financed by high-yield bonds appeared to be ready to go belly-up, spreading fear throughout the bond market. Serious questions surfaced concerning the market manipulations and investment practices of Michael Milken and his firm Drexel Burnham Lambert. [In time Milken, the king of the junk bond market, would plead guilty to trading irregularities and go to jail, followed by the bankruptcy and disbandment of Drexel Burnham Lambert.] Fear stalked the high-yield bond marketplace—fear that these highly leveraged companies would not be able to pay off their staggeringly high debt, fear that without Milken and Drexel trading in junk bonds would be drastically reduced. While Walter Industries was still a profitably operating company, the wide publicity given to the $3 billion asbestos suit gave rise to the possibility that it, too, would go bankrupt and not be able to pay off its bond debts. The price of its bonds plummeted.

It was an unhappy, anxiety-ridden time in the executive offices of Walter Industries in Tampa and at KKR in New York. They were in deep trouble. About half of the Walter Industries bonds had fixed interest rates ranging from 10% to 17 percent, but the other half, approximately $624 million of the senior notes and senior subordinated bonds, had floating rates of interest that were scheduled to be reset as of January 2 of each year. Issued at the start of 1988, the senior bonds paid 14½ percent and the junior bonds paid 16½ percent. Those interest rates were reset easily at an eighth of a point higher at the start of 1989 to ensure that the bonds would be worth 101 percent of their face value. But now with the start of 1990 only a few months away, the market price of those bonds had dropped so precipitously that the reset interest rates would have to be astronomical, if they could be reset at all. Walter Industries could go bankrupt trying to meet the new interest rates.

The only alternative was to persuade the bondholders to give up that reset clause and to exchange their bonds for new ones, which would pay 1 or 2 percent more interest until the following November. That would provide the bondholders a very rich return on their investment, from 15 to 18.6 percent, and would allow KKR enough time to refinance the bonds at more reasonable rates. Mike Tokarz of KKR and Jim Walter and his associates, accompanied by investment advisers and attorneys, journeyed cross-country meeting with bondholders in different cities in an attempt to explain the mutual advantages of their exchange offer—to no avail. The savings and loan and insurance firms which had bought the bonds on Michael Milken's say-so rejected the offer. They thought they could get more.

The reset calculation on the Walter bonds was scheduled for December 2, 1989, to take effect a month later at the start of 1990. The new interest rate was to be determined by impartial experts at two investment houses, Merrill Lynch and Drexel Burnham. As the key date approached, KKR sweetened its exchange proposal, offering some cash and a slightly increased fixed interest rate. This offer was sent out in ballot form to all holders of those $624 million of high yield bonds. Needing 80 percent of the bondholders for approval, it failed by a wide margin. The answer was still no.

When the dreadful reset date rolled around in early December, both investment firms announced the expected dire news: The market price of Walter Industries bonds had skidded so far down (fifty cents on the dollar at that point) that there was no interest rate that would be high enough to bring those bonds up to 101 percent of their face value. There was, in short, no reset rate on those bonds. The incredible had happened. This healthy, viable company with more than $1 billion in annual sales and with operating earnings of $300 million was facing imminent bankruptcy. On January 2, 1990, it would be in default. Bondholders could force the company into liquidation. Some bondholders threatened exactly that.

Once again, the KKR associates and Jim Walter and his colleagues made personal calls and conference calls to various bondholders, imploring them to accept some sort of compromise. "Don't cut off your nose to spite your face," Jim Walter pleaded time and again. Tokarz spoke of coming out of this dilemma with a win/win solution if bondholders would accept a reasonable interest on their bonds for one more year. Otherwise, he warned, if Walter Industries went bankrupt, these unsecured bondholders would be the last of the creditors to receive any money or assets from the company. The bondholders, most of whom were professional investors for the savings and loan and insurance firms, simply would not believe that Henry Kravis would allow one of his buyout companies to go belly-up. He never had before. KKR controlled billions of dollars in various corporate equities and if Kravis so desired, they thought, he could bail out Walter Industries. It would cost him a handsome premium, and the junk bondholders then would make a killing. So went their line of reasoning for refusing KKR's offer.

For KKR, bankruptcy under Chapter 11 of the Federal Bankruptcy Code was certainly an option for handling Walter Industries' debt. It was a form of voluntary bankruptcy under which a company could stop all its creditors from demanding immediate payment while the company continued in business and reorganized its financial affairs. As their attorneys explained, it might be embarrassing and even humiliating, but it could force the junk bondholders to compromise on their demands. They would receive nothing while the bankruptcy continued and that could be years. Chapter 11 under federal law also would supersede the asbestos claims being heard in the Texas state court, the attorneys explained, and that would give KKR a fairer hearing than it could hope to get in Texas. Moreover, the threat of declaring voluntary bankruptcy just might move the bondholders and the asbestos lawyers to agree to some reasonable compromise. So went the thinking at KKR and Walter Industries.

Henry Kravis and Jim Walter had grown close over the past two years and were sensitive to one another's personalities. Since the buyout, they shared in making the key decisions concerning Walter Industries. While Kravis and his investors actually owned the company, it was Jim Walter's name on the building, and on this issue, Henry Kravis wanted Jim Walter to take the lead. One afternoon in December, shortly after the reset had failed, Kravis put his arm around Walter's shoulder and softly asked, "What do you think we should do, Jim?"

"I don't think we have any choice," answered Walter, with a slight shrug. "Our best route now is Chapter 11." It was a painful decision, but logical.

As a "last chance" offer, KKR sweetened a new proposal for the bondholders: a mixture of cash, one or two points higher interest, and a 10 percent share of the stock of Walter Industries. All that would come out of the hide of KKR, which owned 92 percent of the company. A meeting was called summoning the major bondholders to New York to hear the new proposal, as explained by Henry Kravis himself.

At the same time, Kravis dispatched one of his key associates, Perry Golkin, to accompany Jim Walter and attorneys for both companies in a final attempt to reach a compromise settlement with the asbestos attorneys. Golkin was instructed to sound out the plaintiff attorneys on a settlement figure of around $100 to $125 million. To KKR that was the "nuisance value" of clearing the playing field of all the asbestos suits once and for all. No one at KKR truly believed it would be that easy. But it was worth a try.

In an airport hotel in Atlanta, Golkin and the Walter attorneys spelled out their position and their offer to the asbestos litigants. The shrewd product-liability lawyers, each of them representing claimants from different sections of the country, knew they held Henry Kravis and KKR in a bind. Their lawsuit, even while pending, stopped KKR from selling off Walter Industries' assets. Who would want to buy a Walter company and risk being dragged into these asbestos lawsuits? That made it impossible to redeem the bonds, which, in turn, would put the company in default, forcing it into a bankruptcy which would lead to liquidation.

The liability lawyers heard them out and then one of them declared, "We certainly would like to settle this case, but I can tell you now that if you threw $700 million down on the table, we would not take it. We would not settle for that."

"Then we'll see you in court," said Perry Golkin.

Several of the asbestos attorneys left no doubt that they were prepared to fight their claims to the very end, no matter how long it took. One of them taunted Golkin with this outburst: "I look forward to taking the paintings off Henry Kravis's walls. [Kravis, an avid art collector, was reported to have one of the finest private Post-Impressionist art collections in the country.] And I look forward to walking into your home, Perry, and taking *that*, too." This was not going to be a gentlemanly lawsuit.

A few days later, some sixty of the major bondholders gathered in the Wall Street offices of Simpson Thacher, the law firm representing KKR, primarily to see and hear Henry Kravis try to talk his way out of paying off their bonds at a stupendous premium. First, they listened to KKR and Walter attorneys explain their offer to exchange the reset bonds for new bonds of the same face value that would bear higher interest rates, give them a cash bonus, and also give them 10 percent of the shares of stock in Walter Industries. The new exchange bonds would become due and payable the following November. Jim Walter rose to explain that his company was operating at a profit, but that it needed time to either settle its litigation or find some other way to restructure the loans. He promised they would all be paid off in full if they gave his company some more time. The alternative, he told them, was that his company would declare voluntary bankruptcy and the bondholders might have to wait years before the courts straightened it all out. The exchange offer was good for just ten days and would expire at 7 p.m., Wednesday, December 27.

Henry Kravis rose to reiterate most of the points. Speaking softly but earnestly for fifteen minutes he warned the bondholders, "Don't believe for one minute that I am afraid for any reason to declare bankruptcy for Walter Industries. I urge you to accept our latest exchange offer for your bonds. You have seven days to send in your acceptances. I urge you to do it. If this last and final offer is rejected by you, you will be forcing us to seek the protection of the courts under Chapter 11. Rest assured, we will do it, if we have to. The decision is now in your hands, ladies and gentlemen. Act wisely and in your own enlightened self-interest. Accept our exchange offer."

These supposedly experienced and sophisticated bondholders apparently were not accustomed to accepting anything at face value. No one disputed Henry Kravis openly, but the sentiment throughout the room was that Henry Kravis was bluffing. A man of his reputation would never accept the embarrassment and humiliation of part of his empire going into bankruptcy.

When Wednesday, December 27, 1989, rolled around, Tampa was dismal, gray, cold, and cloudy. The hours passed ever so slowly on the executive eighth floor of the twin towers headquarters building. The top managers had gathered in the boardroom, consulting with some twenty different attorneys, going over the stacks of legal documents for the bankruptcy filing for the company and thirty-one of its subsidiaries. A final check on the ballot count at 7 p.m. with Continental Illinois Bank in Chicago confirmed what they already knew: The exchange offer had failed, had not even come close to being accepted. Don Stichter, the company's local bankruptcy attorney, gathered up the necessary papers

and left. The boardroom became eerily quiet. It seemed un-
real. Impossible. But the deed was done. The court clerk had
been alerted to expect a late filing from Stichter for Tampa's
only Fortune 500 industrial company. In the U.S. Bankruptcy
Court for the Middle District of Florida, Tampa Division, the
petition for reorganization under Chapter 11 was filed and
stamped in at 7:15 p.m. Walter Industries, Inc., was indeed
legally bankrupt.

The next day, Jim Walter told the press, "I can safely say
that in my entire business career, which spans forty years, yes-
terday was the saddest day of my life." His plans for retirement were once again put on hold. "I most certainly will be
here for the foreseeable future," he said. "I'm sixty-seven
years old; I'm in good health; I'm certainly not going to leave
the company in the lurch. It's my intention to stay as long as
I feel I can help and am making a contribution."

Now the lawyers took over in earnest. Every interested
party—KKR, Walter Industries, the various bondholder
groups, the banks who had extended loans, the trade creditors, the different groups of asbestos litigants—was represented by at least one, often two, and sometimes three law
firms. Attorneys for KKR and Walter Industries worked furi-
ously over the New Year holiday weekend so that on the first
working day of 1990, they could be first in petitioning the
bankruptcy court in Tampa for a declaratory judgment holding KKR and Walter Industries blameless and not liable for
any asbestos injury claims filed against Celotex or anyone
else. They asked for a declaratory judgment that the corporate veil could not have been pierced between the old Jim
Walter Corporation and Celotex, and that the leveraged buyout had not been, as alleged, fraudulently designed to avoid
the asbestos litigation. They also asked for an injunction
stopping the asbestos litigants from suing any individuals
personally who were affiliated with either KKR or Walter In-

dustries, namely Kravis, Walter, and their associates. In essence, they were asking the bankruptcy court in Tampa to take over the jurisdiction of all asbestos-related cases, including the Texas cases, and to consolidate all the litigation, and decide the case once and for all in Tampa.

Of course, the attorneys for the asbestos injury claimants fought them every step of the way, particularly on venue. But in April the chief judge of the bankruptcy court, Alexander Paskay, ruled that his court should consolidate all litigation affecting the bankruptcy. To allow asbestos suits to be filed in state and federal courts throughout the country, Judge Paskay ruled "would effectively paralyze the entire reorganization process." The asbestos lawyers appealed, but Judge Paskay was upheld in the federal district court and in the U.S. Eleventh Circuit Court of Appeals. Judge Paskay did not say in his venue ruling how he might decide on the more important liability issue, but he did hint that it was up to the asbestos litigants to prove their case. "At this stage it is appropriate and proper to assume that these debtors have no liability for any asbestos-related personal injuries since, as far as it appears from this record (Hillsborough Holdings and Jim Walter Corporation) never manufactured, sold, or distributed to anyone any products containing asbestos." It was a significant victory for Jim Walter as well as for KKR.

Operating a $1 billion-plus business while under the constraints of Chapter 11, however, is a severe strain on anyone's equilibrium. The company could not buy or sell major assets or borrow money without court approval and needed the court's permission to do a host of ongoing business necessities. Any proposed changes that were outside the "ordinary course" of the company's day-to-day operations could be opposed by the creditors, and often were.

Jim Walter continually asked the firm's bankruptcy attorneys how long all this litigation would take, and when the company could expect to emerge from the burdens of bankruptcy. The answer was almost always the same: two years, plus or minus a few months. The answer, however, remained the same as time went on, and became known as "the rolling two years." To cope with conditions under Chapter 11, Walter asked Ken Matlock, chief financial officer, to serve as the company's point man in handling relations with the bankruptcy court and with the various groups of creditors. Walter decided to devote most, perhaps all, of his time to vital Chapter 11 matters. Everyday operations would be managed by Joe Cordell, the company president, aided by Bill Weldon, vice president for finance.

These were deeply distressing times for Jim Walter personally. Never before had he felt so helpless in getting things done, in finding brisk and appropriate solutions to business problems. His days were consumed with legal intricacies that set his nerves on edge; straightforward questions received inconclusive answers; telephone calls at all hours brought far more bad news than good news. He had trouble sleeping through the night. Socially, the bankruptcy was embarrassing. He soon grew tired justifying it to people. His wife, Connie, a native of Tampa whom he had married six years before the bankruptcy and two years after the death of his first wife, soon grew adept at explaining to their many friends and acquaintances that the bankruptcy was not personal, that Jim himself was quite solvent and that the company was not bankrupt in the ordinary way but under Chapter 11 only while seeking to resolve the asbestos lawsuits.

A little more than a year into the bankruptcy, the company and Jim Walter were struck with yet another severe blow. Joe Cordell, thirty-two years at Jim Walter's side, fell ill with cancer. After undergoing major surgery, he failed to regain his usual strength and verve. It came as a shock to his longtime, close colleagues. He was only sixty-three, and it became clear that he could not continue as the company's chief executive officer for much longer.

An executive search firm was put to work to find a successor, and it recommended an ideal candidate for the job: a hands-on, incisive, down-to-earth, self-made business manager. The son of an Illinois coal miner, he seemed to be cut from the same mold as Jim Walter himself. G. Robert "Bull" Durham, at sixty-two, had retired two years earlier as chairman, president and CEO of Phelps Dodge Corporation, the nation's largest producer of copper. Credited with turning around and saving Phelps Dodge from bankruptcy, Durham had been named the 1987 "CEO of the Year" by *Financial World* magazine, which put him in the exalted ranks of Chrysler Corporation's Lee Iacocca, who won the award the previous year, and of WalMart's founder, Sam Walton, who won the following year. The only snag in the executive search was that Bull Durham declined before he even learned the identity of the company looking for a new CEO; he had retired twice from Phelps Dodge and didn't plan on working ever again.

A month later, when the executive search firm called and identified Walter Industries, Durham laughed and said, "Really, frankly, thank you, but no. I've spent my life making sure I didn't get into Chapter 11, and now you want me to come back in and get involved in something like that? Heavens, no!"

A third call, this time identifying Henry Kravis and the number of mutual friends they shared, persuaded Durham at least to meet with the famous financier. At a breakfast meeting with Kravis, Mike Tokarz, and Perry Golkin, Durham was persuaded to meet with Jim Walter in Tampa before he made his decision. A long, candid meeting with Walter in

his Tampa office and a second meeting with Henry Kravis finally convinced Bull Durham that these were the kind of
people he wanted to work with, at least for a couple of years.
Four years later he would say about his decision to come out
of retirement, "I never regretted it for a minute."

Joe Cordell stayed on for several months to escort Durham
through all the subsidiaries, introducing him to the key people, vouching for his character, his integrity, and his fit into
the company. Durham took over as the third chief executive
of the company. He was widely regarded, in the words of
Connie Walter, as a "white knight riding in to save the company just when he was most needed." Company executives
soon realized how compatible Jim and Bull were, how they
seemed to think alike, how smoothly the transition had been
accomplished. Upon reflection, Durham himself has remarked, "I don't think that Jim and I have had a single difference of opinion about the handling of an issue in all these
years." Bull Durham's hand on the wheel quickly revitalized
operations throughout the company. He contributed hands-
on management with regular monthly reviews of operations
at each of the major subsidiaries, attended by himself, Bill
Weldon, and management teams as needed.

The next year, 1992, was as bleak as the year before. The
lawsuits dragged on in bankruptcy court. Joe Cordell succumbed to his cancer. Jim Walter, who had always enjoyed
robust health, was diagnosed with that same dreaded disease.
Life-threatening cancer had affected his vocal chords. Studying his medical options as he would a business problem, he
chose to undergo surgery at a local hospital and radiation in
Houston. He emerged with flying colors, once again in good
health. A few days before his seventieth birthday, he told an
interviewer from the *Tampa Tribune* how he felt about his
company and its bankruptcy:

"Our company has $160 million in the bank. We pay our bills and will continue to do that. We simply must await the outcome of the courts. I am proud of this company and what we have achieved, starting from that classified ad in the *Tribune* forty-six years ago. I would be a hypocrite if I did not admit that. I am proud of my family. I am proud to be a Floridian. I have traveled all over the world and I can say this with all the truth I can muster: I would never, ever, want to live anywhere else. This is my home and it is where we will celebrate my seventieth birthday in a few days, God willing."

He was wrong only as to where he would spend his seventieth birthday. He spent it in New York, where Henry Kravis threw him a surprise private birthday party in the Kravis apartment for fourteen of Walter's closest friends and associates. As a birthday present to a man who has everything, the men chipped in to give him something he did not have: a magnificent oil portrait of Jim Walter in his favorite ranch jacket, painted by Everett Raymond Kinstler, one of the country's leading portraitists and famous for his paintings of four former presidents.

On the business and bond front that year, things went from bad to worse. The junk bond market collapsed and went into a free fall. Several well-known companies financed with Milken/Drexel junk bonds, highly leveraged in their buyouts, went bankrupt. Mike Milken was in jail. Drexel was out of business. Many of the financial institutions, particularly savings and loan associations, which bought those bonds, went bankrupt. The value of all those junk bonds plummeted.

The free fall of junk bond prices gave rise to a new breed of Wall Street wizards who were not so fondly called "vulture capitalists." Quite unlike venture capitalists or leveraged buyout firms, these "vulture capitalists" cared not a whit for helping to start up or to expand needy companies. They instead preyed upon dead, dying, or distressed companies, seeking only to pluck out whatever value remained in them before discarding the carcass. There is nothing illegal about buying the debts of bankrupt and near-bankrupt companies in an attempt to gain a measure of control and then cashing out at face value or close to it. On Wall Street, it is viewed by some as just another sharp way of making money. They call it profiting from special situations. But it is viewed by many with distaste, as any vulture or scavenger would be.

Of this new breed of "vulture capitalists," one of the most successful was a Harvard Business School graduate named Leon Black, who started out as one of Michael Milken's chief lieutenants on mergers and acquisitions at Drexel, helping companies borrow huge amounts of money to buy other companies in the 1980s. When Drexel and Milken went under, Leon Black switched sides. Heading his own investment firm, Apollo Advisors, in New York, he began buying up the securities of distressed, debt-ridden companies for pennies on the dollar and then seeking full payment on the debt in the 1990s. With the backing of the huge French government-owned bank Credit Lyonnais, Black bought the whole junk bond portfolio of the insolvent Executive Life Insurance Company of California, which was seized by the state of California in 1991. In that multibillion-dollar cache were nearly $160 million of Walter Industries bonds, and that made him a big player in the affairs of Walter Industries.

Countless other so-called "vulture" funds followed Leon Black's foray into buying at deep discounts the junk bonds of Walter Industries. Another class of investor was the venerable investment banking firm of Lehman Brothers, then a subsidiary of American Express. There the merger and acquisition department apparently could not resist the opportunity of capitalizing on available Walter Industries bonds put up for sale by the federal government's Resolution Trust Company at a deep discount. The RTC had foreclosed on several failing California savings and loans institutions, including Columbia S&L, as well as Miami-based Centrust, holding huge portfolios of junk bonds. In a highly unusual move for an investment bank, which ordinarily only advises others, Lehman Brothers purchased for its own portfolio $271 million of Walter Industries' publicly traded junk bonds. They paid between fifty to sixty-five cents on the dollar, while Leon Black's Apollo Advisors earlier had paid an average of only twenty cents on the dollar, according to whispered reports on Wall Street. Whatever they paid for the bonds, however, Apollo and Lehman Brothers together owned more than 40 percent of the bonds that had put Walter Industries into bankruptcy. They were a powerful force to be reckoned with. What made the situation particularly bitter was the knowledge that the two firms which now controlled the company's debt had been instrumental in putting Walter Industries into that debt. In the original leveraged buyout, Lehman Brothers had been the investment bank advisers to Jim Walter, while Leon Black had been the Drexel Burnham man raising financing for the LBO. Both of them had been privy to all of the company's confidential data; they knew the company's assets, liabilities, earnings, cash flow, and operations. They knew what those bonds were really worth.

As the asbestos litigation churned on with motions, countermotions, hearings, and discovery proceedings, Jim Walter made it his personal business to appear in court for every session, held one or sometimes two or three times a month for more than five years. They were onerous and boring most of the time, but he felt it his duty to demonstrate his interest, his loyalty, and his steadfastness in representing the company to which he had devoted his life. Judge Paskay recognized

Jim Walter's strong interest and allowed him to sit up front with the attorneys, an almost unprecedented action. Back in the company offices, many longtime employees felt as bitter as their chairman. It hurt to see a company to which you had devoted your life picked apart by a bunch of vultures.

Actually, the company was under attack on two different fronts. The various groups of bondholders wanted to get as much money as they could out of Walter Industries and KKR as soon as possible. Time was the enemy of bondholders. The longer they had to wait, the lower was their rate of return. For the asbestos litigants, time was their best friend. The longer they could hold out and prevent Walter Industries from coming out of bankruptcy, the longer the bondholders would have to wait for their money, the longer Walter Industries would be stymied, and ultimately the larger the settlement they could demand. It was a form of legal blackmail directed primarily at KKR: How much would KKR pay to get rid of this bankruptcy litigation?

KKR and Jim Walter saw eye-to-eye on what they should do. Their interests coincided and neither would jump ship and abandon the other. They agreed that all creditors should be paid in full, including all the suppliers, the banks, and the various bondholders. But not the asbestos litigants. It had become a matter of principle that the asbestos litigants should not be paid off in a settlement, that KKR and Walter Industries, having gone this far, should see the litigation through and, once and for all, put an end to Walter Industries being a target for any more asbestos claims.

After four long, arduous years of legal maneuvering, discovery proceedings, and behind-the-scenes negotiations, the asbestos liability claims were ready to come to trial. The issue, upon which the key officers of the old JWC and a variety of experts had testified to in discovery proceedings, was whether or not the old Jim Walter Corporation had exercised undue control over its subsidiary Celotex so as to "pierce the corporate veil" and thereby make JWC (and Walter Industries) liable for the claims of those made ill by their alleged contacts with asbestos. The trial date was set to begin on Monday, December 13, 1993.

On that Monday, first thing in the morning, an attorney representing Apollo, Lehman, and the other bondholders came into the crowded courtroom, with a startling announcement. On behalf of the bondholders, he declared, the bondholders' committee had settled the claims of the asbestos litigants the previous Friday for $450 million: There was no need for a trial.

Judge Paskay would have none of that. Without the assent of KKR and Walter Industries that $450 million was not the bondholders' money to give away, the judge pointed out. He denied the motion. They had spent four years getting to this point, the judge said, and the trial would begin as scheduled.

The case had turned out to be the longest, costliest, and most complex Chapter 11 proceedings in the history of the Tampa bankruptcy court, and one of the largest in the United States. Thousands upon thousands of pages of legal documents filled almost half the court's storeroom. The trial itself lasted only five days. Judge Paskay took another four months to review all the documents and write his thirty-eight page decision on the key issue. On April 18, 1994, the judge ruled that the "corporate veil" had not been pierced and that Walter Industries was not liable for any asbestos-related claims against its former subsidiary Celotex. The company prevailed on every factual issue.

Jim Walter commented to the press: "I think I speak for all senior management when I say that we feel personally vindicated by the Court's decision. For the last five years, the reputations of various individuals, some now deceased, who spent much of their lives building this company, have been tarnished by the asbestos claimants' unfounded and often outrageous allegations. . . . The record was set straight today."

But that hardly settled matters. In fact, the verdict increased the intensity of the behind-the-scenes bargaining. The asbestos litigants appealed Judge Paskay's ruling a week later. Frederick M. Baron, the lead attorney for the asbestos litigants, announced that without a settlement of the asbestos claims "we've got at least a couple more years of litigation." It was a scarcely hidden threat to KKR that unless his clients were satisfied, at least two more years of litigation would roll on.

All the creditor groups lined up behind the bondholders' plan to pay off the asbestos litigants with $450 million, even after they had lost in court. It was a slap in the face, in effect, to KKR. The plan called for paying off all the creditors at full value with cash, bonds, and equity in the new Walter Industries, giving $450 million to the asbestos claimants to settle all their lawsuits, and giving KKR and the managers of Walter Industries $75 million, which was half of their original LBO investment—but only if they signed on to the creditors' plan. If they did not sign, that $75 million would go to the asbestos litigants, increasing their take to $525 million, and KKR and Walter management would get nothing.

Mike Tokarz renewed his efforts to bring the bondholder groups over to KKR's side. He tried to negotiate a reorganization plan for Walter Industries that would pay all bondholders the full value of their bonds, plus some of the interest accumulated but not paid since the bankruptcy and a value-sharing plan in new equity of the company. He asked the bondholders to stick with Walter Industries just six months longer, by which time the asbestos litigants would have exhausted their appeals and would get nothing and the bondholders would get a share of the benefits.

But the bondholder groups also were negotiating with the asbestos attorneys, who argued that they could and would fight in the courts for years, not six months, and that the case would never be settled without them. The bondholders wanted the payout now, not later, and lined up with the asbestos lawyers. The Lehman and Apollo groups particularly figured their best course was to satisfy the asbestos lawyers and to reap their own profits on the discounted bonds. KKR and Walter Industries responded by asking the bankruptcy court to decide that they did not owe the bondholders any of the unpaid interest accrued over the past four years while the company was under Chapter 11 bankruptcy. That would amount to some $700 million on the original $1.1 billion debt.

Thus, the sides were lined up once again, daggers drawn, as they went into the final battle of reorganizing the financial affairs of Walter Industries so as to pay off creditors and decide who would control the company. Both Walter Industries and the bondholders drew up amended plans for the financial future of the company. Both plans offered full payment to all the creditors. The company plan denied any payments to the asbestos litigants; the bondholders' plan offered $450 to $525 million to the asbestos people and denied ownership to KKR or the management people who invested in the leveraged buyout. Back into court went all the parties to battle over the issue of post-petition (Chapter 11) interest payments and the details of opposing plans for reorganizing the company. The various bank, trade, and bondholder plans were consolidated into one "creditor proponents" plan, similar to the so-called Apollo/Lehman plan.

In August 1994, four months after Judge Paskay's decision denying the asbestos claims, the two reorganization plans were mailed to all creditors and owners of Walter Industries for a crucial vote that would weigh heavily in the ultimate decision of the bankruptcy court. In late September the vote came in overwhelmingly in favor of the Apollo-devised creditors' plan. Back into court once again went the battling parties. This time KKR and Walter Industries argued that Judge Paskay could not possibly find that the creditors' plan was fair because he would then be forcing Walter Industries to pay on asbestos injury claims for which he himself had ruled the company was not liable. The bondholders argued that under law the will of the majority of creditors of the company, as shown by the vote, should determine the ultimate reorganization of a bankrupt company. There was no dearth of legal arguments.

Formal hearings on the opposing plans, the legal question of post-petition interest, and the fairness of the $450 million settlement got under way in mid-October 1994. On the third day of those hearings—Wednesday, October 19, 1994—Judge Paskay looked over his courtroom and noticed that with Henry Kravis present, waiting to testify, all the principals of the opposing groups were there in one room, Jim Walter, Bull Durham, counsel for the asbestos litigants, and various bondholder attorneys from across the nation. Judge Paskay called a recess and summoned the principal players into chambers for conference without their attorneys. He sounded out each group separately. Then, in open court, Judge Paskay made his dramatic announcement:

"For the benefit of all present in the courtroom, it is my considered opinion, and apparently everybody agrees, that a speedy and expedient resolution of this Chapter 11 would be a consensual plan." The judge warned them what would happen if they could not now reach a compromised agreement to end the court battle. If he disapproved the company's plan because they did not have the vote, and disapproved the creditors' plan because it included the asbestos settlement, then, the judge said, the court would be left with no plan at all. That would lead to three undesirable alternatives: a dismissal "which would mean utter chaos and a disaster"; a Chapter 7 liquidation in which some bondholders, the owners, and the asbestos people "would not get a dime"; or a decision to deny confirmation to either plan, which would "start the fight all over again."

Judge Paskay, who had been a Hungarian freedom-fighter during World War II and still spoke with a heavy Hungarian accent, announced he was giving all the parties a "modified *Allen* charge." This, he explained, was "an old shotgun charge from Texas," concerning a deadlocked jury, in which the judge said, "Bailiff, lock them up. No food forever until a verdict." In this case, Judge Paskay said, he was not doing that. But he was giving them just twenty-four hours in which to settle this case once and for all. He instructed them to reach a compromise, to agree upon one consensual reorganizational plan, and to report back to him by 1 o'clock the following afternoon. Or else! Or else, he implied, he would be forced to choose among those three disastrous alternatives.

The warring parties with conflicting interests separated into a number of small office rooms in the courthouse as Henry Kravis, Mike Tokarz, Jim Walter, and their attorneys met with their counterparts in the various creditor groups, moving from one room to another, trying to find a compromise somewhere among the contentious factions. Tensions were high and tempers flared. Conflicts arose even within different groups. Shouting could be heard through closed doors. The building's air conditioning could hardly keep up with the heat generated in the negotiations on how to split the Walter Industries pie valued at $2.6 billion.

KKR fought hard, particularly with the bondholders from Apollo and Lehman who controlled more than 40 percent of the debt. Mike Tokarz argued essentially to this effect:

"Everybody is making money here, hand over fist. Why should everybody give it to the asbestos guys who are getting a tremendous windfall? They don't deserve it; they lost their case. Why should we—the management and KKR—who stuck this thing through for five years operating the company, doing everything we were supposed to do, making money for everybody, why should we come out of this with a loss? It's not fair."

In late afternoon, some of the groups moved from the closing court building to the company's headquarters, and the argumentative discussions continued. When dinnertime approached, they moved to a nearby hotel, then back to the company offices, and, then again, back to the hotel. They battled fiercely over who should get what, dividing up the spoils of a five-year war that had to end with no clear-cut winners. They broke up for a few hours' sleep at about 2 a.m. The KKR-Walter team regrouped for a 6 a.m. breakfast strategy conference, and then all the parties gathered for one last session at 8 a.m. in Don Stichter's office conference room in the bankruptcy court building. All of the representatives of the various groups—bondholders, creditors, asbestos claimants, KKR, and the company's management—were there.

It was not until the hour before the judge's 1 p.m. deadline that the bondholders and asbestos representatives acquiesced to the arguments of Kravis and Tokarz on the thorniest point of contention. They agreed to reduce the settlement on the asbestos claims from $450 million to $375 million (to be paid into a Celotex trust fund) and to increase the KKR/management share from $75 million to $150 million in stock of the company, which was just about their original investment. The settlement was to put an end to these and all future asbestos liability claims against the company. The asbestos liability lawyers would be paid $15 million for their services.

In the last five minutes before the judge's 1 p.m. deadline, KKR wrung a final concession from the other parties. Mike Tokarz came up with the idea that KKR and company management should receive the benefit of any tax deduction on the $375 million being paid to the asbestos claimants. KKR and company management then would receive a total of $250 million in the reorganization, a profit of $100 million.

In essence, as Tokarz later figured it, everyone involved in the final reorganization of Walter Industries came out a winner. The banks and secured bondholders were paid the full principal on their bonds, plus interest plus interest on that interest. The vendors received 100 percent of the money owed them, plus interest. The unsecured bondholders received 100 percent of their principal, but relinquished their right to receive interest as part of the asbestos settlement. No matter how the settlement was analyzed, the outcome was highly unusual in that, unlike most bankruptcy reoranizations, the creditors were paid in full.

When court reconvened at 1 p.m., the exhausted parties reported to Judge Paskay that they had indeed succeeded in reaching a consensual agreement in principle and now needed time to hammer out the details. A happy judge granted the request. A month later, on November 22, 1994, after much contentious wrangling over details, a completed consensual plan of reorganization was filed. Essentially, the agreement also provided that all trade creditors would be paid in cash. The money owed to banks and senior bondholders would be paid in a combination of cash and new Walter Industries common stock. The holders of the $1.1 billion of subordinated bonds would receive their payments within a certain formula in a combination of cash, new senior five-year notes later set at a fixed 12.9 percent interest, or in new common stock which was valued at $22.86 a share. The company would also have a new board of directors for an initial three-year term, consisting of three from company management, three from Lehman Brothers (representing the bondholders), one from KKR, and two independent outside directors selected solely by company management. That configuration essentially gave company management continuing control of the new company. The agreement also provided that if and when Lehman Brothers reduced its holdings in the company, its directors would be replaced by KKR representatives.

The joint plan was sent out for a vote in December; it was overwhelmingly approved and confirmed by the bankruptcy court on March 2, and on March 17, 1995, more than five years after filing for Chapter 11, Walter Industries emerged from bankruptcy.

It was with a sigh of relief and exhaustion that the key people at Walter Industries responded to this dawn of a new era for the company. Many felt they had been put through a wringer, stressed and consumed with unhappy demands forced upon them by the diverse litigants in Chapter 11. One company executive put it this way: "It felt like coming out of a snake pit where we never knew who would take a bite out of us next."

When it was all over, Henry Kravis and his cousin George Roberts reflected on sharing those five years of hardship with the founder of Walter Industries. "Not only is Jim Walter a remarkable businessman, but he is also a terrifically caring and loyal human being," Kravis remarked. "Jim sold his company to us and stayed on as chairman, even though he had profited from the sale and was at normal retirement age. When Walter Industries was forced to file bankruptcy due to the asbestos litigation, Jim worked even harder to ensure that the company remained profitable and emerged intact. I don't know anyone who has more character or better values." George Roberts concurred, adding, "Jim Walter's an amazing man. When he had every reason to 'call it a day' and retire, he stuck with us, his employees, and the company. He never wavered or tired, just persisted, until all was settled and everyone was satisfied."

In the final months, the legal and financial detail work involved in emerging from bankruptcy forced a frenzied six- and seven-day work week upon top management. They had to arrange new financing of approximately $1.5 billion to establish new lines of credit for the company's future operations and to provide for the cash payments to creditors in the reorganization plan. The most bitter aspect of the aftermath, however, was the high cost of the bankruptcy itself. "Never go into a Chapter 11 bankruptcy broke," Jim Walter would advise anyone who asked. His company survived its Chapter 11 only because it had enough money in the bank and was healthy enough to pay all the exorbitant fees involved. Not only did Walter Industries have to pay several firms of lawyers, accountants, and investment advisers to defend itself, but it also had to pay for these services for the various creditors. The total bill came to more than $75 million, and not one cent of that money added to the growth of the company.

Overall, Walter Industries survived in much better condition than most companies undergoing a bankruptcy, voluntary or involuntary. During the five years under the court's direction, the company had been permitted to invest about $70 million a year in capital improvements in order to keep abreast of modern developments. In short, it emerged from bankruptcy as a healthy, profitable, ongoing concern.

It was about half the size it had been before the leveraged buyout because it had sold off many of its subsidiaries, but with sales and revenues where they had been twenty years earlier, the new company was lean, efficient and profitable. Its separate businesses—home building, iron pipe, coal mining, and numerous smaller industrial operations—were all maintaining their market share in their different industries. The home building segment, built around Jim Walter Homes and the Mid-State mortgage servicing operation, still remained the company's core business. It represented 28 percent of the company's net sales and 76 percent of the company's annual earnings.

Jim Walter Homes built 4,331 houses in fiscal 1995, with twenty-eight different models ranging in size from 640 to 1,800 square feet. It financed 97 percent of them. Since the company was founded in 1946, Jim Walter Homes has built more than 320,000 houses. No other builder in the nation has built anywhere near that number. In fact, no other major home builder has been in business that long. Loyalty goes a long way in this division. The nineteen officers in the home building division average 28.9 years with the company, a statistic few companies can match. Today, the company's 90-percent-completed homes range in price from $37,000 to $90,000. But the company still builds and sells the basic shell home for $22,045. At 720 square feet, it is bigger and more expensive than Jim Walter's original 400-square-foot home at $895, but still very affordable. Times have changed, but the original concept has not.

Finally, in mid-1995, with the company free and clear of obstacles, it once again became time to look forward. Jim Walter, who had started this business at the age of twenty-three, could look forward to his retirement at age seventy-three. The old-timers who had stayed on beyond retirement age out of loyalty to him would follow him out the door. Bull Durham and the new board of directors would devote themselves to implementing a new strategy for the growth and well-being of the company. They would also begin a search for a new team of younger managers to lead this unique company into the next century and on to new heights. The enterprise was launched fifty years earlier with the sale of a twenty-by-twenty-foot shell house for $895 and a dream in the imagination of a twenty-three-year-old high school graduate. He and the men he gathered around him built that enterprise into a $2.6 billion business. It remains for the young men and women who will take over to do as well, or better, in the years to come, and to make their own dreams come true.

INDEX

Abrahams, Harry, 52-53
Advertising, 9, 134-35
Alabama. *See* Blue Creek mines
Alabama Power Company, 192, 199, 201, 207, 210
Alex. Brown & Sons, 103
Allied Chemical and Dye Corporation, 146, 147, 148
Almand, Jack, 25, 46, 134
Alston, Jackie, 35
Alston, James O. (Buddy)
    business philosophy, 48-49, 57-58, 88-89
    corporate role, 42, 45, 46, 53, 61, 62, 71, 72, 76, 82, 90-96, 112, 115, 168, 171, 179, 272, 281
    house sales, 18, 19, 21-23, 26-27, 29, 33
    management style, 126, 127, 133, 134-35
    nickname, 85
    partnership, 34-35, 44
    war service, 6, 7
American Express, 317
American Schools and Colleges Association, 81
Apollo Advisors, 317, 318, 320, 322, 324
Asbestos litigation
    background, 183-84
    Celotex suit, 233-34, 235, 258, 264, 265, 303, 304, 320
    Kravis/KKR settlement attempts, 308-9, 311-12
    landmark legal basis, 233
    Manville Corporation bankruptcy, 234-35

    Texas class action lawsuit, 302-4
    trial and consensual agreement, 318-27
    typical lawsuits, 233-34
Asbestos-related disease cases, 233
Asbestos Workers Union, 234
Automatic Sprinkler Corporation of America, 160

Badger, James, 108
Bagasse (leftover product), 98-99
Baker, William Kendall, 25, 34, 62, 244
Bankers Trust, 265, 291
Bankston, Larry, 92, 134-35
Baron, Frederick M., 321
Barrett, Samuel E., 147
Barrett Building Materials, 146-49
Barron's magazine, 80
Beatrice Corporation, 252, 259
Beattie, Richard I., 259, 283, 288
Best Insurors, 54
Billion-Dollar-A-Year Club, 189
Black, Leon, 317, 318
Blake Lumber, 24
Blue Creek coal mines (Alabama), 191-93, 199, 201-12, 213-14, 223-30
Bluhdorn, Charles, 145
Booker Company, 24-25, 46, 133
Borg Warner, 259
Brentwood Financial Corporation, 138-39
Brentwood Savings and Loan Association, 143
    losses, 140, 222
    profits, 143
    purchase of, 139

sale of, 238, 243
Briggs Manufacturing Company, 183, 233, 243
Business Week magazine, 80

CAKE (Courtesy, Appearance, Knowledge, Enthusiasm), 94-95
California Federal Savings and Loan Association, 238
Carey Canadian Mines, Ltd., 183, 233, 243
Carl M. Loeb, Rhoades & Company, 68, 69-70, 101, 102, 103, 110, 162
Carr, William, 204-7, 208, 209, 210, 212, 214-15, 223-24, 225, 228
Carter, John B., Jr., 272, 273, 288
Celanese Corporation, 169
Celotex Corporation
    acquisition and management, 98-132, 137-38, 141-43, 189, 216
    asbestos litigation, 233-34, 235, 258, 264, 265, 303, 304, 320
    Panacon acquisition, 183, 232-33
    product line, 182, 190, 222
    sale of, 263, 301
Centrust, 318
Certainteed, 276
Chase Manhattan Bank, 83
Chemical Bank of New York. *See* Chemical Corn Exchange Bank of New York
Chemical Corn Exchange Bank of New York, 83, 88
Citibank, 83, 204
Citicorp Capital Investors, 274, 275, 280, 281-82, 286
Clement, Henry C., 155
Coal mining operation, 191-93, 199-216, 223-32, 263, 276, 301
Coast-to-Coast Advertising, 134
Cole, Franklin A., 272, 273, 288
Collins, Daisy, 62
Collins, Henry, 106-7, 108-9, 115, 116, 119, 126, 141, 151, 162, 163
Columbia Savings & Loan, 318
Companie S. Gobain, 276
Continental Illinois National Bank and Trust Company, 251, 310

Cordell Award, 228
Cordell, Joe B.
    business acumen, 84-86, 151, 155, 156-58
    buyout role, 260, 264, 266, 267, 270, 272, 274, 277, 279, 281, 284, 290, 294, 295
    Celotex acquisition and management, 102, 103, 107, 109, 110, 112, 113, 114, 115-21, 122-23, 127-28, 141, 302
    CEO appointment, 241-43, 253
    coal development program, 202, 203-6, 207, 211-16, 223-30, 231-32
    corporation presidency, 168, 193-98, 200, 218-19, 235, 236
    illness and death, 313-14, 315
Corporate veil, 303, 311, 320
Crawford Door Company, 131-32
Credit Lyonnais, 317
Croesus Corp., 272

Dahlberg, Bror, 98
Daniels, Danny, 46, 47, 58
Davenport, Lou, 4, 7, 8-12, 17, 19-20, 129
Davenport & Walter, 8-14, 16-20
Deland Naval Air Station, 6
DeLavaud, Dimitri Sensaud, 159
Deloitte Haskins & Sells, 259, 260
Dent, John, 153
DeWitt, William G., 83, 88, 103
Dixie Building Supplies Company, 17, 18, 25, 26, 33
Drexel Burnham Lambert, 317, 318
    asbestos litigation, 302
    long-term financing deal with KKR, 265-66, 291, 292-93
    marketing of JWC mortgage-backed bonds, 296, 297, 298-99, 306
    Milken manipulations, 304, 305, 316, 317
Drummond, Garry, 286
Drummond Company, 276, 280, 281-82, 285, 286, 287, 288, 290
Due diligence evaluation, 258, 260, 266, 275, 276, 277

Durham, G. Robert (Bull), 314-15, 323, 329-30

E. L. Bruce Company, 97, 98
Ellis, Al, 30-32
Emerton, Robert, 260
Everwed Corporation, 229
Executive Life Insurance Company of California, 317

Federal Home Loan Bank, 140
Federal Housing Authority, 66, 73, 134
Federal Trade Commission, 232, 235
Ferro Machine & Foundry, 68, 70-71, 72
FHA. *See* Federal Housing Authority
Figgie, Harry E., Jr., 160-62, 163-64, 165
Finance magazine, 80
Financial Security Assurance Company, 296, 297
Financial World magazine, 314
First National Bank of Atlanta, 153
First National Bank of Chicago, 107-8
First National Bank of St. Petersburg, 88, 139
First National City Bank of New York, 83, 104, 106, 109-10
Fitzsimmons, Henry T., 154-55
Flom, Joseph, 278, 280
Florida Trend magazine, 79-80
Forbes magazine, 199
Forstmann Little & Company, 276
Frazier, Warren, 259, 260, 267, 279, 281
FSA. *See* Financial Security Assurance Company
FTC. *See* Federal Trade Commission

Garrett, Robert E., 160-61, 162-63, 169, 174, 175
Garvey, Richard, 288
Gaynor, Joe, 274, 275
Geneen, Harold, 145
General Discount Corporation, 31-32
Georgia Marble Company, 153-58, 182, 190, 249, 263, 301

Gilbert, Eddie, 97-98, 100, 103, 108, 109
Golden parachute, 253
Golkin, Perry, 283, 295, 314
    asbestos litigation, 308, 309
    role in KKR acquisition of JWC, 260-61, 262, 264, 267
Goodbody & Co., 37, 42
Greenwood, Marvin, 126, 141
GTE, 272
Gulf & Western, 145

Hall of Fame (Jim Walter Homes), 248-49
Halligan, Peter, 151
Hamer Lumber, 243
Harrison, Ben F., 161, 163, 175, 178, 191-98
Heidrick, Gardner, 169
Heidrick & Struggles, 169
Heller, Walter, 53
Herzog, Raymond H., 272
High-yield bonds. *See* Junk bonds
Hillsborough Holdings Corporation, 299, 312
Hires, Tommy, 45, 46-47, 58, 76, 85, 249
Holmes, James E., 103
Home-building operations
    branch offices, 33-34, 45-49, 76-77, 132, 247, 248
    building record, 329
    finished houses, 247-48
    home sales, 132, 301
    housing booms, 143, 240-41
    models and prices, 47, 132-33, 147
    original shell houses, 2-5, 8-14, 16-20, 329
    partially finished homes, 132-33, 248
    profitability, 135, 247, 263
    Walter Construction Company, 20-44
    See also Jim Walter Homes; Mortgages
Horatio Alger Award, 81
Houdaille, 252
Housing. *See* Home-building operations; Mortgages
Hunt brothers, 303
Hyatt, Kenneth, 157, 158, 260

Iacocca, Lee, 314
IBM, 116-17
Institutional Investor magazine, 297-98
ITT, 145

Japanese coal contracts, 199, 200-201, 205, 276
JC Penney Stores, 272, 283-84
Jim Walter Corporation
    acquisitions by, 98-132, 138-39, 141-43, 144, 146-65
    advertising, 134-35
    annual meetings, 58-59
    asbestos litigation, 183-84, 233-35, 258, 264, 265, 303, 312, 319-20
    branch managers, 45-48, 76-77
    building materials division, 146-49
    capitalization plans, 40-44, 50-51, 66-76
    cash flow problems, 51, 63-68, 83-84, 85-86, 133, 236, 238, 239-40, 244, 263, 301-2
    coal mines (*see subhead* mining divi–sion *below*)
    competition, 79, 81-96
    cost reduction program, 216-19, 242-43
    executives, 167-87, 193-98, 216-19
    expansion and growth, 44-59, 76-77, 87-88, 96, 129-30, 135-37, 145, 165, 182-83, 189-90, 249-50
    headquarters, 61-62, 140-41
    home-building operation (*see* Jim Walter Homes)
    incorporation, 44
    indebtedness, 236-44
    leveraged buyout of, 251-99
    mining division, 191-93, 199-216, 223-33, 263, 276, 301
    mortgages (*see* Mid-State Investment Corporation; *under* Mortgages)
    recession impact, 219-23, 231, 235-41
    reorganization (*see* Walter Industries)
    sales and profits, 45, 77, 92, 96, 135-37, 143, 165, 178-79, 184, 189, 199, 200, 211, 230, 241, 242
    stock, 44, 54-57, 70-76, 77-78, 122, 143-

    44, 184, 208, 211, 222, 271, 281-82, 286-87, 288, 289
    work atmosphere, 44-45, 62, 76, 121, 128-29, 181
Jim Walter Doors, 243
Jim Walter Homes, 244-49
    branch offices, 33-34, 132, 237, 247, 248-49
    earnings, 244, 247
    housing boom, 143
    long-term success, 329
    managers, 45-48, 194
    models and prices, 247-48
    mortgage uniqueness, 245-46 (*see also* Mid-State Investment Corporation)
    profitability, 132-35, 247, 263
    sales figures, 301, 329
    sales force, 248-49
Jim Walter Papers, 152, 301
Jim Walter Plastics, 243
Jim Walter Research Corporation, 190
Johns-Manville. *See* Manville Corporation
Johnson, James L., 272
Junk bonds, 43, 265, 292, 293, 297, 298, 304-5, 316
Jurgens, James, 218, 276
JWC. *See* Jim Walter Corporation

Kaneb Services, 227
Katcher, Richard D., 259, 273, 274, 278, 279, 282, 283, 284, 288-89
Katz, Eugene, 138, 141-42, 168-69, 173-74
Kelly, Joe, 62-63
Kinstler, Everett Raymond, 316
KKR. *See* Kohlberg Kravis Roberts & Co.
Knapp, Ernest P., 68, 69, 70-71, 72, 115
Knight Paper Company, 151-52
Kohlberg, Jerome, 252
Kohlberg Kravis Roberts & Co.
    asbestos litigation, 302, 303, 304, 308-9, 311-12, 319, 321, 322, 323-26
    JWC acquisition, 251-52, 254-58, 269-70, 280, 281, 283, 285-86, 287, 288, 289-99
    JWC bonds, 305-10
    Walter Industries bankruptcy, 327

Kravis, Henry
    art collection, 309
    asbestos litigation, 302, 303, 308-9,
        312, 324, 325
    JWC buyout, 251, 252, 253-58, 259,
        261, 264, 264-65, 266, 267, 270,
        283
    relationship with Jim Walter, 307-8,
        314-15, 316, 327-28
    Walter Industries bankruptcy and
        operations, 307-10, 314-15
    See also Kohlberg Kravis Roberts & Co.
Kreher, Alex, 36
Kreher, Karl, 37-38, 39-41, 42, 43, 44, 50,
    66, 70, 71
Kurucz, Don, 236, 296
Kynes, James W., 128, 231, 235, 255
    buyout role, 255, 259, 260, 264, 267,
        270, 272, 275, 277, 279, 281, 284,
        290

Lanzillotti, Robert F., 272
Lazard Frères, 101, 103, 186, 276
LBO. *See* Leveraged buyout
Lehman Brothers, 317-18, 320, 322, 324,
    327
Leveraged buyout, 251-99, 302
Ling, James, 145
Litton Industries, 145
Livingston, Homer, 108, 109
Loeb, John L.
    Barrett Building Materials acquisi-
        tion role, 147, 148
    Celotex acquisition role, 100-101, 103-
        4, 110
    JWC public offering arrangements,
        68, 69-70, 72
    personal background, 69
    U.S. Pipe acquisition role, 164
Loeb Rhoades. *See* Carl M. Loeb, Rhoades
    & Company
Longwall mining, 205, 206, 207, 208-9,
    223-26, 229-30
Lorch chain, 177-78, 228-29
LTV, 145
Luminous Ceilings, 153

M. A. C. Corporation, 87
MacDonald, Thomas C., Jr., 272
Majestic Carpet Mills, 152-53
Malone & Hyde, 252
Manufacturers & Trade Trust of Buffalo,
    83
Manufacturers Hanover Trust, 265, 291
Manville Corporation, 234-35
Marathon Manufacturing Company, 272
Marchich, Michael M., 198, 202-3
Marquette Paper Corporation, 150-51
Marron, Donald, 279, 284, 285
Matlock, Kenneth
    buyout role, 251, 252, 255, 259, 260,
        264, 266, 281, 284, 290, 293, 296
    Celotex management, 116, 117, 118-
        19, 120, 121, 127-28
    as chief financial officer, 198, 221,
        231, 235, 236, 239, 240, 313
Mead, Gary L., 259
Meares, Ted, 36-37, 41-42, 43, 71, 103
Merrill Lynch, Pierce, Fenner & Smith,
    264, 274, 306
"Metaphysical System of Metabolism, A"
    (Kreher), 39
Methane, 227
Metromedia, 259
Meyer, Andre, 186
Miami Carey, 183, 233, 243
Miami Carey of Canada, 243
Michael, Bob, 249
Mid-State Investment Corporation
    financial statements, 240
    founding, 35
    mortgages, 77, 135, 143, 238, 244-47,
        293, 297, 298
    profitability, 245-47, 263, 329
Milken, Michael, 292, 304, 305, 306, 316,
    317
Miller, David F., 272, 283-84
Mining. *See* Coal mining operation
Monsanto Corporation, 169
Moody's Investors Service, 223
Mortgages
    Davenport & Walter, 12-13
    Jim Walter Corporation, 62-66, 77,
        133-34, 135, 143, 238, 244-47, 263,
        296-98

Walter Construction Company, 27-28, 30-33, 35-36
See also Mid-State Investment Corporation
Mustafa, Kamal, 277, 279, 282

Nackie Paper Corporation, 150
National Coal Board (England), 206
Newcombe, USS, 7-8
New Millionaires and How They Made Their Fortunes, The (Wall Street Journal), 80
Newsweek magazine, 79
New Yorker magazine, 99
New York Society of Security Analysts, 207
New York Stock Exchange, 252, 271
    Celotex listing, 100, 103
    JWC listing, 72-76, 122, 271
    October, 1987 plunge, 294, 295-96, 297
Nichelson, Don, 277, 279
Nippon Steel, 200
NV Ryan, 276
NYSE. *See* New York Stock Exchange

Olin Corporation, 169
Operation CAKE, 94-95
Owens-Illinois, 259, 285

Pacific Holdings, 276
PaineWebber, 274, 275-88, 290
Panacon Corporation, 183-84, 232-35
Paskay, Alexander, 312, 318-19, 320, 321, 322-24, 326
Paul Weir and Associates, 204
Penzoil, 304
Perfect Polishers, 229
Perkowsky, Jack, 275, 277, 279
Petro, Pete, 177, 228-29
Phelps Dodge Corporation, 314
Philip Carey, 183, 232-33, 234
Pizzitola, Betty, 172
Pizzitola, Frank J., 169-87, 193, 194
Pogo Producing Company, 272
Poison pill, 253
Prescott, Barney, 66-67

Prescott, Edward P., 67-69, 72
Prescott & Company, 67, 69
Price Waterhouse, 84, 85, 102, 116, 259, 260
Profit Improvement Program, 176-77

Raether, Paul, 283, 295
Rapid American Corporation, 183
Republic Water Heater, 233
Resolution Trust Company, 318
Riklis, Meshulam, 183
RJR Nabisco, 302
Roberts, George, 252, 283, 285, 288, 289, 302, 327, 328
Robinson, Bill, 45-46
Robinson, James Douglas, 153
"Rocket" offers, 42-43
RTC. *See* Resolution Trust Company
Ruberoid Company, 98, 100, 103, 109

Salomon Brothers, 297
Saraw, Arnold, 168, 272, 281, 290
    JWC formation, 42
    sales and mortgages, 26-27, 28, 62, 244
    stock holdings, 72
    Walter Construction Company partnership, 34-35, 44
Savings and loan institutions. *See* Brentwood Savings and Loan Association
Searle, Daniel C., 272
Securities and Exchange Commission (SEC), 73-74, 122
Shackleford, Farrior, Shannon & Stallings, 41
Shackleford, Farrior, Stallings and Evans, 259, 272, 279
Shearson Lehman Brothers, 70, 273, 275, 276, 280, 281, 282, 285, 288, 289, 290
Siddall, Frank H., 155
Simpson Thatcher & Bartlett, 259, 260, 267, 283, 288, 295, 309
Skadden, Arps, Slate, Meagher & Flom, 278

South Coast Corporation, 102, 132, 140, 143-44
Southeastern Bolt & Screw, 243
South Shore Oil and Development Company, 102, 132
Specification Roof, 147-48
Spencer, William I., 104-6, 110
Springs State Bank, 8
Stagflation, 221
Stallings, Norman, 41, 44, 73, 103
Standard & Poor, 223, 249
Stewart, Ernie, 17
Stichter, Don, 310, 311, 325
Stock market. *See* New York Stock Exchange; *subheading* stock *under* Jim Walter Corporation
Stock market crash (October, 1987), 294, 295-96, 297
Susman, Steven D., 303
Sweat equity, 29, 52
Synergism, 130, 145-46, 148, 150, 232

Tampa Shipbuilding and Engineering Company, 39
Tampa Tribune, 315-16
Tarvia (road paving material), 147
Tate, Sam, 155
Texaco, 304
Texas, class action asbestos-injury lawsuit, 302-4
Thornton, Tex, 145
Time magazine, 80
Tokarz, Michael
    asbestos litigation, 302, 304
    bondholder efforts, 305, 306, 314, 321, 324-25, 326
    buyout role, 251-52, 255, 256, 260-61, 262, 264, 265, 267, 283, 288, 294, 295, 296, 298
Townsend, David, 271

Uniroyal, 259
United Mine Workers, 206, 225
United States Pipe and Foundry Company, 263, 301
    Alabama coal mining rights, 191-93

Harrison presidency, 196
history, 158-62
JWC acquisition of, 158, 162-65
Pizzitola management, 174-75, 177-78
profitability, 190, 249
technological improvement expenditures, 182
University of Florida, 272
U.S. Gypsum, 118
U.S. Homes, 198
U.S. Pipe. *See* United States Pipe and Foundry Company

VA. *See* Veteran's Administration
Venture capital, 43, 72, 316
Vestal Manufacturing Company, 131
Veteran's Administration, 66, 73, 134
Vulture capitalists, 316-17

Wachtell, Lipton, Rosen & Katz, 259, 273, 279-81, 283, 286, 288, 289
Wall, Anders, 272, 281
Wall Street Journal, 80
Walter, Connie, 313, 315
Walter, Ebe, 2-3, 4, 5, 14, 31
Walter, Ebe, Jr., 3
Walter, James W.
    asbestos litigation, 302, 303, 312, 318-21, 323, 324
    business acumen, 63-65, 71-72, 130, 131-32, 139-40, 144, 146-65
    businesses (*see* Davenport & Walter; Jim Walter Corporation; Jim Walter Homes; Walter Construction Company; Walter Industries)
    business style and reputation, 41, 42, 48-52, 53, 59, 87, 113, 126
    buyout role, 253-55, 257, 258, 264-65, 266-67, 269-70, 272, 273-74, 275, 277-78, 279-80, 281, 284-85, 290, 293, 294, 295, 298
    Celotex acquisition and management, 100-132, 141-43
    childhood, 5

coal development program, 199-212, 213-16
corporate bankruptcy, 305-28
corporate responsibilities, 167-87, 193-98, 216-19
first house sales, 2-14
illness, 315
marriage and family, 2, 14-16, 313, 315
media attention, 79-81, 199
personality, 11, 112-13, 128-29, 223, 237-38
retirement, 241-42, 311, 329
war service, 1, 5-8
Walter Construction Company, 20-38
cash flow problems, 13, 19, 32, 36
demise, 40-42, 44
expansion, 33-34
mortgages, 27-28, 30-33, 35-36
partnership, 34-35
Walter E. Heller & Company, 51-53, 272
Walter Industries, Inc., 301-30
asbestos litigation, 302-4, 308-9, 311-12, 318-27
bankruptcy, 310-27
bankruptcy aftermath, 328-29
bondholders, 305-10, 321-27
vulture capitalists, 316-18
Walter, Monica Saraw (Monty), 2, 14-16, 25, 26, 35, 313
Walton, Sam, 314
Warren Industries, 138, 142
Waters, Stephen, 273, 274-75, 283, 285-86, 288, 290
Wedlo, 228-29
Weir, Jack, 206
Weldon, William
Celotex role, 116, 117, 118-19, 120, 121, 128
as financial officer, 235, 260, 276, 281, 290, 296, 313, 315
WesRay Capital Corp., 276
Willer, Richard, 108
Wometco, 252
Woodfin, Gene, 138, 162
Barrett Building Materials acquisition role, 148, 149-50
Celotex deal, 101-2, 103-4

KKR buyout negotiations, 272, 273, 278, 282-83, 288-89
personal background, 101
Wright, Jim, 303

Ziegler, Norman, 46